TRUE LIES

· · ·

Anthony Lappé
and
Stephen Marshall

with additional reporting
by Ian Inaba

Guerrilla News Network

A PLUME BOOK

PLUME
Published by the Penguin Group
Penguin Group (USA) Inc., 375 Hudson Street,
New York, New York 10014, U.S.A.
Penguin Group (Canada), 10 Alcorn Avenue,
Toronto, Ontario, Canada M4V 3B2 (a division of
Pearson Penguin Canada Inc.)
Penguin Books Ltd, 80 Strand, London WC2R 0RL, England
Penguin Ireland, 25 St Stephen's Green,
Dublin 2, Ireland (a division of Penguin Books Ltd)
Penguin Group (Australia), 250 Camberwell Road, Camberwell,
Victoria 3124, Australia (a division of Pearson Australia Group Pty Ltd)
Penguin Books India Pvt Ltd, 11 Community Centre,
Panchsheel Park, New Delhi – 110 017, India
Penguin Books (NZ), Cnr Airborne and Rosedale Roads, Albany,
Auckland, New Zealand (a division of Pearson New Zealand Ltd)
Penguin Books (South Africa) (Pty) Ltd, 24 Sturdee Avenue,
Rosebank, Johannesburg 2196, South Africa

Penguin Books Ltd, Registered Offices: 80 Strand,
London WC2R 0RL, England

First published by Plume, a member of Penguin Group (USA) Inc.

First Printing, October 2004
1 3 5 7 9 10 8 6 4 2

Copyright © Guerrilla News Network, 2004
All rights reserved

Excerpt from *The Collected Essays, Journalism and Letters of George Orwell,
Volume IV: In Front of Your Nose 1945–1950*, copyright © 1968 by Sonia
Brownell Orwell and renewed 1996 by Mark Hamilton, reprinted by
permission of Harcourt, Inc.

Ⓟ REGISTERED TRADEMARK—MARCA REGISTRADA
CIP data is available.
ISBN 0-452-28531-3

Printed in the United States of America
Set in Galliard

Endorsements for the Guerrilla News Network

"GNN reaches and moves young people looking for the real story behind the spin. It's a hard-hitting, hot, and effective new style of investigative journalism. I love it."

—John Stauber, founder, PR Watch, and
author of *Weapons of Mass Distraction*

"As a former *60 Minutes* producer and founder of the Center for Public Integrity, it is painfully apparent that much of the American mainstream is in major denial. Their project is, in other words, absolutely crucial, not to mention timely."

—Charles Lewis, founder, Center for
Public Integrity, and author of *The
Buying of the Presidency 2004*

Anthony Lappé is a writer and television producer. He has written articles for more than twenty publications, including *Details, Paper, The New York Times, New York* magazine, and *Salon,* among many others. He's tracked down an American fugitive who hijacked a plane to Cuba, hung with L.A. gang-bangers fighting a new war in El Salvador, and was given a tour inside an underground pot farm in Manhattan. In television, he received a grant from the U.S. government to help set up a Palestinian television station in the West Bank. In addition, he has worked as a correspondent for The New York Times Video News International, and as a producer for Worldwide Television News, MTV News and Specials, and Fuse. He has a master's degree in journalism from Columbia University and a bachelor's degree in politics from New York University.

Stephen Marshall is a founding partner and creative director of GNN, as well as a writer and Sundance Award–winning director. His critically acclaimed VHS magazine project, Channel Zero, was one of the first successes of the small-format video revolution. In 1997, Stephen was the host and producer of Voice of Free Nigeria, a pirate radio show that was part of a covert movement to overthrow the regime of Sani Abacha. Since cofounding GNN, Stephen has written on subjects ranging from media monopolies to the Homeland Security Act. "Coca-Karma," his investigative report on Coca-Cola's unreported multibillion-dollar copyright infringement lawsuit, has drawn over 500,000 readers to the site. Stephen has also directed controversial music videos for Ad Rock, Eminem, and 50 Cent.

Ian Inaba produces and directs investigative documentaries and music videos for GNN. He has spent the past three years producing news videos for GNN and developing GNN.tv. Ian holds degrees from the University of Pennsylvania's School of Engineering and Wharton School of Business.

For all the guerrillas
who made GNN.tv their own

Acknowledgments

▪ ▪ ▪

GNN would like to especially thank our editors Trena Keating, Emily Haynes, and Jake Klisivitch at Plume for their faith and patience. Our agent Ian Kleinert at the Literary Group for his cool head and sage words. Researchers Jennifer Bleyer and Kate Pickert for their diligence and insight.

Clarice Lappé and Lisa Kawamoto Hsu for their love, wisdom, and courage.

We also deeply appreciate the contributions of the following people, without whom this book wouldn't have been possible: Anna Lappé, Bev Harris, Blaise Bess, Blaine Machan, Brian Will, Gen. Buck Kernan (Ret.), Carol Park, Christina Nova, Cynthia McKinney, Ellen Proctor, Eric Schlosser, Felipe Armesto-Fernandez, Frances Moore Lappé, Frank Albayati, Col. Frederick Rudesheim, Gert Van Langendonck, Greg Palast, Hesham Barbary, Jack Weiss, Jason Tlaloc, Jen Reed, Jesse McKinley, Judy Browne, Joe Strummer (RIP), Gen. Joe Ralston (Ret.), Marc Lappé, Mark Benjamin, Mary Blizzard, Matthew Cole, May Ying Welsh, Melissa Blizzard, Dr. Meryl Nass, Michael Fitzpatrick, Noam Chomsky, People of Iraq,

Peter Dale Scott, Raed Jarrar and Emaar, Rana Al Aiouby, Cap. Sandra Chavez, Scott Peterson, Sherif Sadek, Stephanie Pasvankias, Tom Lesser, People of Shanksville, Vanessa Grigoriadis, Vern Grose, and all the guerrillas on the forum.

Also thanks to NYFA (New York Foundation for the Arts), NYSCA (New York State Council for the Arts), Nathan Cummings Foundation, Jerome Foundation, Pacific Pioneer Fund, and North Star Fund.

In addition, we'd like to express our gratitude to all the people we interviewed and consulted, too numerous to list, who generously gave their time and shared their knowledge.

And lastly, a tip of the old tumbler to Christopher "I can't believe I'm a hawk" Hitchens for the ultimate inspiration: the prospect of utter failure.

. . . we are all capable of believing things which we know to be untrue, and then, when we are finally proved wrong, impudently twisting the facts so as to show that we were right. Intellectually, it is possible to carry on this process for an indefinite time: the only check on it is that sooner or later a false belief bumps up against solid reality, usually on a battlefield.

George Orwell, "In Front of Your Nose"

Contents

■ ■ ■

Foreword

Blind Man's Burden

■ ■ ■

OUR MEDIA SUCKS. But you already knew that.

In *True Lies*, Stephen Marshall and Anthony Lappé don't offer up another cranky complaint. There's enough of those to knock down half the rain forest in Belize. Instead, they give you a new view into the satanic machinery of the information factory that tells you what you want to eat, what you want to wear, who you want to invade, and, ultimately, what you believe in.

In other words, it's about empire and the culture of deception that has allowed us to enter a new age of conquest without ever seeing it coming.

But the problem is, America is very bad at empire. Unlike the bloody Brits, where Winston Churchill could speak of his nation's colonial sprawl with a tear in his eye, Americans don't want to be imperialists; they would never tolerate a policy that puts empire-building above catching a rerun of *Friends*. So we have a cartoon empire, Disneyfied with fancy graphics and a president hopping around on an aircraft carrier like Daffy

Duck quacking, "Mission accomplished! Mission accomplished!"

The real cost of empire is hidden. The dead are mourned way off camera, while the media elite suck down sushi at black-tie dinners, guffawing as the commander in chief cracks jokes about the reasons we went to war: "Those weapons of mass destruction have got to be somewhere!" Ha, ha, ha.

But the damage is not hidden to Marshall and Lappé.

True Lies traces the digital Don Quixotes and their perambulations around the globe. Along the way, you meet heroes and geniuses, the paranoid and the plain perplexed about the new America in which a president who was never elected gets accolades on Fox television that would have made a Soviet broadcaster blush. From the poisoning of our own soldiers to the turning over of the most fundamental act of democracy to shady corporations to the unanswered questions of 9/11, the authors examine what has become a cultural phenomenon of mass denial. As an Oxford historian explains to them, Life is lubricated by lies. The tagline for our times, if ever there was one.

True Lies is Marshall and Lappé's virgin dive into print from the Web platform of their Guerrilla News Network, one of the Net's hottest sites, and one of the few places to get the hard info that Dan and Tom and Peter won't let through the electronic Berlin wall. That's how I originally met these two.

I am a journalist. Like Marshall and Lappé, I'm of a dying journalistic tradition. We're those old-schoolers who still believe (call us naive) that journalism is a public service, that journalists' first job is to give voice to the voiceless.

When I met these guys, I had just broadcast reports for BBC Television on the nasty little details of how Jeb Bush fixed the 2000 election in Florida for his big brother. See, he'd found this neat trick: Knock off tens of thousands of black voters from the rolls by declaring them convicted felons. Only, it turns out—whoops—a lot of them were quite innocent. If you were living in the United States at the time, unless you read about this on Guerrilla News or other samizdat outlets, you wouldn't know about it.

When Dan Rather appeared on my show, *Newsnight in the UK*, he made this confession: On American television he couldn't ask tough questions of his leaders. He feared he would be necklaced. "You will have a flaming tire of lack of patriotism put around your neck."

Burned in public as unpatriotic? Silence as patriotism? Ugh.

Marshall and Lappé are not afraid of the auto-da-fé. They have the guts to give us full frontal coverage from the front lines of the new empire crafted by our armed and dangerous clownocracy. And we're all better for it. George Orwell once said, "In an age of universal deceit, telling the truth is a revolutionary act."

Viva la GNN revolution.

—Greg Palast, author
The Best Democracy Money Can Buy

Introduction
Paradigm Drift

*If the nineteenth century was the age of the editorial chair,
ours is the century of the psychiatrist's couch.*
—Marshall McLuhan

Guerrilla News Network is an independent media project
that launched in the summer of 2000. Collectively, we are
writers, filmmakers, designers, DJs, and music-video directors,
but most of all, we are journalists. We have reported from the
jungles of Congo, the barrios of Havana, and the back streets
of Bangkok. We have been published everywhere from the
New York Times to two-page anarchist handouts. We are suspicious, analytical, and increasingly aware that journalism, the
calling we have dedicated our lives to, appears to be caught in
a downward spiral.

When we started GNN four years ago, on a shoestring
budget with computers and video cameras cobbled together
from a busted dot-com, we never imagined it would come
this far.

The idea was simple: provide a serious platform for important global stories that we felt were under-covered, or simply
ignored by the corporate media. We would take no advertising. We would try to hold the left as accountable as the right.
Our target audience would be a generation that had tuned out

traditional news sources and was now getting most of its information from people like Michael Moore and Jon Stewart. Since we weren't that funny, we came up with the idea of supplementing our coverage with a series of highly designed, music-driven short documentaries we called NewsVideos, featuring music from some of the biggest names in pop music, from Peter Gabriel to Eminem.

The idea seemed to catch on. We won a Sundance award for our NewsVideo looking back at the CIA's drug-dealing operations in Central America during the 1980s. *USA Today* made us a "hot site of the day," saying, "It's times like these, when questioning government policies is characterized as near treasonous, that one appreciates the skillful dissent displayed by the Guerrilla News Network."

The *Times* of London said we were "required reading for news hounds." Thousands of people packed indie movie houses and college auditoriums to watch and discuss our documentaries. By the time the U.S. invaded Iraq in March 2003, we were getting more than a quarter million unique visitors a month—all through the viral, word-of-mouth network of the Internet. We had no advertising budget; the entire project was financed through working second jobs and the modest sales of our DVDs. Our readers were our inspiration. Like kids brought up on Pop-Tarts and Kool-Aid, our primarily high-school- and college-age audience was hungry for nutrients in its media diet—raw information, historical context, and alternative opinions from around the world that they were being deprived of in the processed, packaged, low-carb corporate media.

GNN has become part of a global phenomenon of independent bloggers, discussion forums, and news sites that bypass Big Media and provide what many increasingly consider a critical facet of an authentic democracy—information free of corporate filters.

But for us, there had always been something missing from GNN's Net-based reportage—a depth of analysis that our blogs, our Web-length articles, and our short videos could not satisfy. We yearned for the ability to travel and to delve head-first into some of the biggest questions facing our nation in the post-9/11 era. So we dusted off our passports, bought some flak jackets, and hit the road.

Over the course of a year, the four of us (this book was reported by GNN's Josh Shore, Ian Inaba, Anthony Lappé, and Stephen Marshall and was written by Lappé and Marshall) traveled from small-town America to the banks of the Tigris. Along the way, we interviewed some of the world's preeminent historians, political philosophers, media critics, and even high-ranking military officers on the front lines of the "war on terror." We also sought out other reporters who were trying to make a difference, in an attempt to understand the complex calculus that determines why some stories get covered and others get left out of the national frame.

The stories we investigate are some of the biggest issues of the day, yet we found an almost universal lack of awareness in the body politic: they were not part of the national discourse. Yet consider the fact that on the morning of September 11, the future chairmen of the Joint Congressional 9/11 Inquiry had breakfast with Mahmoud Ahmed, an alleged moneyman behind the hijackers. Or that while George W. Bush was campaigning on an isolationist platform in the 2000 election, a small junta of right-wing intellectuals was drafting a policy whose core mission for the Bush presidency was to win "multiple, simultaneous major theater wars." Or that when an outspoken congresswoman questioned the profits a major defense contractor was making from the fallout of the September 11 attacks, she was literally run out of office. Or that the American military may be poisoning its soldiers with radioactive weapons and dubious drugs. Or that Republican-connected firms are implementing voting technology that may imperil the most sacred act of our democratic process.

Stop the Presses

We began with a simple yet disturbing premise: America has become a fortressed island of self-delusional globalists bent on empire, who are corroding the foundations of a democratic republic while expanding their economic and military supremacy to an extent that dwarfs that of any other civilization in history. The rest of the world sees it. Many groups and individuals are rising up against it. But Americans are somehow blind to what is being perpetuated in their own name.

Simply put, journalism, that great fourth estate* of any healthy republic, is failing us. In fact, the industry is facing nothing less than a structural crisis. The very integrity of the tradition is being challenged in a way that threatens to make "news" irrelevant for future generations. Conventional wisdom points to a new economic paradigm, one that was crystallized in a maxim Francis Cairncross, former media editor of *The Economist*, once told us: "Facts are expensive; opinions are cheap."

And she's right. It's no surprise there are no Watergate-like scoops coming from today's bottom-line-driven newsrooms. News organizations, and their corporate owners, can no longer

---

*The term *fourth estate* is generally attributed to Thomas Carlyle (1795–1881), a Scottish historian who referred to it in his celebrated work, *The French Revolution*: "Alas, yes: Speculation, Philosophism, once the ornament and wealth of the saloon, will now coin itself into mere Practical Propositions, and circulate on street and highway, universally; with results! A Fourth Estate, of Able Editors, springs up; increases and multiplies; irrepressible, incalculable."

afford to pay for in-depth investigative reporting. *CBS News'* Bob Simon said flatly in 2002, "We are no longer a news-gathering organization."[1] The reigning stars of the postmillennial mediasphere are puffed-shirt personalities with little or no journalistic experience, like Bill O'Reilly, whose background was the TV tabloid *Inside Edition*. Some of the country's highest profile journalists have come to rely solely on press releases handed to them by the government or corporations. As a demoralized Dana Milbank, the *Washington Post*'s White House correspondent, told *The New Yorker*, "It's more of a stenographic kind of job." Or for the more unscrupulous fiction, as long as they can get away with it.

No matter how much the establishment media wants to pin the blame of the collapse of American journalistic integrity on a few overeager fantasists, Stephen Glass, Jayson Blair, and Jack Kelley are all just symptoms of the crisis facing journalism, not the cause of it. The real issue is cultural and, we would argue, psychological. It is a problem embedded deep in the complex geography of the American consciousness.

The Theory

Everyone knows *the theory*. Whether you're progressive or conservative. Libertarian anarchist or National Socialist. Left wing or right. We all know *the theory*:

The media is controlled by economic and political forces that seek to frame the national dialogue, create the parameters for our debate, and limit the spectrum of possibility for outside interests to gain access to the vast realm of psychic real estate that is the American mass consciousness.

The reason? Because, we have been told, an informed public is dangerous to the economic and political elites of this country. Information must be controlled, just as the few must control the many, as they have done from time immemorial.

We've heard it all before.

But for the majority of Americans, and the corporate media stars who speak to them from establishment papers and television, this thinking is merely the intellectual conspiracy theory of a jealous minority who are, themselves, seeking to get access to the public mind. In their view, the public has never, in the history of our world, had access to more information.

For the average person, the notion that the media is somehow controlling the national discussion, and thus our democratic system, is not only silly, but it is impossible as well. The media is the facilitator of our democracy, the information superstructure that allows the public to operate in their full capacity as citizens of the most functional democracy on the planet. With the sheer flow of breaking stories and images from crisis centers around the world, who could blame the people for feeling overwhelmed. How could they possibly deal with any more . . . *news*?

And yet, those of us who have been inside the temple and studied the media, and its natural process of filtering stories, know that the theory has validity. The major news entities, all of which are owned by major corporations, uniformly frame the worldview of their audiences in a way that excludes specific information and perspectives from the national consciousness.

In the past, liberal and conservative media critics have developed their own theories to explain why their ideological opponents are not reporting on issues that would hurt their party's cause. Throughout the Clinton administration, conservatives like Rush Limbaugh and Sean Hannity and publications like the *National Review* decried a liberal bias in the media that protected the Democratic president from any real degree of objective analysis or critique.

Likewise, during the most recent Bush administration, progressives like Eric Alterman, Al Franken, and Norman Solomon created a virtual cottage industry exposing what they believe to be the emergence of a dominant right-wing, conservative media bias. Tagged as the "Fox effect"—after the ratings-dominant cable network created by Roger Ailes (the former Republican communications strategist to Presidents Nixon, Reagan, and George Bush Sr.)—critics saw the bulk of the major networks and papers shift right, and become feverishly patriotic, demonstrating an alarming lack of critical scrutiny during the administration's military incursions in Afghanistan and Iraq.

No matter which party is in control, there is a sense that the media will rally around and protect those in power. It's almost axiomatic. With the vicious competition between networks and newspapers, none can risk alienating the administration and losing access to it as a source of information. Even more critically, the broadcast media, with its need to constantly exploit new markets and increase audience share, is totally dependent on the Federal Communications Commission (FCC) and its politically appointed officers. It is not surprising that the major networks dutifully parrot the party line, especially during periods in which the FCC is considering a new phase of deregulation. Or when the nation is going to war.*

At least, that is how it works, *in theory*. Stories are buried; scandals are glossed over. Kobe Bryant, Scott Peterson, and Michael Jackson are elevated to front-page status while serious explorations of the corruption of power is pushed to the far end of the public's attention span.

However, there is a fundamental disconnect between *the*

---

*These government pressures on mainstream media—namely, proposed deregulation at a time of war—were made even more real by the fact that George Bush's FCC commissioner is Michael K. Powell, son of Secretary of State Colin Powell.

theory and the functional reality of the media business. The intellectual foundation for *the theory*, which views the media as a monolithic, singular-minded entity, fails to account for the supremely competitive, ego-driven individuals who populate it. Are we to imagine that Tom Brokaw sits with his bosses in some back room, taking instructions on which stories he can, and which he cannot, tell his audience? Is Dan Rather getting brown bags of cash to follow the marching orders of the corporate and political elite? Do the editors of the *New York Times* coordinate with their opponents at the *Washington Post* to decide which headlines they will be featuring, and which they will bury?

We don't think so. And neither, for that matter, do the most articulate proponents of *the theory*.

Noam Chomsky's most famous work, *Manufacturing Consent* (coauthored with Ed Herman), offers a model for understanding the forces that shape media bias in the United States. His critique identifies the institutional pressures that act on individual journalists, gradually conforming their values and opinions until they reflect the interests of the elites. According to Chomsky, it is a process of internalization. One that, like an ideological version of *Star Trek*'s all-encompassing Borg, takes over the individual until that person instinctively applies a framing construct to his or her perception, naturally excluding ideas and critiques that challenge power and its dominion over the republic.

Talking to us in his small Cambridge, Massachusetts, office, the iconoclastic MIT linguist explained that journalists develop a psychology of denial that shields them from their culpability.

Correspondents for the New York Times *like Anthony Lewis or Tom Wicker get very angry when people say,*

"Look what you're doing—you're subordinate to power."
They say no one is telling them what to write. And that's
right—nobody is telling them what to write, but if they
weren't writing those things, they wouldn't have the columns.
They wouldn't make it through that system.

While Chomsky accepts that there are still Western journalists who courageously speak truth to power, he sees them as
anomalies, destined to be marginalized and suppressed. Or, at
least, to remain below the surface of managerial power.

"Systems of power and dominance are by and large not going to like or tolerate people who are going to undermine
them. They'll admire and support and honor those who are
supporting them . . . so, in a way, the outcome shouldn't
come as a surprise."

As most people now realize, media corporations like Fox and
Clear Channel use histrionic patriotism as a shrewd ploy to simultaneously increase ratings and score points with the administration. In Fox's case, the corporation has even appropriated
two of journalism's hallmark maxims, *fair* and *balanced*, and
incorporated the words into its trademark. Progressive media
critics moan about Fox's brazen contempt for the journalistic
virtues. We have learned to see this disdain as a positive thing.

Fox News Channel is the first ironic news network. How
else could you explain a "news" network that runs promos like
this:

Washington, Jefferson, Lincoln. They were America's
greatest presidents. Some are saying George Bush ranks
right up there with them. Find out why. *

*Actual Fox News Channel promo, February 2004.

In Fox's caustic news culture, we see a menacing but accurate reflection of the American society, where an entrenched classism and bitter partisan rivalry have erupted like millennial hot lava, bursting through the crust of the republic's vulnerable facade.

The rest of the networks and major newspapers still promote—and presumably labor under—the illusion that they present an objective, unfiltered perspective to the American people. And in that sense, they are far more dangerous to the health of the entire journalistic enterprise than the so-called Fox effect. Sadly, Fox News Channel may be the closest thing to honesty we have left in this culture of denial that has enveloped the American people and the media that is the lifeblood of their democratic system.

Despite our profound respect and indebtedness to thinkers like Noam Chomsky, it is no longer sufficient to deconstruct the economic, social, and political forces that have made modern journalists into a high-priced intercom for the elites. At some point we have to realize there is little to be learned by leveling an institutional critique when that institution is already a crumbling ruin. To understand how and why the media is failing us so horribly, we have to hit the road.

1

Meet the Press

How to Make Friends and Influence People

■ ■ ■

You can crush a man with journalism.
—William Randolph Hearst

Park City, UT

Al Gore is sitting in front of us, crying like a baby.

We're at Sundance with two of our short films in competition and have been invited to pitch Gore and his team on our vision for their "progressive news" channel. Seated around the kitchen table of multimillionaire—and Gore confidant—Joel Hyatt, in his mountaintop chalet, the group is eating bad pizza and decompressing. Gore is still talking about *S-11 Redux*, our satirical short that features, among other things, video-scratch cuts between George Bush Jr. and the retarded banjo-playing inbred from *Deliverance*. But when we ask about Florida, the mood turns more serious.

"It must have been such a ride. If you don't mind us asking, how did you feel at the end of it all?"

Gore pauses for a second and looks straight ahead. We shift in our seats, trying to will away the silence that has enveloped the table. Then, suddenly, and with perfect timing, Gore drops his shoulders, screws up his face, and lets out a high-pitched wail that, at first, catches us off guard:

"Waaaaaahhhhhhh . . ."

The whole table breaks out laughing. It was a brilliant bit of self-mockery that we would never have expected from the stiff candidate we saw during the 2000 election. As it turns out, Gore is funny. And if there are Democrats around the country who are still obsessed with his crushing loss to Bush, Gore is at least able to project the image he isn't one of them. But he does have his war stories.

"We know that Welch was in the control room at NBC on election night," he explains between bites of cold salami pizza. "We just couldn't get our hands on the tapes to prove it."

Gore is referring to controversial allegations that Jack Welch, then CEO of NBC's corporate parent General Electric, had influenced the network's election coverage by pressuring *NBC News* to call Florida for Bush before all the tallies were in. The charges came directly from NBC sources, who told Waxman that Welch, a high-profile Republican, standing in the control room alternatively "cheering" and "hissing" when George W. Bush surged ahead or fell behind Gore. At one point, according to witnesses quoted by Waxman, the GE patriarch turned to a key official at the network's "decision desk" and asked him, possibly only jokingly, "How much would I have to pay you to call the race for Bush?"[1]

The scandal did not make national headlines until Congressman Henry Waxman (D-Fla.) publicly demanded NBC turn over videotapes that purportedly showed Welch bullying the *NBC News* staff to call the election in favor of Bush.

The issue of the tapes was first raised at a February 2001 congressional hearing of the House Energy and Commerce Committee, where Representative Waxman extracted a commitment from NBC president Andrew Lack to release tapes shot by their internal promotions department on the night of the election. But after months of deflection by NBC,* Waxman issued an ultimatum to the network: Either turn over the tapes or face the risk of a congressional subpoena.

Despite the explosive drama of the Waxman–NBC battle, only one U.S. journalist was covering the story: Ted Hearn, a writer at a small TV trade publication called *Multichannel News*. And so, the intrigue of a corporate CEO using his power to affect his network's coverage of the election remained far off the national radar.

It's not hard to understand why. By this point, Americans were justifiably sick of news about the election and wanted to hear about something other than dimpled chads and voter rolls. Not to mention the fact that the last thing corporate media will report on is the manipulation of news by corporate executives.

More to the point, there was a widely held public perception that Bush had won the election and that Gore's protest was merely a case of partisan sour grapes. To rub it in, during the Florida recount, Bush supporters sold thousands of bumper stickers labeled *Sore Loserman*, a parody of the Gore–Lieberman campaign sign. The last thing the media wanted to do was remind audiences of, or bind itself to, that collective national shame.

Which, according to Representative Waxman, was exactly the point. In an op-ed published in the *Los Angeles Times*, the congressman noted:

---

*NBC argued that releasing the tapes would impinge on the First Amendment, which protects media from government interference. Waxman said he "could not disagree more strongly that a congressional investigation jeopardizes the First Amendment. To the contrary, this is an instance where investigation may be necessary to preserve the independence of the media."

For all the controversy over what did or didn't happen in the last election, one fact is absolutely clear: The pivotal presumption that George W. Bush won the election was the result of the calls the major television networks made on election night.[2]

In *two* of those calls, network decisions were influenced by high-level Republican supporters.

One week after the polls closed, *The New Yorker* magazine dropped a bombshell on the national news media. Writer Joan Mayer detailed how John Ellis, a cousin of George Bush Jr., was working that night as a Fox News senior election analyst. Ellis, a respected journalist who had previously worked at NBC and the *Boston Globe*, bragged to Mayer about his close ties to the Bush brothers. On election night, Ellis claimed, the cousins were back and forth on the phone all night. Mayer wrote:

At 2 A.M. Ellis called his cousins and told them, "Our projection shows that it is statistically impossible for Gore to win Florida." It was just the three of us guys handing the phone back and forth—me with the numbers, one of them a governor, the other the president-elect. Now, that was cool.[3]

As Eric Boehlert wrote in *Salon*,* Fox's decision to be the first network to call Florida for Bush would play a crucial role in how the events would play out. That decision, Boehlert wrote, "created the false impression that Bush had won the general election. Ever since, the Bush camp has been playing the 'we won' card; Fox's call made it a participant in the elec-

---

* *Salon* was one of the only media outlets to extensively cover all aspects of the Florida election debacle, from the electronic disenfranchisement of black voters to the Supreme Court's judicial gymnastics.

tion, not merely an observer."[4a] This becomes especially clear when you consider the effect it had on Jack Welch.

According to Waxman's sources, Welch had posted himself next to NBC's director of elections, Dr. Sheldon R. Gawiser, almost immediately after arriving in the studio early on election night. Gawiser was in charge of interpreting the data coming in from the since-disbanded Voter News Service (VNS), and Welch apparently wanted to be as close to the source as possible. Witnesses described Welch as "hovering" over Gawiser and refusing to leave.[4b]

After a crash course on interpreting VNS raw vote counts from Gawiser, Welch started doing his own calculations. With Florida data coming in, he concluded that Bush had taken the state and began demanding that NBC's staff make the call. As Representative Waxman describes it, the scene was out of every journalist's worst nightmare as Welch, "the head of the corporate owner of NBC, an individual who was one of the most widely respected and powerful CEOs in the world, became a participant in NBC's analysis of the election results."[4c]

At almost this same time, John Ellis over at Fox News called both the Florida and national election for his cousin, George W. Bush. According to the eyewitness sources,

> *immediately after this announcement, Mr. Welch was observed standing behind Mr. Gawiser with a hand on his shoulder, asking why NBC was not also calling the election for Mr. Bush.*[4d]
>
> *Shortly after this, Dr. Gawiser informed the control room that NBC would declare George W. Bush the winner. NBC subsequently did so.*[5]

Sitting in his Los Angeles office three years later, Representative Waxman summed up the whole sordid affair for us, saying if Welch was guilty of what the eyewitnesses reported, it was a "real violation of the separation of the corporate owners from the news decision on something of enormous significance— the determination of who was going to be president of the United States."

So it was hard to blame Gore for feeling a little cheated. Hell, you don't need a "vast right-wing conspiracy" when you have a few take-charge operatives in key positions. The entire episode raises an even larger question. Can we still define journalism by the same standards that were used in the past? When powerful partisan players insert themselves into the process of covering a story that will influence the fate of the country, if not the world, then can we still call it reporting?

As *Salon*'s Boehlert observed, the media's framing of the postelection controversy was based on the perception that Bush had won Florida. Gore was portrayed as somehow trying to tack extra minutes onto the fourth quarter of a game he had already lost. It seemed downright "un-American." When, in reality, the networks' own election guidelines determined that the margin was too close to make an official call.

Had the networks not called it for Bush, the results would have been seen as a tie, with each side entering the "overtime" equally vested in the recount and write-in ballots. In the long run, Ellis's and Welch's influence played a pivotal role in the nation's psychological imprint of the election.

Far from admitting his influential role in NBC's decision to call the election for Bush, Welch mocked the intelligence of anyone who asserted it, telling the Associated Press, "It's just pure crazy. . . . The idea that I had anything to do with the election is—on its face, for people with IQs over fifty— beyond belief."[6]

If anyone understands the value and impact of broadcast news on the public psyche, it's Jack Welch. Many argue that the fact that General Electric, one of the world's largest weapons manufacturers and notorious polluters, owns a network like NBC is no accident. It is, one might argue, a line of last defense. This was not the first time Welch is alleged to have used his corporate leverage to mold news coverage when it served his interests. During the 1987 stock market crash, Welch called then–*NBC News* chief Larry Grossman and told him to stop using negative language to describe the crash.* As Grossman said, "We were describing it as Black Monday and the 'plunge' . . . he thought we were making it worse and undercutting the stock value of the company."[7] Or, worse, fueling the sell-off that drove the market to the largest one-day drop in American history.

Can we really blame Welch for having such a vested interest in NBC's reporting? After all, as CEO, Jack Welch had a fiduciary responsibility to generate profits for shareholders of General Electric. It was his neck on the line, if the company didn't turn a profit. He didn't become one of America's most powerful CEOs by sitting back on his heels. Fortunately, Welch's employees at *NBC News*, the reporters who had been covering the Democrat and Republican candidates, were still bound by the journalistic ethos of objectivity and nonpartisanship. This was a point that Representative Waxman wanted to make clear in a letter written to NBC CEO Bob Wright, stating, "Mr. Welch's reported conduct in no way impugns the integrity or independence of Tom Brokaw, Tim Russert, or any other news reporters at NBC."[8]

But, as we were about to learn, there may have been other reasons to doubt the integrity and independence of one of NBC's star reporters.

---

*Less than one year after Black Monday, Larry Grossman was fired by Jack Welch.

Pin the Tail on the Elephant

Back at Sundance, the table is littered with pizza crusts and half-finished cans of soda. Intoxicated with this proximity to a former vice president, our lunch has turned into an impromptu press conference, Guerrilla News–style. Gore is starting to look tired, but he tells us we can have one more question before we go.

We want to know if there is really such a thing as media bias. Has he ever seen evidence of influential reporters themselves betraying an internal bias or agenda that would negate their professional claim to objectivity?

Gore leans in like he has a secret. In unison, we all push our heads across the table.

According to Gore, he and Bush had been invited to speak at the Al Smith Dinner a few weeks before the 2000 election. A prestigious fund-raiser held annually in New York, the event attracts a high-profile crowd, one of which was Tim Russert, moderator of *NBC News'* top-rated Sunday news program, *Meet the Press.*

As one of America's most influential, and highest-paid, broadcast journalists, Russert has interviewed every major political figure in the United States since the early 1980s. With a pugnacious face and a sharp, savvy political intellect, he is often referred to as the ultimate objective, nonpartisan interrogator. As it turns out, apparently he only plays one on TV.

At one point in the evening, Gore explains, Russert approached the candidates. As Gore was closest to him, Russert respectfully shook his hand and then moved on to Bush. Thinking that Gore had turned away, Russert shook Bush's hand and, mischievously, turned over his jacket lapel to reveal a Bush campaign pin hidden under the fold.*

---

*An *NBC News* spokeswoman flatly denied it ever happened, telling us it was an "urban myth."

There is no malice or anger in his voice. Just a modest resignation and shrug of the shoulders. Clearly this is something he has learned to accept as part of the game. A factor that could have, just as easily, played into his election campaign, had Russert been wearing a Gore–Lieberman pin. Looking back, Tim Russert—for NBC—was repeatedly the go-to guy for Bush administration officials who needed a platform to stump from, or defend themselves in a time of crisis.

For example, when George W. Bush needed to get some national face time after chief U.S. weapons inspector David Kay exposed the lie of Iraqi WMDs in February 2004, the White House chose Russert as the vehicle. Watching the rare prime-time Bush interview,* we could see why.

For over an hour, six million viewers were treated to one of the biggest journalistic letdowns of the election year.[9] With so much on the table—from the nonexistent WMDs to the Iraqi quagmire to accusations that Bush was AWOL from the National Guard—Russert could have hog-tied the president and left him twisting in the wind. Instead, he let him off easy, failing to counter Bush's dodges with obvious follow-up questions.

Even conservative *Wall Street Journal* columnist Peggy Noonan could not ignore Bush's lackluster performance, writing "[t]he president seemed tired, unsure and often bumbling. His answers were repetitive, and when he tried to clarify them he tended to make them worse. He did not seem prepared."[10]

Far be it for Noonan, a former speechwriter for Reagan and George Bush Sr., to criticize Russert for being soft on a

---

*By April 2004, Bush had given just twelve solo press conferences. At the same point in their administrations, Bill Clinton had given forty and George Bush Sr., seventy-five.

Republican president. But she did manage to imply that the questioning was less than incisive: "When [Bush] was thrown the semi-softball question on his National Guard experience—he's been thrown this question for 10 years now—he spoke in a way that seemed detached. 'It's politics.' Well yes, we know that. Tell us more." Which is what Russert should have said. But he never pushed the issue. And Bush walked through the interview unscathed.

In a way, Russert's tough-guy image provides him with the perfect cover. A day after his Bush interview, the *New York Times'* Jim Rutenberg analyzed Russert's dominance over his competitors. In the piece, titled "To Many Insiders, Russert Has Hottest Seat," Russert explained how he was able to get access to the president at such a critical time:

> *I continued to make the case that if you really want to have an opportunity for serious people across the country in the millions to listen to you and make a judgment about serious issues, you need a credible forum.*[11]

After Bush took over the White House, Russert negotiated a new, ten-year, multimillion-dollar contract. Shortly after, Jack Welch retired as CEO of General Electric.*

The Benefit of a Downward Spiral

Driving down the icy, winding road from Joel Hyatt's mountain chalet, we're emotionally and mentally spent. Gore's juicy

---

*Two years later, in October 2003, G.E. announced a merger with Vivendi Universal to create one of the world's largest media companies, with an estimated value of $43 billion.

stories of corporate manipulation and alleged journalistic bias are exactly the kind of evidence we have been seeking, but did they bring us any closer to a deeper understanding of the way that media works to obscure certain issues from the American public?

The Welch story raises important questions about corporate influence over news divisions, and how that influence breaches the "wall" that is supposed to divide them. But it does not explain how the political, social, and economic biases of corporate owners impact the news-making process on a direct, day-to-day level. If anything, it shows how nakedly they have to exploit their media properties to effectively stamp their footprint on the world.

Given Gore's account of Russert's alleged partisan bootlicking, he should not be granted the assumption of journalistic neutrality that goes along with his role as "moderator" on *Meet the Press*. But, in the end, he is only a symptom of a much larger problem. In a corporatist system, only those who play along, get along. If it wasn't Tim Russert, it would be somebody else. They're all interchangeable cogs in a mechanized system that has replaced the individual pursuit of journalistic excellence with a deceptive confidence game, where the audience is left to guess which shill is hiding the truth. This probably isn't a startling revelation for most people who get their news from the independent media. They already believe that through bias and obfuscation, the critical flow of information for an informed electorate is being filtered, polluted, or simply deflected.

As *The Washington Monthly*'s Nicholas Confessore put it, "one of the great challenges for critics of the 'corporate media' is that their arguments—which are generally thoughtful and germane—must often rest on isolated, abstract, or even hypothetical conflicts of interest."[12]

In the end, it's not about a pin on some guy's lapel. Nor is it about some rabid CEO grabbing control of his network's election desk. All those stories prove is that the media is run by rich, powerful men who like to get their way. We already know that. It's not even about elephants and donkeys and conservatives and liberals.

Breaking it down that way works fine for explaining why networks will try to sway the public's perception of this economic policy or that bill on media ownership. Or why newspapers will cover one candidate more favorably than another. But what about when journalists fail to report on issues that impact the well-being of all Americans, including themselves? How do we explain the failure of reporters to directly challenge the government on a lie, even when everyone knows they are lying? What are the forces that compel media to act monolithically, so that there is a lateral exclusion or distortion of a story that we all have a vital and democratic interest in knowing?

And so, if *the theory*—that is, that corporate media is a tool of control rather than liberation—is to have any relevance to those outside the small intellectual cabal of social theorists, media critics, and news junkie netizens, we will need to explain how it works on meta-scale, how it frames what is, and is not, allowed to be said. Whose stories are to be told and whose stories are left on the proverbial editing-room floor. We need to look deeper into this process of "framing" and ask what subtle, psychological forces are at play.

Vital Lies

In his groundbreaking book *Vital Lies*, Daniel Goleman[13] studied the psychology of self-deception as it applies to both individuals and social groups. His thesis centered on the mind's ability to "dim awareness" and create "blind spots" to prevent itself from experiencing anxiety. This process leads to a form of self-deception that affects individuals as much as the "collective awareness of the group," where there is a tacit agreement not to question those ideas or values that are considered sacred or fundamental. The overall effect is that "dissent, even healthy dissent, is stifled." This has an intriguing applicability to the way that media acts on the national psyche.

Applying Goleman's theory to the culture of news broadcasts, the parallels are fascinating, specifically the

> *notion that the mind packages information in "schemas," a sort of mental code for representing experience. Schemas operate in the unconscious, out of awareness. They direct attention toward what is salient and ignore the rest of experience—an essential task. But, when schemas are driven by the fear of painful information, they can create a blind spot in attention.*

According to Goleman, these "schemas"—which, for our purposes, can be likened to headlines or news broadcasts—are an important foundation for the "social construction of reality. Shared schemas are at work in the social realm, creating a consensual reality. This social reality is pocketed with zones of tacitly denied information. The ease with which such social blind spots arise is due to the structure of the individual mind. Their social cost is shared illusions."*

---

*While, for Goleman, the cost of distorted awareness is "shared illusions," the benefit is a sense of security that is "an organizing principle operating over many levels and realms of human life." The instinct becomes politically hazardous when our group mind uses the power of self-deception to cushion itself from anxiety, thus

Noam Chomsky would call them necessary illusions, reminding us that "it is the task of the media, and the specialized class generally, to ensure that the hypocrisy 'walks Invisible, except to God alone.'"[14]

And there is no better example of this phenomenon than in the perceptual disconnect that has been forged between America and the rest of the world. In the two short years after the September 11 terrorist attacks, America's political elite took an unprecedented degree of world sympathy and transformed it into seething anger and contempt. When Mexican soccer fans began chanting "Os-am-a, Os-am-a" during a match between their national team and the United States, it should have been an indicator something has gone seriously wrong. But, for the majority of the American public, this open display of hatred from America's southern neighbor was inexplicable, so distanced were they from any sense of how the Bush administration's actions were being interpreted beyond American borders.

Washington, D.C., peace activist John Judge sees the post-9/11 paradigm as emblematic of the media's inability to level with the American people, who were told,

> *the reason they bombed the Trade Towers and the Pentagon is that they hate us because we're a democracy. Because we're a pluralist society. Because we have an open society, and they can't stand that. Or because we're large and have a great deal of wealth. Well, if that's the case, then why aren't they bombing Canada? Canada is a pluralist,*

---

distorting our sense of reality and our ability to make informed decisions. In a democracy that thrives on information flow, a media that tacitly denies "uncomfortable truths" becomes the most powerful ally of authoritarian structures that seek to exploit them.

large society... but it has a much different foreign policy, doesn't it?

Judge and others argue that the mainstream media has become disabled by a form of mass self-denial that prevents American viewers from seeing a critical picture of who they are, which interests their government really serves, and what their nation represents to the world at large. One need look no further than the UK media's coverage of the 2000 presidential election scandal, in which Greg Palast, a BBC reporter and author of *The Best Democracy Money Can Buy*, broke the story of a racial targeting system implemented by Republican party operatives to purge black citizens from the Florida voter rolls. Reporting for the UK *Guardian* and the *Observer*, as well as the BBC, Palast showed how eighty thousand predominantly Democratic voters were disqualified from participation in the election. The *Washington Post*, a once-proud symbol of American investigative journalism, did not publish Palast's story until seven months after the election. Are we to assume it was a cover-up? Or that the *Post*'s esteemed editors simply deemed it less than relevant for their national audience? Either way, the case points to an alarming tendency for Big Media to block out uncomfortable truths, which, according to Goleman, leaves "a gap in that beam of awareness which defines our world from moment to moment." What could be more troubling to the American psyche than knowing its democratic process had been tampered with in a way that purposely disenfranchised black voters. It strikes at the core of our identity as a politically and socially evolved society.

The situation worsened after September 11, as the media rolled over and allowed a series of actions to be undertaken by the Bush administration that have had a devastating effect on the American democratic institution, as well as the delicate balance of our global geopolitical position; respectively, the passing of the USA Patriot Act and the subsequent invasion of Iraq.*

While this is certainly not a new phenomenon, where individuals and communities will subvert their interests and silence their voices in deference to power, it is something that began to happen in a more concentrated and crude way after the September 11 attacks. It was at that time, when the nation was suffering the effects of a debilitating collective trauma, comparable only to the Kennedy assassination, that many began to sense the American news media had finally lost its center of gravity altogether, becoming little more than outposts of a larger state media apparatus. As legendary blue-collar commentator Jimmy Breslin wrote, America witnessed the "the worst failure to inform the public that we have seen; the Pekingese of the press run clip-clop along the hall to the next government press conference."[15]

While it is generally understood that media will uncritically embrace the government in a time of war, few administrations have taken such ruthless advantage of the press's malleability than that of George W. Bush. Nor have they been so openly hostile and threatening to those whom they consider their enemies. Just weeks after the attacks, *Politically Incorrect* host Bill Maher offered a comparison between the U.S. military and the 9/11 terrorists, saying, "we have been the cowards lobbing cruise missiles from two thousand miles away. That's cowardly. Staying in the airplane when it hits the building, say

---

*The USA Patriot Act, which many civil rights advocates allege was drafted long before 9/11, was passed into law just six weeks after the attacks. In the heightened sense of danger and patriotic fervor, which were only intensified by an anthrax scare targeted at the Congress, mainstream media barely subjected the legislation to a basic degree of scrutiny. According to Riva Enteen, executive director of the San Francisco National Lawyer's Guild, the effect was a wholesale "shredding of 200 years of constitutional law."

what you want about it, it's not cowardly."[16] The following week, White House spokesperson Ari Fleischer responded, warning all Americans "to watch what they say, watch what they do. This is not a time for remarks like that; there never is."[17] Eight months later, ABC canceled Maher's show, citing as its reason, a decision "to go with straight entertainment programming in late night."[18]

Fleischer's ominous warning was not uncalculated. The Bush administration knew this kind of strong-arming would have a profound effect on the corporate media, which had already begun to swing right with the increasingly pro-government reportage coming from Rupert Murdoch's high-rated Fox News Channel. One of the most shocking revelations to come in the wake of the media's unprecedented, "embedded" access to the Iraq War was respected war correspondent Christiane Amanpour's admission to a practice of "self-muzzling." Speaking with Tina Brown on CNBC, Amanpour said, "My station was intimidated by the administration and its foot soldiers at Fox News. And it did, in fact, put a climate of fear and self-censorship, in my view, in terms of the kind of broadcast work we did."[19]

But the intimidation was not restricted to coverage of the war. *ABC News* star Peter Jennings was warned in advance that his story on a senior White House official "better be good." As Jennings told the *New Yorker*'s Ken Auletta, "It wasn't a threat, but it didn't sound like a joke. There is a feeling among some members of the press corps that you are either favored by the administration or not, and that will have something to do with your access."[20]

Which takes us back to Tim Russert who, as *New York* magazine's Michael Wolff explained, "was a political operative before becoming a journalist."[21] Modern media stars like Russert understand the game has changed and the key to strong journalism isn't integrity—it's proximity. Success depends on the degree of trust that can be engendered between journalists and the Washington elite they want to cover. Of Russert's skills as a reporter, Wolff does not mince words, saying, "He isn't a journalist so much as a player, a mover and shaker among the Washington set." This makes him an icon in the press domain, the one to beat. Suddenly the idea of hiding a Bush pin under his lapel doesn't seem so cheap and meretricious. He was just hedging his bets. And judging from his access to key administration officials, it paid off.

2

The Road to Shanksville

Post-traumatic Press Disorder

■ ■ ■

Did we shoot it down or did it crash?
—GEORGE W. BUSH
September 11, 2001

Shanksville, PA

"IS THIS THE PHONE NUMBER *for the Guerrilla News Network? If it is, well then, we've got some information for you.*"

The message on our cell phone is garbled and ominous. We're not sure if it's because the man's voice cuts out intermittently from bad reception, or because of the way he says *infer-may-shun*. It's our first callback since arriving in the small rural hamlet of Shanksville, Pennsylvania, but we're disappointed, nonetheless. The townspeople have not shown us their most welcoming face, and this is no exception—he hangs up before leaving a callback number.

We can't help feeling that we're lost somewhere in between the *X-Files* and *Deliverance*. We're twenty miles west of the Pennsylvania Turnpike, where barren postindustrial wastelands give way to gently sloping farmland, dotted with brown and white cows chomping on green herbicide-ridden grass.

Shanksville, population three hundred, is just like any other small American town. There is a main road, lined with double-story houses, that leads to a small intersection. At the corner is Ida's, a small convenience store that sells ice cream and flies the American flag. Next to that stands the ubiquitous red-brick firehouse complete with commemorative plaque. The only difference between Shanksville and other small towns is that on September 11, 2001, United Airlines (UA) Flight 93 crashed into an old strip-mining field just two miles from here, forever changing the character and destiny of the town and its people.

In the immediate aftermath of the 9/11 attacks, the nation went into a form of collective shock, buckling under the weight of its communal grief. We turned inward and looked up from the frail ground, seeking strength from their leaders and shelter within the authoritarian structure of the government. Those who threatened the cocoon of security were viciously attacked. Trauma proved to be a powerful inhibitor of dissenting viewpoints.*

The national media went into a state of receptive transmission. There was no room for interpretive discourse, let alone investigative reporting. They simply looped images of the falling towers and repeated whatever information was given to them by the White House and Pentagon. In the midst of the shock and grief, the story of Flight 93, in which a band of heroic passengers rose up to overcome their hijackers, became a symbol of courage and strength for a broken nation.

But as we would find out, the story of Flight 93 might have more to do with what we collectively wanted to believe than with what really happened.

---

*The phenomenon is exemplified in a letter to the U.S. military newspaper *Stars and Stripes,* which reported Rep. Barbara Lee's dissenting vote against the September 15, 2001, bill authorizing President Bush to use "all necessary and appropriate force" against anyone associated with the terrorist attacks of September 11. One frustrated reader wrote, "In times like this, is it not essential that good-hearted, right-thinking citizens not be subjected to dissenting viewpoints that could lead some to question their unblinking support of our leadership?"[1]

We walk over to Ida's and look in the window. On a wall behind the ice-cream dispenser is a display for Flight 93 paraphernalia. There are trucker hats and T-shirts emblazoned with commemorative designs that read SHANKSVILLE—FLIGHT 93, PROUD TO BE AN AMERICAN and LET'S ROLL, the universal battle cry for America's revenge on those who perpetrated the worst act of terrorism on American soil.

We hear someone shout, "Guerrilla News!" A man waving his arms in drunken disjunction motions for us to come over. We don't have much else to do, or any leads to follow, so we cross over to him. A few minutes later, we are standing in the shade of an open garage, swilling beer with three middle-aged local men. We're curious about how they were able to recognize us.

"We make it our business to know who's in town. Did you get our message?"

The town is getting even more surreal. "We did. You have some information for us?"

"Well, John might." The man nods at a burly dude with short cropped hair.

Realizing for the first time who we are talking to, we ask, "You're John Fleegle?"

He nods and downs the rest of his Bud.

It is all becoming more clear. We have been calling Fleegle for the past few days, trying to set up an interview but, until now, hadn't received a reply. He was one of the first people to arrive at the crash site that day and, as we were told by one of his coworkers, Fleegle claims to have evidence Flight 93 was shot down. But when we ask him what he knows about Flight 93, he plays coy, taunting us with the implication that he has a bombshell to share with us. "I can't talk about it now."

Unsure how to proceed with the drunken trio, we're interrupted by the arrival of a minivan. The side door slides open, revealing a pretty youngish mother and three spiky-haired boys.

"It's the boss." Fleegle turns around and smiles sheepishly. Nodding at his wife, he turns back to us with his poker face. "You can try me tomorrow."

"When?"

Fleegle gets into the minivan and shuts the door, leaving us standing with his two drunken friends. We ask them if there is anyone else in town who was an eyewitness to the crash and who might want to talk. One of them slurs, "Nobody's going to talk to a couple of journalists. They're all too busy making money off of it."

He looks up and shrugs. "Specially with the anniversary coming and all."

On September 11, 2001, United Airlines Flight 93 took off from New Jersey's Newark International Airport at 8:42 A.M., flew for fifty minutes along its route to San Francisco, then suddenly banked hard to the left, completing two ninety-degree turns, and headed toward Washington, D.C. Twenty minutes later, after a series of frantic cell-phone calls from passengers and crew alerted United Airlines and (North American Aerospace Defense Command (NORAD) to the flight's probable hijacking, New Jersey businessman Todd Beamer rallied a small band of mutineers with his legendary sign off, "Let's roll." Eight minutes later, at 10:06 A.M., Flight 93 slammed into an open field in Somerset County, narrowly missing the small town of Shanksville, Pennsylvania. Thirty-seven passengers, five flight attendants, and two pilots were dead.

In the days following 9/11, as family members began to speak about the last words they shared with loved ones, a heroic story began to develop. Deena Burnett recounted her husband's courageous declaration that, despite knowing "we're all gonna die, there's three of us who are going to do something about it." Jeremy Glick told his wife that the passengers had taken a vote to attack the hijackers. Moments later, screams could be heard on Glick's open phone line. But it was not until September 16, when reports surfaced of Todd Beamer's call to a Verizon operator, that the "hero story" became front-page news, galvanizing the mourning nation behind his famous two-word exhortation "Let's roll" before heading to the cockpit.

The next day, newspapers and television networks heralded *Let's Roll** as the post-9/11 shibboleth, cementing Flight 93's heroic legacy in the annals of national lore. In an editorial emblematic of the public sentiment, the *Pittsburgh Post-Gazette* declared, "It is fitting, and wonderfully American, that the first organized counterattack in the war against terrorism was conceived, organized and executed by a sales manager on a business trip, and others like him. Way to go Todd Beamer, Jeremy Glick, Thomas Burnett, and Mark Bingham."[2] Later that week, during President Bush's September 20 State of the Union address, Todd Beamer was mentioned in the fourth sentence. The camera cut to a pregnant, mournful Lisa Beamer sitting in the gallery.[3]

From that point on, for the mainstream media, Flight 93 was a closed book. The story provided them with a perfect antidote to an otherwise tragic debacle. It was the crucial dramatic reversal to restore national confidence and give readers, viewers, and listeners alike the kind of "feel-good feeling" that helps sell cars, Viagra, and the image of a resourceful nation bouncing back from an almost unfathomable abyss. And that is where they left it. In December 2001, *Vanity Fair* magazine said Flight 93 "may be remembered as one of the greatest tales of heroism ever told."

However, if the *New York Times*, *Dateline NBC*, or any of

*In one of the more egregious examples of commercialization of the tragedy, "Let's Roll" became the slogan for the Florida State football team for their 2002 season.

the other bastions of American journalism had sent their reporters to Shanksville, they would have found a complex story that did not fit so neatly into the heroic tale presented to them by the administration. Not everyone could accept the government's story of a last-minute midair rebellion. As it turns out, initial reports of the UA 93 crash were indecisive and seemed to hint at a bomb explosion as the cause. On the night of the September 11 attacks, the Associated Press quoted Glenn Cramer, a 911 emergency dispatcher who spoke to a frantic man from the bathroom. (The man was later identified as Edward Felt.) According to Cramer, Felt said he heard some sort of explosion and saw white smoke coming from the plane. "And we lost contact with him," said Cramer.[4]

Skeptics of the hero story find the more they study the facts, the less they believe the "official" explanation of events. On the ground near Shanksville, eyewitnesses reported the plane flying erratically before impact. One woman told local reporters she saw a fireball, smoke and then the plane "nose-diving" to the ground.[5] Another described hearing a loud bang before seeing the plane take a sharp downward turn.[6] Several more claimed to have seen the plane either "wobbling" or "flying upside down" before crashing.[7] Several eyewitnesses placed a second plane above the crash site moments after UA 93 went down.[8] While some described it as a commercial aircraft, others were sure it was a fighter jet. Adding fuel to the fire, Shanksville was abuzz with gossip of candid reports from local police officers and military families who were told UA 93 was shot down by a fighter jet.

The rumors of a shoot-down were even fueled by reports from mainstream media sources. On September 13, *ABC News* reported that a Pentagon official, when asked if Flight 93 had been shot down, replied, "We have not ruled out that."[9] Meanwhile, on the same day, the Associated Press leaked statements by a flight controller in Nashua who, in defiance of a gag order on FAA employees, claimed that an F-16 fighter jet was flying close enough to UA 93 that it had to make 360-degree turns to stay in visual range of the hijacked plane. Of his proximity to the crash, the controller said the F-16 pilot "must've seen the whole thing."[10]

These accounts, combined with reports of the plane's erratic trajectory before impact and evidence that, despite relatively light winds, debris had been scattered as far as eight miles from the crash site,[11] were enough to cause widespread speculation that Flight 93 had been "intercepted" by U.S. military aircraft. With the emerging "shoot-down" theory reaching critical mass, on September 12 NORAD was forced to issue an official denial.[12] Four days later, Vice President Dick Cheney appeared on Tim Russert's *Meet the Press* to confirm reports that President Bush had given a shoot-down order but that it had not been necessary due to the "courageous acts of those on Flight 93."[13]

Cheney's assurance was not enough to quell the conspiracy theories. In the weeks after the crash, an entire underground culture devoted to the investigation of UA 93 was formed. Relying on information gathered from mainstream news sources, government statements, and eyewitness accounts, the Flight 93 crash skeptics constructed a parallel narrative based on the possibility that the plane was shot down—a narrative more rigorously researched than the "hero story" championed by mainstream media who had simply bought the government version without any independent verification. Traditionally ridiculed and outcast by establishment journalists, suddenly the conspiracy researchers had a forum and an audience. Sites like www.flight93crash.com became primary outlets for those who did not trust the government's version of events.* For many Americans, they represented the only truth-seeking, muckraking journalistic culture left after 9/11. It was only a matter of time before the shoot-down theory would reach critical mass and crack through the facade of the mainstream media's hero story.

A "Scrappy" Paper

Will Bunch is the senior writer of the *Philadelphia Daily News.* Dressed in an oversize polo shirt, loose jeans, and running shoes worn through on the toes, Bunch is an old-school journalist who shrugs off the celebrity culture that has overtaken his industry. Walking through the busy newsroom, he describes the *Daily News* as a "scrappy paper that gives its reporters a lot of freedom, more than you might find in a larger paper, like the [*Washington*] *Post.*"

Bunch became curious about Flight 93 shortly after September 11, 2001, when a friend asked if he thought the plane had been shot down. Bunch said he had heard the rumors but not read anything convincing enough to prove the government was covering up the truth. At first he thought nothing of it, but then, after spending some time on the Internet reading the work of independent researchers and Web sites dedicated to investigating the crash, Bunch became convinced there were enough inconsistencies in the official story to warrant a trip out to Shanksville. He pitched the story to his editors, and they bit.

Sitting with his back to a large window overlooking the

---

*One of the most informative and well-organized Web sites dedicated to Flight 93. The site includes hundreds of links to mainstream and independent media reports as well as a discussion board that features posts from Shanksville residents arguing over the story.

newsroom, Bunch recalls the emotionally charged atmosphere of post-9/11 America. It was a difficult time to be a journalist, he explains, because so many of his peers had been swept up into the patriotic fervor of compliant progovernmentalism, and this affected mainstream coverage of the shoot-down story.

"I think the reason that reporters weren't exploring the possibility back in September or October of 2001 was that the government and the FBI told them it hadn't been shot down. There was something about September 11 that caused reporters to accept any statement coming out of the White House at complete face value. . . . As a journalist, it was kind of disheartening to see."

In preparation for his story, Bunch did an in-depth study of the independent research that had evolved on the Internet. He was struck by the level of factual and evidenciary analysis that had been applied to the study of Flight 93, and how clearly it illustrated the mainstream media's total blackout of the story, which relegated the story to a status of nonimportance, or sheer fantasy. It's one or the other, explains Bunch, "there is either all or nothing. Either something happened or it is called a 'conspiracy theory.' And if something is called a conspiracy theory, then by definition, it's something that didn't really happen."

But the more he studied the crash data, what little had been released to the public, the more he understood how people might suspect a massive cover-up. One of the oddities of the story was there was not much of a fire after the crash. According to Bunch, local authorities "monitored the ground water underneath it afterwards and they never really found much in the way of fuel from the aircraft."*

---

*Wallace Miller, coroner of Somerset County, made this observation of the crash site: "The interesting thing about this particular case is that I haven't, to this day,

To make his point, Bunch compares Flight 93 to the planes that crashed into the World Trade Center. In both of those cases, there was clearly tons of unevaporated jet fuel, "enough to cause the buildings to collapse and yet, you have to wonder why this dry wooded grassy area didn't catch fire with the same intensity that the WTC did."

Even more striking for Bunch was the crash's far-flung "debris field," in which papers and pieces from the aircraft were blown as far as eight miles away. One of the most cited aspects of the shoot-down theory is that a one-ton piece of the engine was found over a mile from the crash site.[15] Of the weather that day, Bunch tells of a local resident who "snapped a picture after the plane impacted and there's a big black cloud of smoke going straight up. . . . It looks like an almost windless day, so you have to wonder. . . ."

Bunch lists some of the other anomalies that made him suspicious. Chief among them was the eight-minute gap between the last cell-phone call made from the plane and the time of the crash. Emergency dispatcher Glenn Cramer lost contact with a passenger who reported an explosion on the plane at 9:58 A.M., but the aircraft did not crash until 10:06.[16] Bunch's curiosity was only magnified by the FBI's initial refusal to release data from the so-called black boxes, the Cockpit Voice Recorder (CVR) and the Flight Data Recorder (FDR). Finally, there was the sheer number of Shanksville residents who believe the plane was shot down. As Bunch explains, "it was a kind of strange phenomenon that the closer I got to Shanksville, the more people didn't believe the official story."

---

eleven months later, seen any single drop of blood. Not a drop. The only thing I can deduce is that the crash was over in half a second. There was a fireball fifteen to twenty meters high, so all of that material just got vaporized."[14]

On November 15, 2001, the *Daily News* published Will Bunch's story "We Know It Crashed, But Not Why." Though he did not make any definitive conclusions about the validity of the shoot-down theory, Bunch's article immediately became a lightning rod for online conspiracy researchers who saw vindication in the first mainstream investigation of the crash. The text became part of a massive viral e-mail campaign, attracting an even larger following to the community of Flight 93 skeptics. And while the vast majority of corporate media journalists continued to ignore the story, it eventually led to a major blip on the mainstream radar when nationally syndicated columnist Michelle Malkin cited Bunch's findings. In a March 8, 2002, article titled "Just Wondering—Unsolved Mysteries about September 11," Malkin reported,

> *Many folks in Shanksville, PA . . . believe the plane was shot down. Eyewitnesses reported seeing a small unmarked jet flying overhead immediately after the impact; others are convinced they heard the piercing sound of a missile.*[17]

A week later, Malkin appeared on Fox's *O'Reilly Factor* to defend her story. Once he had her safely secured in the No Spin Zone, Bill O'Reilly wasted no time getting down to business. Eyeing Malkin suspiciously, he asked, "Do you really believe that?"[18]

Malkin replied, "I definitely think that the question should be raised and asked. It's been more than six months, and it seems almost sacrilegious to raise questions like this, but, I mean, that's part of our job. And there's plenty of unanswered questions out there, and a lack of disclosure by the government."

Progressive media pundits have valid critiques about Bill O'Reilly and his brand of "balanced journalism." But, to his credit, O'Reilly provided the only substantive coverage of the shoot-down theory for American television audiences. As one of the top-rated news programs on cable, the *O'Reilly Factor* put a spotlight on a potentially major government cover-up. If proved, it would have been the biggest story since the 9/11 attacks, but not one other major U.S. news organization touched it. Instead, it was left to foreign journalists to expose the story to their domestic audiences.

In August 2002, the UK *Independent* sent reporter John Carlin* to Shanksville where he filed a well-researched article on the crash, ultimately predicting "the story of Flight 93 may come to acquire the morbid mystique of the Kennedy assassination."[19] One month later, the UK *Mirror*'s Richard Wallace reported from Shanksville, where George Bush was present for the one-year anniversary of the tragedy.[20] In a broad investigation of the crash, Wallace determined that much of it was still a mystery and the president "was one of only a handful of people who know what really happened to the 40 innocents and four hijackers aboard the doomed United Airlines Boeing 757-200."

On September 16, 2002, while Lisa Beamer's *Let's Roll* was riding the *New York Times* best-seller list, Will Bunch broke another story questioning the official story about the crash. Working from government-prepared transcripts of the Cockpit Voice Recorder, he compared the time the tape went silent, 10:03 A.M., to seismic data that confirmed the time of the crash at 10:06 A.M.[21] Since the CVR typically stops on impact, and cases for electrical failure are rare, the three-minute discrepancy indicates a potential loss of information about the fi-

---

*In John Carlin's story for the *Independent*, he wrote, "The shortage of available facts did not prevent the creation of an instant legend—a legend that the US government and the US media were pleased to propagate, and that the American public have been eager, for the most part, to accept as fact."

nal moments of Flight 93. In Bunch's report for the Daily News, he reported "the FBI and other agencies refused repeated requests to explain the discrepancy."

On the Internet, this report fueled more speculation that the FBI had scrubbed or manipulated the tapes to cover up the evidence of a shoot-down. In the mainstream media, there was again no mention of it, at least not until over eighteen months later, when Gail Sheehy included the data in her February 2004 report on the 9/11 widows for the New York Observer. Like shouting into an echo chamber, Sheehy asked the now-rhetorical questions, "Did a U.S. fighter shoot down Flight 93? And why all the secrecy surrounding that last flight?"[22] For Bunch, the answer has become obvious.

The plane being shot down, who wants to hear that story? In my mind the possibility that Flight 93 was shot down is an incredible story. But on the other hand, in the minds of a lot of people, TV producers, magazine editors, this story that emerged instead, of heroism by the passengers, is a re-markable story. It's been the basis of two best-selling books, it was featured on Dateline NBC, *several of the top news-magazine shows.*

Bunch leans forward in his chair and does his best impression of a network television producer, "We have a *great* story here! Why would we want to muck around and mess it up with a *different* story when people *like* this story?" Leaning back, he resumes his contemplative posture, "I think to come out now and say that 'Let's roll' is meaningless—I don't think people could handle that."

Bunch is describing a behavioral pattern elaborated by the social psychologist Leon Festinger in his theory on cognitive dissonance. Writing in 1957, Festinger described cognitive dissonance as the traumatic mental state in which people "find themselves doing things that don't fit with what they know, or having opinions that do not fit with other opinions they hold."[23] It was his belief that the avoidance characteristic of this state was as natural to human beings as the need to find food and shelter. Perhaps the mainstream media's obfuscation and denial of the Flight 93 shoot-down theory has as much to do with an instinctual drive for order and familiarity as with a need to placate their government masters. Once the conventional wisdom was set, they simply could not fathom its alternative reality.

Down the Rabbit Hole

It's a beautiful morning as we drive into Shanksville. We're about three hours early for our meeting with John Fleegle, which is fine, because we have also arranged to meet Ernie Stuhl, Shanksville's mayor, at the Flight 93 Memorial that has been constructed at the crash site. Despite the early hour, people are out in their front yards, sitting in lawn chairs hawking Flight 93 paraphernalia.

About two miles from town, we turn right onto a gravel road and drive over a hill that drops into a gently sloping valley. It's hard to ignore the aura of solemn gravity that hangs over the site. The feeling is simultaneously tragic and anticlimactic. Apart from the simple memorial display and makeshift parking lot to its left, all that remains of the crash is a pile of dirt near the edge of a sparsely wooded forest. We can't help thinking, it's an excellent place to put down an airplane.

The memorial is a somber place. Winds gust intermittently through the valley, ruffling hundreds of little American flags pinned to the three-panel wall that serves as a shrine to the memory of those lost in the crash of Flight 93. Visitors walk meekly past, reading notes written by people from all over the world. At the far corner, a group of people are listening to an elderly man who is tracing a line in the sky with his finger, showing the path of the plane before it crashed. Seeing us approach, the mayor nods and excuses himself from the group.

In his late seventies, Ernie Stuhl has lived in Shanksville all his life, and he talks in the slow drawl of an elder rural statesman.

We have been greatly anticipating our interview with Mayor Stuhl. When Will Bunch came out to Shanksville to write his article, Stuhl was one of the first people he met. And though he aggressively disavowed the notion of a shoot-down, Stuhl simultaneously fueled the conspiracy theory, saying "I know of two people—I will not mention names—that heard a missile. They both live very close, within a couple of hundred yards. . . . This one fellow's served in Vietnam and he says he's heard them, and he heard one that day."[24]

But when we ask him about the shoot-down theory, he glares at us. "Sure, there are stories like that floating around. Yeah, I've heard that the plane was shot down. No, it wasn't."

We prod him, quoting eyewitness reports of a second plane in the sky directly after the crash. Stuhl looks at us with weary eyes, like someone who has been asked the same question one too many times. "The word we got was that the fighter planes that were sent to shoot it down were at least two minutes from Shanksville when it crashed. And two minutes don't seem like long when you fly at the speed that they do, but that's what they said."

With that Stuhl excuses himself, citing a bad back. We want to ask him more questions but decide not to press our luck. When it comes to theories on the crash of Flight 93,

Shanksville is a community divided. Stuhl's version of the story directly contradicts that of three high-school students we met the day before who said "ten seconds" after the crash, "a big fighter plane came and flew right over the school." Epitomizing the deep divisions in the town, each of the three kids offered a totally different opinion about the crash—with one believing the hero story, a second the shoot-down theory, and the third citing a combination of both, in which a jet shot down Flight 93 as passengers mounted a rebellion.

With time to kill, we drive a few miles down the road to Jim and Linda Shepley's house. Linda Shepley is one of the few eyewitnesses to see Flight 93 in the final moments before it crashed. It is still something she remembers vividly. Sitting under the shaded roof of her front porch, holding a small lap dog in her arms, she tells us about that morning.

I had taken the last load of clothes outside to hang them up, and I thought I heard a noise in the sky. I looked up and saw an airplane and I thought, "What's up with this plane? Is something wrong with it?" It was lower than normal, and the flight path, it was not [like] any other airplane that I've seen. And then, all of a sudden, it made a turn. And just as soon as it turned, it went down.

When we ask her if she saw the second plane reported by other eyewitnesses, Shepley shakes her head. "No. They said there was a Learjet that went down to see the crash—but I didn't see it. I watched for a few minutes, but I really didn't see it." She is indignant at the suggestion of a shoot-down.

A lot of people said it was shot down, and I said, "Did you see the plane actually fly over?" They said "No," and I said, "Then how can you say that plane was shot down? I stood there and I watched that plane go out. If it was shot down, there would be debris falling from it, there would have been a ball of fire, there would be some indication that that plane was shot down."

Twenty minutes later, we're racing back toward Shanksville for our much-anticipated meeting with John Fleegle. So far, we haven't gathered much groundbreaking evidence from the townspeople and, after hearing his promises of a bombshell tip on the crash, we are eager to get something on record. When we arrive, Fleegle is working on the back lot of his property, dragging wood into a bonfire with his wife, Lynette. Their three sons hover around, listening as their father recounts his story.

Fleegle is a manager at the Indian Lake Marina, which is approximately 1.5 miles from the crash site. He remembers standing around the television with the rest of the staff, watching the WTC Towers billowing smoke over New York City. Suddenly, Fleegle explains, "the lights flickered in the building. About that time we heard the engine roar and we took off out of the building. As we were coming up from the office, the ground shook and we heard a big boom. Then we saw the big ball of fire up in the air."

Fleegle immediately jumped into his pickup and "followed the fire and smoke" until he found the crash site. Driving with two of his coworkers on the bed of his truck, Fleegle remembers they were getting hit by debris all the way, another indication there may have been substantial damage to the plane before it crashed. They arrived "before any fireman or paramedics or anybody. When we got there, there was a plane flying up above and he was smart, he flew straight for the sun so you couldn't look at it and see exactly what type of plane, if it was a fighter or what it was."

Despite the pilot's maneuvering, Fleegle claims that he could tell that the plane "was decent sized. It wasn't just a little private jet or something like that, from what we could see."

When we ask him about his evidence of the shoot-down, Fleegle tells us a story about being in Atlanta for a training course last winter. After introducing himself to the rest of the class, some expressed curiosity about the crash of Flight 93. According to Fleegle, as soon as he told them about the lights in the marina flickering before impact, a man sitting nearby stopped him. Explaining that he was a retired air force officer, the man told Fleegle, "That plane was shot down."

When Fleegle asked how he knew, the man replied, "Well, when your lights flickered, [it was because] they zap the radar frequency on everything before they shoot. Your lights didn't flicker from the impact—your lights flickered because they zapped the radar system before they shot it."*

Fleegle smiles triumphantly. Behind him, his kids start to fidget. Somehow his story doesn't feel like the kind of bombshell evidence he had promised us back at the garage when we first found him guzzling beers. We ask if he knows anyone who saw the plane get shot down. Fleegle nods, adding:

> But he changed his story. There was one person who worked out where the plane crashed. I heard it from friends of his, some other people talking [that] at first he said that it was definitely shot down. But as soon as he said it was shot

---

*To vet Fleegle's story, we contacted Buck Kernan, a retired four-star general who consulted CBS during the Iraq War. Kernan told us, "In answer to your question regarding an aircraft engaging an airborne target having an electrical disruption on the ground, no, this would not be a result of lock on or any electromagnetic pulsing. It is possible that overpressure from explosions could momentarily disrupt microwave connections or cause sensations on ground relays, wiring, et cetera, that might result in the conditions you describe."

*down, the FBI took him and had him all day. And when
he got out that night, his story was changed.*

Fleegle is referring to Lee Purbaugh, who was working at
the garbage dump that looks over the valley where Flight 93
went down. As the closest eyewitness to the crash, Purbaugh
was interviewed by every major media source covering the
story. It was his account of the crash that became the dominant version presented to the American public. Intrigued by
Fleegle's allegation, we make the short trip over to Somerset
to meet him.

Purbaugh remembers the day vividly. The first thing he
tells us is that the plane crashed on its own. "That plane was
not shot down. It was coming over more or less the height the
trees, coming over the top of my head, I could see everything
on the plane."

When we ask him about the second aircraft, Purbaugh
nods. "I seen it immediately as I was running down. I looked
up and said, 'Oh no, not another one.'"

But, as Purbaugh explains, it turned out the plane was doing circles trying to locate the precise location of UA 93. This
is the official explanation of the second plane,* verbatim.
Next, we ask Purbaugh if he was approached by FBI or law enforcement after the crash, he nods affirmatively. But when we
push the issue, asking if they fed him any information about
the incident, he shakes his head and quietly says, "No."

Once we finish, Lee Purbaugh's behavior becomes erratic.
Purbaugh's wife takes him aside, and they begin to talk in

---

*What no government source has explained is why a private jet was still flying
forty minutes after the FAA grounded all aircraft in the continental United States.
Additionally, there is no official record of who owned the private jet.

hurried, hushed tones. As we are getting into the car, Purbaugh comes back over and asks us for some identification, to
prove that we are journalists. Unsure of the effect it will have,
we show him our GNN cards. He nods at us, looks back at his
wife, and then says good-bye.

As the single most referenced witness to the crash of Flight
93, Lee Purbaugh represents the linchpin of the hero story.
Without another credible eyewitness who was as close as he
was to the crash, the validity of the shoot-down theory is
shaky at best. We had exhausted all our contacts, and it was
beginning to look as if there would be no conclusive challenge
to the official version. Just as we were about to leave Shanksville, we got a call from a person whose story rivaled anything
we had heard so far. A caregiver for special-needs children, Su-
san McElwain was driving home just before the crash when an
aircraft flew directly over her car. Of all the townspeople we
interviewed, McElwain was the least opiniated about the
"truth" of Flight 93. Ironically, she may hold the key to un-
locking the mystery.

It's late afternoon. McElwain is retracing her steps from the
morning of 9/11 and explaining the series of bizarre events that
occurred in the moments before and after the crash. Rolling
down her window, she slows the car and points toward a de-
serted intersection.

"When I got up here, almost to the stop sign, this small
white plane went over top of me, barely missing the van."

At first McElwain could only get a quick glimpse because it
flew directly over her. "I saw it first, that belly, it was tubular.
Then I ducked."

But then, after it passed, she was able to get a better look at
it. She describes the plane as small, without any visible markings. "I'm looking at the fin, or the spoiler. I was looking at
that and it was as wide as, or almost as wide as, the van. Then

it just banked to the right and went over and went down behind those trees."

McElwain gets out of the car and walks over to the stop sign.

"And after it went over top of me, I thought, 'That plane is gonna crash,' and I said it like two times because I remember saying it out loud. Then I saw the big plume of smoke; so [I thought] it had crashed."

Convinced that she had just witnessed the downing of a small commercial plane, McElwain left her car at the intersection and rushed to the nearest home to call 911. It was there that she first heard about the terrorist attacks on the World Trade Center and the Pentagon. But it wasn't until later that afternoon, when she returned home and turned on the television, that she realized the crash she had witnessed was connected to the planes in New York and Washington.

"We got to watching it on TV, and they kept saying it was a large plane, like a 757. And I was like, 'No what I saw was like a little jet . . . a big jet would have blown me off the road, being that close.'"

She then did some calculations and realized that the direction the small plane had flown was not the same as that being described for Flight 93:

So I said to my husband, "Will you go up and tell the police that I had seen another plane, if they wanted to come and talk to me about it." So at about 11:30 that night, the FBI came and wanted to talk to me. They kept asking me how big the plane was, and I said it was small, that it wasn't much bigger than my van that I saw. That it went over top of me, and he said, "You don't know what a 757 looks like." And I said, "Don't be condescending towards me. If you don't want to believe me, that's fine, but I thought I should report what I saw. You ought to know there was something

*else in the air at the same time this was going on. We want
to make sure it was ours and not somebody else's." And
that's when he did seem to get a little nicer. Told me that it
was a white Learjet. Somebody was taking pictures. And I
said, "Before the crash?" and he says, "Well, we've got to
go," and that was the end of it.*

Since 9/11, McElwain has told her story to law-enforcement
officials, the FBI, and several reporters. The only American
journalist to cover her story was Jeff Pillets from the *Bergen
Record*, a small paper in northern New Jersey. McElwain was
one of five people Pillets interviewed for a September 14,
2001, story titled "In a rural hamlet, the mystery mounts."

McElwain is not sure why the media have ignored her story.
But she does have a theory about the government. "Why
doesn't the government want to know? Maybe because they
know and they just don't want us to know."

The Making of a Legend

There will never be a public hearing or government inquiry
about the fate of Flight 93, because unlike every other major
airplane crash in modern history, Flight 93 was not given a
National Transportation Safety Board (NTSB) investigation.
Considering this was the most tragic hijacking since the beginning of American commercial aviation, this was a very unusual development.

Vern Grose is a former NTSB member and one of America's most respected air-disaster analysts. A regular contributor
to the major networks, he was called to Fox News Channel the
morning of September 11 and was on-air when Flight 93 went
down in Pennsylvania. Grose acknowledges the process of

investigating the crash was "fairly unique in the way it was handled."

Grose's wall is covered with pictures of airplanes and Ronald Reagan, who appointed him to the NTSB. A massive cast-iron eagle sits on his desk. He explains:

> *First of all, after any aircraft crash, the NTSB launches what they call a "go team" within two hours and that go team will have up to twelve people on it. Specialists in airframe, in engines, in electronics, in human factors. And these folks all go to the scene—they isolate the scene. From that point on, it's the NTSB's responsibility. In this particular case, it's my understanding that it did not occur exactly like that. They may have launched an NTSB crew, but it never took the same course a normal investigation would have.*

According to the NTSB, none of the four 9/11 plane crashes has been given a formal investigation due to the fact they were "criminal acts," and thus placed under the jurisdiction of the FBI. Grose is highly critical of that answer, saying that though the NTSB statute states the leadership of the investigation will defer to the FBI, the NTSB has still completed formal investigations into crashes deemed criminal acts. One example he gives is that of Egypt Air 990, in which a pilot crashed the plane in an apparent suicide attempt. Given the seriousness of the 9/11 crashes, Grose describes the absence of any credible investigation as "unacceptable."

Despite his proximity to the Washington establishment, Grose is not afraid to describe the "heavy political and public pressures" that have influenced the handling of Flight 93. Grose hints at the possibility of external influences that have put the investigation of Flight 93 beyond the potential of realization.

I doubt the NTSB will release a report on 93 much like they've done on others, because this is in a class all by itself. We want the NTSB to be objective. We want the people to trust the U.S. government. But people are people are people, and wherever they are—whether they're in government or industry or business or whatever—they can be pushed, unfortunately.

While he does not rule out the possibility of a shoot-down, Vern Grose does not interpret the unprecedented dismissal of an NTSB investigation into the crash of Flight 93 as a cover-up, either. Rather, for him it is indicative of the nation's need to preserve a national legend that has "built up around this particular crash, that didn't build up over the Pentagon or over either of the towers in New York."

The mainstream media coverage of Flight 93 points to a troubling possibility: Journalists may have chosen to obscure or spin the story because of economic, political, or ideological reasons.

The official story of Flight 93 is an inspiring account of American heroism and wherewithal on a day that saw the rest of the country rendered impotent and defenseless. If the public would rather buy into a myth that has less factual basis than the reality, which is potentially more frightening, that is their choice. But if the news media, who are the primary conduit for information that fuels the democratic process, engages in the same practice of self-deception, then we are facing a crisis. No matter how difficult the truth may be, society depends on journalists not to shrink away from the difficult questions, especially those that challenge our national myths and legends.

Selling September 11

9/11 Was a Smash Hit, but Was It the Real Thing?

■ ■ ■

It is a reflex that springs from the survival instinct: protecting your own "reality" seems to be crucial for survival. The "norm" holds our values to be stable and a cult movie sends shocks to the very foundations that society is built upon, like an earthquake.
—*IDN* magazine

THE STORY FOR 9/11 had all the makings of a multimillion-dollar blockbuster film. An innocent nation heading back to work on a sunny Tuesday morning. An evil, cave-dwelling villain who hatches a brilliant plot that breaks through the world's most technologically advanced military defenses. Apocalyptic destruction that rivals any Bruckheimer disaster movie. But, like all great Hollywood films, 9/11 had its uplifting second act. Everyday heroes fighting back against all odds. A humble president who rises to lead his country out of its darkest hour, warning rogue nations, "You are either with us or against us."

This blockbuster, packaged for mass consumption by the mainstream media, transformed the presidency of George W. Bush who, before 9/11, had been presiding over what looked to be a one-term administration. In the period before the terrorist attacks, Bush was increasingly being held up for ridicule by the mainstream media. His job approval rating was at 51 percent, the lowest of his tenure.[1] Ten days later, as Bush embraced the nation as a "war president," it reached 90 percent, a record for an American president.[2] Overnight, his timid, monosyllabic stammering took on the air of authority that Americans seek in their leaders.

Two days after the attacks, Bush made a televised phone call to New York City mayor Rudy Giuliani and New York governor George Pataki. Speaking from the Oval Office, Bush articulated the mission that would later come to define his presidency. "Make no mistake about it, my resolve is steady and strong about winning this war that has been declared on America." In a short press conference after the call, Bush characterized the terrorists' motives for attacking the United States, saying, "These people can't stand freedom; they hate our values; they hate what America stands for."[3] These words would become his mantra in the months following 9/11.

For many on the left, this interpretation of the terrorist's raison d'être is a dangerous oversimplification of a complex sociopolitical legacy. It typifies the failure of the American public to grasp the consequences of a half century of unchecked imperial aggression and exploitation of weaker, less self-reliant nations, as well as the corporate media's complicit parroting of the economic and political elite's revisionist propaganda. As the United States moved onto a war footing, this perspective became the frame through which the progressive and establishment left media critiqued the Bush administration's vengeful, knee-jerk reaction to the attacks.

LIHOP

There is another, even more skeptical group of Americans, for whom 9/11 and Bush's rapid military response signals a more underhanded and nefarious reality, delivering an all-too-providential justification for the neoconservative American leadership to position its military in the geostrategically vital nations of Afghanistan and Iraq. They see the blockbuster version of 9/11 as a well-choreographed fiction, camouflaging a dark legacy of ties between U.S. intelligence agencies and the terrorist network responsible for the attacks. They trace a pattern of unheeded warnings about the potential of a widescale terrorist attack, which indicates that if the administration was not complicit in 9/11, it had at least allowed it to happen. In the subculture of America's media underground, an alternative narrative has been constructed to explain the events of 9/11, one that plays more like a cult horror film than the big-budget blockbuster being sold to the American public.

Like *The Rocky Horror Picture Show* or *Texas Chainsaw Massacre*, the cult version of 9/11 never hit the mainstream. Attracting a devoted fan base, it gained popularity slowly through a network of like-minded fans who held a basic distrust for the superficial trappings of the mainstream account that played through the corporate news. Unlike Todd Beamer, Donald Rumsfeld, and George W. Bush, who are the stars of the blockbuster film, the cult version of 9/11 features a cast of characters who emerge from the dark netherworld of alternative research, claiming to have indisputable proof that the official version is a complex lie being used to further American imperial aspirations. Of these, perhaps none is as well known as Michael Ruppert, a former Los Angeles police officer who became one of the Internet's most prolific independent researchers after 9/11.

Using his popular Web site, From the Wilderness, as a platform, Ruppert began to publish controversial investigative articles just hours after the terrorist attacks. Viral messages about Ruppert's work drove huge traffic to stories linking Osama bin Laden to the CIA, suggesting records of insider trading that netted huge profits for investors who had fore-knowledge of the attacks, and attributing the true source of Bush's War on Terrorism to a phenomenon called "peak oil," which asserts that global oil production has peaked and will subsequently decrease, driving prices up and instigating a trans-global race to claim and protect oil reserves. Less than two weeks after the 9/11 attacks, Ruppert told us, "I absolutely be-lieve, at this moment, that the United States government had foreknowledge of the attacks and allowed them to occur."

For mainstream America, this assertion is preposterous, even dangerous. The months following 9/11 were a fragile time for the American psyche. Flags were waving from nearly every window, and dissent of any form, whether against the planned invasion of Afghanistan or America's support of the World Trade Organization, was considered unpatriotic. But Ruppert's essential thesis was one familiar to many in the un-derground media. It eventually became known by its acronym, LIHOP, or Let It Happen On Purpose.

Naturally, there are various interpretations of the level of government complicity in the terrorist plot. Some of the more extreme conspiracy theorists claim the planes had not been flown by hijackers but, instead, by remote flight control de-vices installed in large commercial aircraft, ironically, to re-cover them from hijackings. Others argue that the WTC towers were demolished with explosives, not from the impact of the two planes. While still another faction contends the Pentagon was hit by a missile,* not a commercial aircraft. These theories go on and on. But there are also moments of

---

*In *The Horrifying Fraud*, French author Thierry Meyssan claimed the Pentagon was not hit by a plane, but by a guided missile fired on orders of far right-wingers inside the United States government. The book rode the best-seller list in France for a short time after its publication.

eerie clarity and historical precedent. One fixture of the 9/11 cult movie circuit is Alex Jones, the Texas-based radio and television broadcaster who is one of the more charismatic figures in the conspiracy underground. With his raucous Southern accent, Jones comes off like a sonic doppelgänger for conservative radio host Rush Limbaugh. In *Waking Life*, indie filmmaker Richard Linklater's animated feature film, a red-faced Jones drives through an urban wasteland, barking antiestablishment slogans from loudspeakers on top of his car. At one point, the cartoon Jones yells, "What a bunch of garbage: liberal, Democrat, conservative, Republican. It's all there to control you! Two sides of the same coin. Two management teams bidding for control, the CEO job of Slavery, Incorporated!"

Alex Jones does not shy away from absolutist statements about fascistic elites. As he told us, "Governments always get caught engaging in terrorist attacks against their own populations to rally them for war or for domestic crackdown." His take on 9/11 is that it was engineered from within the U.S. government as a "modern-day Reichstag fire," referring to the blaze set by Nazis to give reason for martial law in Germany. Jones sees a historical pattern at work that traces back to the Spanish-American war, when, he alleges, William McKinley's navy blew up an American ship in Havana harbor to use as a pretext for war with the Spanish government.*

Jones is also quick to cite newly released documents proving the American military had intercepted Japanese communiqués regarding their imminent attack on Pearl Harbor. Some believe that President Franklin Delano Roosevelt may have provoked the Japanese and then allowed the attacks to

---

*While historians believe the Spanish had nothing to do with the explosion, whether it was merely an accident that was exploited by the United States or something more sinister, as Jones claims, is still hotly debated.

happen, knowing the outrage would create public support for U.S. participation in World War II.* There's more.

Sitting in his Austin television studio, Alex Jones is in his element. "One of the best examples we have of the U.S. government planning terrorist attacks against its own institutions is the Northwoods Document. This is a confirmed admitted document declassified just a few years ago."

In *Body of Secrets*, his best-selling exposé of the National Security Agency, author James Bamford revealed a harebrained scheme by a group of top U.S. military officials to frame Fidel Castro by committing acts of terrorism in the United States. The plan, code-named Operation Northwoods, was conceived by Gen. Lyman Lemnitzer, head of the Joint Chiefs of Staff under President John F. Kennedy, as a means of tricking the American public into supporting a war against Cuba. Among its various recommendations, Northwoods called for innocent people to be shot on American streets, a wave of violent terrorism to be launched in Washington, D.C., and for a U.S. ship to be blown up in Guantánamo Bay.

Alex Jones nods at us and closes the deal. "And they say in the Northwoods Document: 'Casualty lists in U.S. newspapers would cause a helpful wave of indignation.' We certainly saw a helpful wave of indignation after September 11!"

Another popular star in the cult film version of 9/11 is William Rivers Pitt, who edits Truthout.com. In one of the first major articles written about LIHOP, Pitt deconstructed the theory's foundation and its most alienating principle. "At the core of the LIHOP Theory lies motivation—what possible purpose could be served by the Bush administration allowing

---

*Author Robert Stinnett spent sixteen years reviewing more than 200,000 documents released by the navy. In his book *Day of Deceit*, he presents evidence that he suggests shows that FDR knew the Japanese were coming but did nothing to warn the naval officers at Pearl Harbor. Other historians have discounted the claims.

a terrorist attack to take place on American soil? It is flatly inconceivable to most Americans that Bush and his people could demonstrate such callous disregard for American lives, and accusations that they allowed an attack to happen reek of the worst kind of poisonous partisan politics."

But for Michael Ruppert it has nothing to do with politics. He sees it as a strategy that has been developed over successive administrations. Talking about the invasion of Afghanistan, he explains, "This war was coming for a long time."

To prove his point, Ruppert holds up a book written in 1997 by Zbigniew Brzezinski, former national security adviser to the Carter administration and cofounder of the Trilateral Commission. Titled *The Grand Chessboard: American Primacy and Its Geo-Strategic Imperatives*, the book is one of the cornerstones to Ruppert's LIHOP theory. Fingering a worn copy of Brzezinski's book, Ruppert points to the underlined text, "In three specific places in this book, he says that the key to America's control of the world in the 21st century is the control of Eurasia."

In *The Grand Chessboard*, Brzezinski claims that after the collapse of the Soviet Union, America became the world's "first truly global power" whose "global primacy" would be dependent on its ability to control the Eurasian continent. To support this assertion, Brzezinski elaborates, "A power that dominates Eurasia would control two of the world's three most advanced and economically productive regions and about three-fourths of the world's known energy resources."

According to Brzezinski, the problem with America is it's "too democratic at home to be autocratic abroad." This is a key point for Ruppert. He sees in Brzezinski's writing a "protofascist aspiration" to manufacturing the right conditions for public compliance with what Brzezinski calls the "external projection of American power." Piecing together a series of selected quotes, Ruppert builds on Brzezinski's thesis.

> *What he's saying is that without an attack on the order of Pearl Harbor or without a direct external threat, there was no way that the American people would support the "imperial mobilization" necessary to control central Asia. And in this book, Brzezinski had a map of where the next world conflict was going to be, and you look at this map in the book and it is exactly where we are fighting now.*

Brzezinski didn't advocate Eurasian war—in fact, he's criticized the war in Iraq—but his book eerily predicts what has happened since 2001.

Other LIHOP theorists, or "9/11 skeptics"—as they prefer to be called, offer more recent, and direct, evidence of the Bush administration's naked ambition to control Eurasia's abundant resources, specifically the oil wells of the Middle East. The "U.S. National Energy Policy Report of 2001," authored by Vice President Dick Cheney, formerly CEO of Halliburton, which still pays him a yearly "deferred" salary of nearly $200,000 a year, recommended a priority on "easing U.S. access to Persian oil supplies." Published four months before the 9/11 attacks, the report does not make clear the administration's strategy for achieving that goal. However, in a report submitted to Cheney in April 2001, the Council on Foreign Relations (CFR) *makes clear* the vital America interest in shaping the destiny of the region.

> *Americans face long-term energy delivery challenges and volatile energy prices. . . . As the 21st century opens, the energy sector is in critical condition. A crisis could erupt at any time from any number of factors and would in-*

*evitably affect every country in today's globalized world.
While the origins of a crisis are hard to pinpoint, it is clear
that energy disruptions could have a potentially enormous
impact on the U.S. and the world economy, and would affect U.S. national security and foreign policy in dramatic
ways. . . . The world is currently precariously close to utilizing all of its available global oil production capacity. . . . The American people continue to demand plentiful
and cheap energy without sacrifice or inconvenience.*[4]

And while it would not require a conspiratorial mind-set to
understand how the Cheney and CFR reports may have impacted the Bush administration's foreign policy objectives,
specifically in their approach to Iraq and Afghanistan, it is a
long cry from the LIHOP claim that they conspired to allow
the 9/11 attacks to occur. William Rivers Pitt acknowledges
that "LIHOP is, of course, the purest breed of conspiracy theory, involving high-ranking members of government from
both parties, as well as the CIA, FBI, and NSA." But Pitt admits, "like all good conspiracy theories, LIHOP is surrounded
by disturbing facts and bits of evidence that are difficult to
ignore."[5]

Actionable Intelligence

During the 2004 National Commission on Terrorist Attacks
hearings (also known as the 9/11 Commission), as more and
more information regarding the government's level of awareness and failure to act before 9/11 came to light, it became increasingly clear that some of LIHOP's conspiracy theories
were being held up as irrefutable truths.

One of the pivotal aspects of the 9/11 blockbuster is that

the government could not have predicted terrorists would use airplanes as weapons of mass destruction. The myth was crystallized by National Security Adviser Condoleezza Rice in May 2002 when she told reporters, "I don't think anybody could have predicted that these people . . . would try to use an airplane as a missile, a hijacked airplane as a missile."[6] However, this may be the most disputable facet of the official story. As it turns out, the administration had ample warning and opportunity to prepare for the attacks. Reports of terrorists planning to use planes as missiles began to surface seven years before 9/11. Looking back chronologically, the first warning came in 1994 when French commandos killed a group of Algerian hijackers on the tarmac in Marseilles. Their plan: to crash an Air France flight into the Eiffel Tower.[7] Then came "Operation Bojinka," uncovered by Philippine authorities after the capture and interrogation of would-be terrorist Abdul Hakim Murad in 1995.[8] Following a suspicious explosion in his Manila apartment, Murad admitted to a plot to crash a small plane rigged with explosives into the CIA headquarters in Langley, Virginia. He also confessed to being part of a larger plan to blow up eleven American airliners simultaneously over the Pacific Ocean. Less than a year later, U.S. officials banned planes from flying within a three-mile radius of the 1996 Olympic Games during events because of the potential danger of terrorists using small aircraft as missiles.[9]

Then, in 1999, a report prepared for the National Intelligence Council warned that terrorists might hijack and "crash-land an aircraft packed with high explosives" into government targets.[10] The report noted that Ramzi Yousef, an al Qaeda operative first arrested in the Philippines in 1995 and later convicted in the 1993 World Trade Center bombing, had talked specifically of a suicide jetliner mission: "Suicide bomber(s) belonging to al-Qaida's Martyrdom Battalion could crash-land an aircraft packed with high explosives (C-4 and Semtex) into the Pentagon, the headquarters of the Central Intelligence Agency, or the White House." One year later, in October 2000, the government staged mock rescue exercises, preparing for a scenario in which a plane was crashed into the Pentagon.[11]

But it was not until the first half of 2001 that warnings specific to the 9/11 terrorist operation began to flow into U.S. intelligence agencies, many originating from foreign services, including Jordan, Russia, Germany, Egypt, and Italy. Most significantly, the German daily *Frankfurter Allgemeine Zeitung* (FAZ) reported that, at least three months before 9/11, German agents warned the CIA that "Middle Eastern terrorists were planning to hijack commercial aircraft to use as weapons to attack important symbols of American culture."[12] And in July 2001, responding to reports from Egyptian intelligence, the G8 Summit in Genoa, Italy, was ringed with antiaircraft missiles because of warnings that terrorists might attempt to kill President Bush and other leaders "by crashing an airliner" into the Summit.[13] Finally, and most directly, it was revealed by the *Washington Post* that just one month before the 9/11 attacks, "President Bush and his top advisers were informed by the CIA . . . that terrorists associated with Osama bin Laden had discussed the possibility of hijacking airplanes."*[14]

If the administration did not take the intelligence seriously enough to actively prevent the loss of civilian lives, certain of their officials made sure to protect their own. *Newsweek* re-

---

*When reports of the now-infamous August 6, 2001, Presidential Daily Briefing (PDB) first surfaced, they caused a minor scandal in Congress, with some senators calling for a bipartisan commission to investigate the intelligence breakdown on 9/11. In response, Vice President Dick Cheney warned his "Democratic friends in Congress . . . to be very cautious not to seek political advantage by making incendiary suggestions, as were made by some today, that the White House had advance information that would have prevented the tragic attacks of 9/11." He called such criticism "thoroughly irresponsible . . . in time of war."[15]

ported that on September 10, "a group of top Pentagon officials suddenly canceled travel plans for the next morning, apparently because of security concerns."[16] But they were not
the only ones who received advance warning about the dangers of flying. Author Salman Rushdie, who is the target of a
fatwa (an Islamic legal decree) issued by former Iranian leader
Ayatollah Khomeini, said he believed that U.S. authorities
knew of the imminent attacks when they "banned him from
taking internal flights a week before the attacks."[17] San Francisco mayor Willie Brown, who was scheduled to fly to New
York on September 11, was slightly more cryptic about his advance knowledge. Brown told media he received a phone call
from his "security people at the airport," cautioning him
about risks to air travelers.[18] The next morning he woke to the
apocalyptic image of New York's Twin Towers crumbling to
the ground.

For advocates of the LIHOP theory, the sheer volume of
information being funneled into U.S. intelligence agencies
prior to 9/11 is proof that the administration knew the attacks were coming and did everything in their power either to
ignore the intelligence reports or, if that failed, thwart the
earnest and patriotic individuals who tried to warn their superiors about an imminent, catastrophic strike. While this logic
never translated to a credible theory in the corporate media,
there was a steady procession of whistle-blowers who brought
the issue of prior warning to the forefront of the national
consciousness, and to the front pages of every newspaper in
America.

On May 21, 2002, Minneapolis-based FBI agent Coleen
Rowley sent the now-famous *j'accuse* memo to FBI director
Robert Mueller, lambasting the FBI hierarchy for obstructing
the investigation of the so-called twentieth hijacker, Zacarias
Moussaoui, who was arrested in August 2001 after trying to

learn how to fly, but not land, a 747. Despite warnings from French intelligence that Moussaoui had connections to al Qaeda, the FBI's Minneapolis office was refused permission to search Moussaoui's laptop, which was later found to contain information regarding the 9/11 terrorist attacks. In its original handwritten request for permission to search Moussaoui's computer, Rowley's office stated he was the "type of person that could fly something into the World Trade Center." *[19]

In a sign of how little she trusted her own superiors, Rowley flew to Washington to hand-deliver two copies of her memo to members of the Senate Intelligence Committee. In the blistering letter, Rowley came very close to calling Mueller an outright liar, saying, "I have deep concerns that a delicate and subtle shading/skewing of facts by you and others at the highest levels of FBI management has occurred and is occurring." Even more damaging, Rowley later criticized Mueller's post-9/11 comments that the FBI had no prior warnings, claiming they should be immediately revised.

Two weeks after she delivered her memo to Washington, Rowley testified in front of the House and Senate Intelligence Committees' joint inquiry into the attacks. With the spotlight firmly on FBI director Mueller, he finally admitted the bureau might have been able to prevent 9/11 if it had responded to a variety of intelligence reports. But even though this concession further proved there was some level of prior warning, at least on the part of intelligence agencies, it still did not satisfy the LIHOP enthusiasts, who saw the administration easily

---

*In May 2002, another FBI memo was leaked, adding more heat to Rowley's accusations. The so-called Phoenix memo referred to a July 2001 FBI report, warning that bin Laden operatives might be taking flight training in the U.S. so that they could launch terrorist attacks on American targets. Like Rowley's pre-9/11 warnings, it was ignored.

compartmentalize it to the failure of FBI officials. For their part, the corporate media parroted the government line, keeping any blame for the tragedy of 9/11 far from the administration's manicured lawns. Without any credible, first-person evidence that Bush's team had failed to protect the country despite direct warnings of imminent terrorist attacks, the media wouldn't touch it. And even then, the story would have to come from an insider. Eventually, it did.

In March 2004, the issue of prior warning slammed through the national media apparatus when Richard Clarke, Bush's former national counterterrorism coordinator, appeared on *60 Minutes*. It was a big week for the onetime "Terrorism Czar" who hit the networks as part of a strategically brilliant PR campaign around the release of his tell-all book, *Against All Enemies: Inside America's War on Terror*. As a career federal bureaucrat who had dutifully served under three successive presidents, Bush I, Clinton, and Bush II, before retiring in disgust at the Bush administration's handling of the War on Terror, Clarke was as dangerous as he was credible, especially with the release of his memoir coming right before his testimony in front of the 9/11 Commission.

During his interview with *60 Minutes* correspondent Lesley Stahl, Clarke recounted his efforts to warn administration officials of an "impending al Qaeda attack," including a January 2001 memo to Condoleezza Rice requesting a cabinet-level meeting to deal with the issue.[20] As Clarke told *60 Minutes*, that urgent memo "wasn't acted on," and he was continually diverted to lower-rung officials until a cabinet-level meeting was finally convened on September 4, eight months after his initial request.

But Clarke was not the only experienced counterterrorism expert warning the administration about al Qaeda. In his testimony before the 9/11 Commission, Clarke asserted CIA director George Tenet* had been equally committed to creating a "sense of urgency" about the imminent threat, only to be ignored by President Bush and Condoleezza Rice, the national security adviser.

Even more damning was Clarke's admission that the concept of terrorists commandeering planes to use as kamikaze weapons was not unfamiliar to him. As Clarke told the committee, it was he who issued the warning to protect the 1996 Olympic Games from airborne attacks. In a chilling moment of testimony, Richard Ben-Veniste raised the issue of Coleen Rowley's buried Moussaoui search request, and its potential significance, and whether Clarke had known "that there was a jihadist who was identified, apprehended in the United States before 9/11 who was in flight school acting erratically. . . ."

Clarke replied, "I would like to think, sir, that even without the benefit of twenty-twenty hindsight, I could have connected those dots."

When Clarke hit the airwaves with his incriminating portrayal of the administration, Bush's team responded much more energetically than it had to his repeated warnings about threats posed by Osama bin Laden and al Qaeda. Dick Cheney and White House spokesman Scott McLellan both went on the attack, characterizing Clarke as an opportunist and, as Cheney stated on Rush Limbaugh's conservative radio show, "not in the loop," regarding his role in the Bush administration's counterterrorism policy-making process.†[22]

---

*Later that week, Clarke appeared on Tim Russert's *Meet the Press*, telling the story of George Tenet sitting in Rice's office in the months prior to 9/11 with his "hair on fire." Said Clarke of Tenet, "He was about as excited as I'd ever seen him. And he said, "Something is going to happen."[21]

†In his TalkingPointsMemo blog, Josh Marshall clarified the idiocy of Cheney's claim: "Clarke was the counterterrorism coordinator at NSC. That means he *ran* the interagency process on terrorism issues. Cheney says Clarke wasn't in the loop, but that means that he actually *ran* the loop.

But in the end, it was left to National Security Adviser Condoleezza Rice to answer Clarke's criticism. After all, in many ways, the responsibility of 9/11 fell on her shoulders. When Clarke wrote that Rice gave him "the impression she had never heard of [al Qaeda] before," he struck her a vicious blow. With the administration's initial reluctance to allow her to testify at the 9/11 Commission hearings on the basis of executive privilege, she used the mainstream media as her platform of rebuttal. Writing an op-ed in the *Washington Post*, Rice stuck to her mantra about prior warnings of airborne attacks, arguing, "Despite what some have suggested, we received no intelligence that terrorists were preparing to attack the homeland using airplanes as missiles, though some analysts speculated that terrorists might hijack planes to try and free U.S.-held terrorists."*[24]

But that only broke a new dam of controversy and unveiled another whistle-blower waiting patiently for her turn in the sun.

In a story published by *Salon* just days after Rice's op-ed, Sibel Edmonds, a former FBI wiretap translator, claimed the national security adviser's statements were "an outrageous lie. And documents can prove it. . . ."[25] Edmonds, who had been hired by the FBI to translate taped conversations and documents seized by agents from suspected terrorists, first hit the national spotlight in 2002 when she publicly accused the bu-

---

If he was out of the loop on the central points of what the White House was doing on terrorism, that means there was a complete breakdown of the interagency process. Saying Clarke was out of the loop is less a defense of the administration than an indictment of it.[23]

*One day after Condi Rice's op-ed, Defense Secretary Donald Rumsfeld echoed her assertion, telling the 9/11 commission, "I knew of no intelligence during the six-plus months leading up to September 11 that indicated terrorists would hijack commercial airliners, use them as missiles to fly into the Pentagon or the World Trade Center towers."

reau translations department of misconduct and gross incompetence. Edmonds told *Salon* that after her report, the FBI offered her a substantial raise and a full-time job if she did not go public with the information she had gathered in the translations. When she refused, Edmonds alleges in *Salon*, she was harassed and then fired by the FBI.

In order to prevent her from going public, John Ashcroft got a judge to place her under a gag order, stating State Secrets Privilege—invoked to "block discovery in the name of national security." Undeterred, Edmonds filed for the documents under the Freedom of Information Act, but the government refused to comply, and the request was turned down. Left with only one viable option, Edmonds sued the FBI for release of the files. But, during an in-camera session with the judge, federal lawyers once again cited the rarely invoked "State Secrets Privilege," and the court ruled against her.

As Edmonds told *Salon,* the documents contained "specific information about use of airplanes, that an attack was on the way two or three months beforehand and that several people were already in the country by May of 2001."

In February 2004 she was back, giving three hours of damaging testimony to the 9/11 Commission. Though the public was not allowed access to the incriminating documents, Sibel Edmonds had broken through the veil of silence and pushed a final nail into the coffin of the government's executive privilege. Besieged by questions raised by Richard Clarke's damaging allegations and with 9/11 commissioners now publicly clamoring for Rice to testify under oath, the White House had no choice but to concede. On March 30, 2004, after months of stonewalling, George Bush announced that Condoleezza Rice would meet the 9/11 Commission in a public hearing.

Rice's eventual testimony before the 9/11 Commission on April 8 gave further evidence that the government had prior knowledge that an attack was imminent. Although she stuck to her argument that "there was no silver bullet that could have prevented the 9/11 attacks," she could not avoid questions about the now-infamous August 6 PDB. Democratic Commissioner Richard Ben-Veniste drew first blood, raising the issue of prior warning as it specifically related to an August 6 PDB presented to George Bush while on vacation at his Crawford ranch.* Though the PDB was still classified, the commission had been given access to a heavily redacted copy of the document, and Ben-Veniste took full advantage of it.

"Isn't it a fact, Dr. Rice, that the August sixth PDB warned against possible attacks in this country? And I ask you whether you recall the title of that PDB?"

Rice smiled and looked at the ceiling, "I believe the title was, 'Bin Laden Determined to Attack Inside the United States.' Now, the—"

Impatient, Ben-Veniste cut her off, sending the interrogation into a Mametian downward spiral.

"Thank you."

"No, Mr. Ben-Veniste—"

"I will get into the—"

"I would like to finish my point here."

"I didn't know there was a point."

Though Rice would not submit to Ben-Veniste's charge that the brief contained enough information to warrant more urgent response from the administration, the August 6 PDB was now on the table and a public demand had been made for

---

*Ironically, it was the August 6, 2001, PDB that had been the source of a May 2002 report by the *Washington Post* "that terrorists associated with Osama bin Laden had discussed the possibility of hijacking airplanes." It was in response to this report that Rice had made her original statement, cited above, that she didn't "think anybody could have predicted that these people . . . would try to use an airplane as a missile, a hijacked airplane as a missile."

its declassification. Perhaps unsure whether the administration would take that grave step, a second Democratic commissioner, former senator Bob Kerrey, went one step further and did it himself, unilaterally declassifying the brief by quoting it on national television.

"In the spirit of further declassification, this is what the August sixth memo said to the president: "that the FBI indicates patterns of suspicious activity in the United States consistent with preparations for hijacking.'"*

The expression on Rice's face was one of restrained astonishment. Without pause, she assured Kerrey that those patterns were "checked out and steps were taken through FAA circulars to warn of hijackings," but again took issue with the implication that the administration could have done anything more to protect the country.

"I think it is really quite unfair to suggest that something that was a threat spike in June or July gave you the kind of opportunity to make the changes in air security that could have been—that needed to be made."

While the damaging revelations of government whistle-blowers and testimony before the 9/11 Commission validate some of the skepticism regarding the government's claim of no prior knowledge and subsequent justifications for failing to prevent the attacks, some LIHOP theorists see an even darker implication. These skeptics believe the hijacked planes could have been at least engaged with a basic deployment of the FAA's standard operating procedures, effective in the event of a hijacking. Instead, these rules were broken or ignored throughout the entire morning of September 11. Given the

---

*On April 10, 2004, the White House released a heavily redacted version of the memo to the public. The original was said to be eleven and a half pages long. The redacted version was one and a half.

administration's now-admitted emphasis on hijackings and the warnings about potential air attacks from al Qaeda in the months prior to 9/11, skeptics contend, the failed military response to the four simultaneous hijackings indicates some level of complicity from the government or military command.

Response Time

According to skeptics, there was ample time for NORAD to scramble fighter jets before the hijackers reached the World Trade Center and Pentagon. The fact that no jets reached either target before they were struck has been interpreted as evidence of a military stand-down, engineered to allow maximum damage to be inflicted on American targets by the terrorist hijackers. Whether the theory is tenable or not, it is hard to explain how the military, with all its billions in funding, could have failed so dramatically on the one day it was most needed.

Standard operating procedures for the Federal Aviation Administration (FAA) dictate that as soon as a plane flies off course, air-traffic controllers contact the plane to determine the reasons for its diversion. If the aircraft cannot be reached, the FAA immediately informs NORAD, which scrambles fighter jets to intercept the plane and evaluate the situation. The maximum time allotted for this reaction by NORAD is fifteen minutes.

One well-known example of this procedure in action is the case of pro golfer Payne Stewart, whose private jet flew off course and later crashed due to cabin pressure failure in October 1999. Following standard operating procedures, NORAD dispatched two fighter jets when the plane failed to respond to air-traffic control. Flying at above-average speeds, they reached Stewart's plane within twenty minutes of the time the FAA lost contact. By applying these same standards to the multiple hijackings on 9/11, it is easy to see how some people have become skeptical of the official story.

Take the first plane to strike the World Trade Center, American Airlines Flight 11, which took off from Boston's Logan International Airport at 7:59 A.M. and hit the North Tower at 8:46. Air-traffic control's last routine contact with the plane came at 8:13. Soon after that, flight controllers suspected something was wrong but did not determine that Flight 11 had been hijacked until 8:20. Contrary to FAA regulations, the controllers did not notify NORAD of the problem. By 8:25, the plane had radically diverted from its course and was heading south toward New York. Even more alarming was the fact that, over the open radio line, flight controllers could hear the hijackers broadcasting a message to the passengers, "We have some planes. Just stay quiet and you will be OK." Despite this clear indication of a major commercial hijacking in U.S. airspace, the controllers still did not follow standard procedures and contact NORAD until fifteen minutes later, at 8:40.[26]

According to the official timeline, in response to the alert, NORAD waited six minutes before ordering two F-15 jets to scramble from Otis Air National Guard Base, which is about 188 miles northeast of New York. It took another six minutes for the pilots to board the planes and take off, making them airborne by 8:52 A.M. According to one of the F-15 pilots, Lt. Col. Timothy Duffy, he flew his jet "full-blower all the way," which is military slang for top speed.[27] NORAD claims it took the fighters nineteen minutes to reach New York, meaning they flew less than an average speed of 600 mph, which is just over what the military refers to as the F-15's "cruising speed," and well below the supersonic speeds the jet is capable of.

For skeptics, this time difference is critical, especially when they consider the complete 9/11 timeline. Flight 11 crashed into the North Tower at 8:46 A.M., making it impossible for the F-15s to intercept it given all the FAA's delays. However, had the fighters actually flown "full-blower," skeptics argue, they might have had a shot at reaching New York by the time United Airlines Flight 175 crashed into the South Tower at 9:03 A.M. When journalists questioned the military about this time lag, they allowed officials to contradict the official story and let the most basic mathematical errors go unchallenged. In an interview with NBC's *Dateline*'s Mike Taibbi, Maj. Gen. Larry Arnold stated the F-15s left Otis at 8:46 A.M., six minutes off the official timeline, were flying between 1,100 and 1,200 mph and were still eight minutes away when Flight 175 hit the South Tower at 9:03 A.M.[28] But if Major General Arnold's take-off time and air speed are correct, even when accounting for acceleration and deceleration, the planes would have reached Manhattan in around thirteen minutes, or at 8:59 A.M.—four minutes before the fatal impact. And how come no one at *Dateline* discovered the mistake?

The difference between minutes and seconds during a crisis situation is meaningless, and the 9/11 skeptics know it. What they assert is that there has been a consistent effort to obfuscate the breakdown of standard military procedures on 9/11. And the mainstream media simply filtered this misinformation through to the public without even a collegiate level of journalistic verification.

One of the most cited examples is a *Dallas Morning News* report on the statements of Maj. Gen. Paul Weaver, director of the Air National Guard. According to the *Morning News*, Weaver said the F-15 "pilots flew like a scalded ape, topping 500 mph, but were unable to catch up to the airliner."[29] A scalded ape? At 500 mph, the F-15s would have been flying at a little over half their low-altitude maximum velocity, according to a retired high-ranking military official we spoke to—

about as fast as Flight 11 when it hit the North Tower! Even a basic background check on the specs of an F-15 fighter would have thrown up red flags for any reporter. Instead, the American public was fed the analogy of a scalded ape, conjuring images of a high-tech military jet red-lining it to defend New York City. Nothing could have been further from the truth.

Assuming the first two planes caught the FAA and NORAD off guard, causing a major breakdown in communications and deployment of standard operating procedures, the delayed reaction to the 9/11 hijackings can be reduced to human error. But it is more difficult to justify the failure of the U.S. military to defend the Pentagon, which was hit more than thirty minutes after the second WTC tower was struck by United Airlines Flight 175.

In the case of Flight 77, which took off from Washington's Dulles International Airport, air-traffic control lost contact with pilots at 8:50 A.M. Once again, the FAA is inexplicably delayed in relaying information to NORAD, which claimed the first notification they received about Flight 77's hijacking was at 9:24 A.M., over a half hour after the FAA decided Flight 77 had been hijacked, and more than twenty minutes after a second plane smashed into the World Trade Center. The delay is even more astonishing considering that, by this time, the plane has already turned around and was ominously heading toward Washington, D.C. Pushing standard operating procedures aside, given all that was happening over domestic airspace, the response to Flight 77's hijacking is incomprehensible.

During the 9/11 Commission hearings, FAA officials disputed the NORAD account, claiming that, although the official notification came at 9:24 A.M., "information about the flight was conveyed continuously [between the agencies] before the formal notification." This assertion is backed up by a *New York Times* report published just after 9/11 that asserted, "During the hour or so that American Airlines Flight 77 was under the control of hijackers, up to the moment it struck the west side of the Pentagon, military officials in a command center on the east side of the building were urgently talking to law enforcement and air traffic control officials about what to do."[30]

Despite all that was happening, it wasn't until 9:30 A.M., six minutes after they were notified, that jets took off from Langley Air Force Base, 150 miles south of Washington, D.C. That delay would prove costly. Had the F-16s flown an average speed of 850 mph (their maximum low-altitude speed is Mach 1.2, or 910 mph, according to military experts), they still wouldn't have been able to reach the Pentagon in time.

But they might have come close. Flight 77 crashed into America's military headquarters at 9:37 A.M. The fighters didn't arrive in Washington airspace until 10:00 A.M., making their average speed a leisurely 300 mph. For the skeptics, given the urgency of the mission, this bizarrely lackadaisical pace was evidence enough that something was rotten at the core of the nation's command structure.[31]

One explanation offered by 9/11 skeptics is that the statements from NORAD and air force pilots concerning scramble times are fabrications, created to cover up a military standdown that was ordered by the highest levels of the U.S. government. To substantiate this theory, skeptics point to the Senate Confirmation hearing of Gen. Richard Myers, who was appointed to the position of chairman of the Joint Chiefs of Staff, the highest military post in the country. Held just two days after the attacks, Myers's appointment is worthy of scrutiny, considering he had just presided over the single worst failure of military defense in United States history. But even more suspicious to skeptics is what transpired during the general's testimony. When asked by Sen. Carl Levin when the first fighter aircraft were scrambled on 9/11, Myers replied, "that order, to the best of my knowledge, was after the Pentagon was struck."

If General Myers is to be believed, then, as Paul Thompson wrote in his definitive analysis of the 9/11 air defense failures, "the level of incompetence this implies is breathtaking."[32]

Deep Politics

For some LIHOP advocates, the issue of intelligence failure and foreknowledge are merely smoke screens deployed to cover up a sinister intelligence coup that has its origins in the shady, nebulous realm of transnational covert ops. As editor of *The Center for Research on Globalization*, Michel Chossudovsky is another star fixture in the LIHOP constellation. With a day job as professor of economics at Canada's University of Ottawa, Chossudovsky is more suave than Mike Ruppert and less radical than Alex Jones, or at least a little less radical.

Explaining his red herring theory on prior warning and foreknowledge, he deconstructs:

> *I think that intelligence failure is not the issue. The issue is political deception. It is, in fact, the complicity at the top levels of the Bush administration in what happened on September 11. That does not say that they actually ordered it, but they have agencies and entities and intelligence assets which perform on their behalf.*

In his view, the 9/11 attacks were the result of a covert partnership between al Qaeda and the CIA, both of which, he alleges, remained tactical partners at the end of the Afghanistan war. In the blockbuster version of 9/11, as the corporate media has sold it, this idea is a delusive heresy. Al Qaeda is America's mortal enemy, dedicated with bloodthirsty vengeance to the destruction of the United States and its infidel population.

According to Chossudovsky, however, the murky world of covert action is a complex web that, in order to be understood, requires careful attention to the details of history and the global network of intelligence agencies that were built to fight the Cold War. Through Chossudovsky's lens, this is a vast, interconnected world of shared alliances that operate in a parallel sphere to that of the day-to-day, civilian paradigm of mainstream America. Covert operations are called *covert* for a reason; they almost never make the front page of the newspaper.

To help us understand his thesis, Chossudovsky takes us back to the Soviet–Afghan War of the 1980s, when the Unite States was secretly funding and arming the Islamic mujahideen guerrillas to fight the Russians. Because the war was being financed covertly, the United States needed a middle man through which to funnel money and entrust adequate military training for the mujahideen soldiers. In this capacity, Pakistan's own CIA, the Inter Services Intelligence (ISI) agency, served as the critical link between American agents and front-line rebel groups, one of which was Osama bin Laden's nascent al Qaeda network. The partnership was extremely successful. After ten years of brutal fighting, the Russians retreated from Afghanistan, broke and demoralized. Nine months later, the Berlin wall fell, signaling the end of the Soviet Union's superpower status.

As the official story goes, Osama bin Laden returned to Saudi Arabia and then, without any other significant first-world power to hate, turned his fanatical army on the generous hand of his former master. In other words, bin Laden was a classic case of *blowback*, a CIA term defined by Chalmers Johnson as "a metaphor for the unintended consequences of the U.S. government's international activities that have been kept secret from the American people."[33] According to 9/11 skeptics like Chossudovsky, this was a conveniently simplistic story for the mainstream media to digest, but the reality was far more complex. He argues that throughout the 1990s, the ISI remained tactically associated with al Qaeda,* while the United States continued to aid the terrorist network's overseas military adventures.

The single most visible U.S.–al Qaeda alliance came during the Yugoslav war, when President Bill Clinton authorized collaboration between U.S. military forces and the Kosovo Liberation Army (KLA) in 1998. When Robert Gelbard, United States special envoy to the Balkans, first encountered the KLA, he said, "I know a terrorist when I see one, and these men are terrorists."[35]

In two successive reports by the Senate Republican Policy Committee (RPC) published between 1997 and 1999, the Clinton administration was criticized for its unwillingness to "come clean with the Congress and with the American people about its complicity in the delivery of weapons . . . to the Muslim government in Sarajevo." The report goes on to allege that beyond the "thousands of mujahedin ('holy warriors') from across the Muslim world" who had been filtering in to Kosovo to fight alongside American soldiers, the Clinton-backed KLA "is closely involved with terrorist organizations

---

*In 2001, the *New York Times* reported that the ISI "had an indirect but longstanding relationship with Al Qaeda," to the extent that Pakistan was using "al Qaeda camps in Afghanistan to train covert operatives for use in a war of terror against India."[34]

motivated by the ideology of radical Islam,* including assets of Iran and of the notorious Osama bin-Ladin."

It does not take an investigative sleuth to Google the now-infamous pictures of U.S. Gen. Wesley Clark and Secretary of State Madeleine Albright, shaking hands and smiling alongside KLA leader Hashim Thaci. These telling images and the above-quoted allegations, ironically from the Republican party's own policy report, embolden Chossudovsky to assert that "the al-Qaeda network is considered by the CIA to be an intelligence asset, and intelligence assets are controlled by their sponsors. That does not of course mean that al-Qaeda is necessarily pro-American. It means that al-Qaeda is being used to perform certain functions for the U.S. intelligence apparatus, and it goes through a whole complex group of intermediaries."

For Chossudovsky, and the legions of 9/11 skeptics that have found resonance with his publications, the name of Gen. Mahmoud Ahmed is a critical piece of the puzzle linking the ISI–CIA–al Qaeda axis. As the head of Pakistan's ISI, General Ahmed was on an official visit to Washington from September 4 to 13, 2001. During that trip, he held meetings with his counterparts in U.S. intelligence agencies and then, on the morning of September 11, he attended a breakfast meeting with Sen. Bob Graham and Rep. Porter Goss, the chairmen of the Senate and House Intelligence Committees. This meeting would have been historically unremarkable if not for a startling revelation. In October 2001, the *Times of India,* citing Indian intelligence and FBI sources, reported General Ahmed had authorized a $100,000 wire transfer to Mohamed Atta,

---

*Of postwar Kosovo, the *Wall Street Journal* reported, "the only real development that may be said to be taking place there is the rise of Wahhabi Islam—the puritanical Saudi variety favored by bin Laden—and the fastest growing variety of Islam in the Balkans."[36]

the alleged ringleader of the 9/11 hijackers.*[37] According
to the *Times of India*, the information was leaked from an official intelligence report of the Indian government that had
been delivered to Washington. Despite the story's undeniable
intrigue, mainstream media did not cover it. The only direct
mention of the story came from Chossudovsky himself, who
wrote about the *Times of India* report in the *Philadelphia City
Paper* in December 2001.[38] In his article, Chossudovsky
quoted an Indian government source who told the Agence
France-Presse the evidence gathered on General Ahmed was
"of a much wider range and depth than just one piece of paper
linking a rogue general to some misplaced act of terrorism."

Commenting on the significance of the *Times of India*
story, Chossudovsky wrote:

> *it suggests that the September 11 attacks were not an act of
> "individual terrorism" organized by a separate Al Qaeda
> cell, but rather they were part of coordinated military-
> intelligence operation, emanating from Pakistan's
> ISI. . . . precisely at the time when [Ahmed] and his dele-
> gation were on a so-called "regular visit of consultations"
> with U.S. officials.*

Some might question the two sources of this report, India
and France. India is the chief geostrategic enemy of Pakistan
and would rejoice at the prospect of an American overhaul of

---

*In his bestselling book, *Who Killed Daniel Pearl*, French author Bernard-Henri
Lévy takes it one step further. After an extensive investigation that took him into the
heart of the terrorist network in Pakistan, Lévy asks was the *Wall Street Journal* reporter killed because he was getting too close to the al Qaeda connection to the ISI?
Lévy finds evidence that the mastermind behind Pearl's sensational beheading was
Omar Sheikh, the man General Ahmed is alleged by Indian intelligence to have used
as a conduit to send Atta the $100,000. Lévy concludes, "The possible Pakistani re-
sponsibility in the September 11 attack remains the great unsaid in George Bush and
Donald Rumsfeld's America."

the ISI, which has been co-coordinating guerrilla warfare efforts against Indian forces in the disputed province of Kashmir. France became the primary source for conspiracy theorizing and anti-American political rhetoric after 9/11. But the way the Bush administration handled the Ahmed allegations would only add to the skeptics' suspicion that there was something to the ISI allegations.

One day before the story broke internationally, and just hours before the launch of a U.S.-led invasion of Taliban-controlled Afghanistan, General Ahmed was fired by Pakistan's President Pervez Musharraf. Reporting on the sacking, the BBC floated the official line, saying that it reduced "the influence of pro-Taliban supporters inside the army." Of course, this would have been a strong reassurance to American officials who were already weary of the ISI's tacit support of the Taliban and Osama bin Laden. Some intelligence experts suggested that the U.S. ordered Musharraf to fire General Ahmed. Why, they ask, the sudden shift after Ahmed's high-profile meetings in Washington, D.C.? According to Chossudovsky, it is necessary to look at the mission he was given while stranded in America after the 9/11 attacks.

During a series of meetings held with Deputy Secretary of State Richard Armitage on September 11 and 12, General Ahmed guaranteed Pakistan's loyalty to America in the War on Terrorism. Later that month, the *Washington Post* reported that "at American urging, Ahmed traveled . . . to Kandahar, Afghanistan. There he delivered the bluntest of demands. Turn over bin Laden without conditions, he told Taliban leader Mohammad Omar, or face certain war with the United States and its allies."[39] The official account of this meeting was that it ended in failure, with the Taliban's mullah Omar telling General Ahmed, "Osama will be the last person to leave Afghanistan."

The 9/11 skeptics believe that meeting was meant to fail. With the American military forces already in full motion, and the nation hungering for blood after losing three thousand innocent civilians on September 11, the last thing the administration wanted was the body, dead or alive, of Osama bin Laden. Chossudovsky writes that would have denied them a "pretext for military intervention which was already in the pipeline. If Osama had been extradited, the main justification for waging a war 'against international terrorism' would no longer hold. And the evidence suggests that this war had been planned well in advance of September 11, in response to broad strategic and economic objectives."

And so, with the first bombs of America's global war on terror dropping on Afghanistan, there was no major report, or investigation, of the ISI allegations. Nor did the mainstream media make any effort to find out from Sen. Bob Graham or Rep. Porter Goss, what the general had discussed with them over breakfast during the very hours the attacks he allegedly aided were occurring. Later, Graham and Goss were chosen to lead the initial joint House–Senate investigation into intelligence failures surrounding the 9/11 attacks.

September 11 skeptics see a pattern of containment and cover-up that points to a larger framework of American complicity. At the very least, Chossudovsky believes, the sheer proximity of top-level administration and intelligence officials to General Ahmed justifies a modicum of skepticism.

The question you have to ask, Chossudovsky says, is: If Ahmed is in Washington and at the same time reportedly sending money to terrorists, "does that not suggest that senior Bush officials should at least give us some answers of what they were doing with this guy?"

It's not an invalid question. Of course, it is expected that the head of a major national intelligence agency would take

meetings with his American counterparts. There is hardly anything verifiyingly incriminating about General Ahmed's presence in Washington at that time, but the White House's
reaction to questions about Ahmed are suspicious.

During a May 2002 White House briefing, an accredited Indian journalist dared to ask the question no American reporter
would. Addressing National Security Adviser Condoleezza
Rice, the man asked, "Are you aware of the reports . . . that the
ISI chief was in Washington on September 11, and on September 10, $100,000 was wired from Pakistan to these groups here
in this area? And why he was here? Was he meeting with you or
anybody in the administration?"[40]

Rice answered, "I have not seen that report, and he was
certainly not meeting with me," and the question passed without remark by other journalists in the room.

As national security adviser, it is hard to imagine that Rice
would not have seen the reports about General Ahmed's alleged financing of the terrorist hijackers, especially considering his high-level visits with Colin Powell, Richard Armitage,
and George Tenet in the days before and after the attacks.
More alarming is the administration's attempt to scrub the
record after the fact. What follows is an excerpt of the transcript of that same meeting, as provided by the official White
House Web site.

Q: Dr. Rice, are you aware of the reports at the time that
[deleted] was in Washington on September 11th, and
on September 10th, $100,000 was wired to Pakistan to
this group here in this area? While he was here meeting
with you or anybody in the administration?

DR. RICE: I have not seen that report, and he was certainly not meeting with me.

Note that the critical words *ISI Chief,* were deleted from the official White House record. Now look at the CNN transcript of the same briefing:

QUESTION: Are you aware of the reports at the time that (inaudible) was in Washington on September 11. And on September 10, $100,000 was wired from Pakistan to these groups here in this area? And while he was here, was he meeting with you or anybody in the administration?

RICE: I have not seen that report, and he was certainly not meeting with me.

It does seem inconspicuously coincidental that the two major sources for the transcript omit any reference to General Ahmed. Listening to the audio recording of the briefing, the words *ISI Chief* are clearly recognizable. While the potential reasons for the deletions are debatable, the net effect is to render the transcript unintelligible, so that the contacts between an alleged 9/11 moneyman and the Bush administration are forever muddied and obscured from the historical record. It is precisely this type of "political deception" that Michel Chossudovsky sees as evidence of a larger cover-up.

If the 9/11 skeptics had any hope of exposing the links between the ISI, al Qaeda, and the Bush administration to the American public, they had their chance during the 9/11 commission hearings on March 24, 2004, when Deputy Secretary of State Armitage testified in place of Rice.* Remember, it was Armitage who met with General Ahmed several times before dispatching him to Afghanistan with an ultimatum for the Taliban.

---

*National Security Adviser Condoleezza Rice had originally refused to testify under oath in front of the commission. Under intense public pressure, President Bush relented and sent Rice to testify on April 8, 2004.

Armitage has deep ties to Pakistan and the ISI going back to his role, as Ruppert writes, as "one of the main architects behind U.S. covert support to the Mujahedin and the 'militant Islamic base' both during the Afghan–Soviet War as well as in its aftermath.*

A holdover from the Reagan–Bush era, Armitage is a colorful character with an even more colorful past. Described by Bob Woodward as looking like a "cross between Daddy Warbucks and a World Wrestling Federation champ,"[41] Armitage was a famously gung ho commando in Vietnam who went to run covert operations across Asia. During the 1980s, he helped arm the ISI-connected Afghan mujahideen in their guerrilla war against the Soviets and is alleged to have played a role in illegal missile sales to Iran to fund the Nicaraguan Contras. His notoriously evasive Iran-Contra hearing testimony was sufficient that, in 1989, he had to request that his nomination for assistant secretary of state be withdrawn. But his record was clean enough to be nominated deputy secretary of state in 2001, when Bush named him to the position, under his mentor Colin Powell.[42]

In a surreal moment, glossing over his controversial past, Armitage told the 9/11 commission panel under oath, "I'm the only honest person in Washington."

Instead of questioning Armitage about General Ahmed, the commission stuck to the script, focusing on the issue of prior warning and whether the administration had done enough to prevent the attacks. By choosing to avoid the historical evidence of an ISI–CIA–al Qaeda axis, the commission conveniently side-stepped what for many skeptics was a key piece of the puzzle. Had the panel asked Armitage to discuss the activities of General Ahmed and the ISI, the American public may have

---

*In the late 1990s, Armitage's connections were fresh enough that his firm, Armitage Associates, was hired by American oil giant Unocal to help them land a pipeline deal with the Taliban. The contract was never finalized.

been given a brief glimpse into the complex web of agencies that work below the radar of Congress, not to mention the corporate media. Instead, the information remained buried in the cult film version of 9/11, out of reach for the American public and beyond the perimeter of official history.

September 11 was a watershed moment for conspiracy theory in American popular culture. Not since the assassination of JFK have so many felt so deeply that something had gone terribly wrong, and that neither the government nor the media had given them a plausible explanation for the tragedy. But instead of looking at the rise of post-9/11 conspiracy theory as a reaction to the lack of a credible narrative, establishment journalists describe it as a symptom of some latent madness infecting the margins of American society. This is consistent with their treatment of conspiracy research, where the theorists are branded heretics in a manner that is reminiscent of the Salem witch trials, or the Spanish Inquisition. Only now, instead of being burned at the stake, the offending practitioner is maligned publicly by credible, official sources so that they will never be taken seriously again.

The mainstream media has a responsibility to filter out the myths and misinformation that are presented as truth to the American public. Their job is made all the more critical with the rise of the Internet and the wide dissemination of radically implausible and unsubstantiated theories posited as factual deconstructions of current events. There is no doubt that many of these are totally delusional if not dangerous, should they ever become part of the public's perceptual framework of reality. But in compartmentalizing all 9/11 skeptics together as one mass of raving lunatics, Big Media has cut itself off from a vital source of information that could provide a more coherent and believable picture of the events that have brought America into the worst foreign policy disasters since the Vietnam

War. Even worse, establishment journalists were so dazzled by the blockbuster version of 9/11, they failed to question those elements of the government's story that were just as specious and unbelievable as those of the hard-core conspiracy theorists. As with the controversy surrounding the assassination of JFK, the level of government secrecy and deception associated with 9/11 has set the scene for decades of doubt and suspicion. Echoing the sentiments of the 9/11 cult-film crew, Alex Jones told us "the most audacious conspiracy theory is the one coming out of Washington, D.C."

4

Cynthia's War

The Fall and Rise of a Maverick Congresswoman

■ ■ ■

*Did she say these things while standing on a grassy knoll
in Roswell, New Mexico?*
—CHRIS ULLMAN, SPOKESMAN, CARLYLE GROUP

Stone Mountain, GA

ON THE EAST SIDE of DeKalb County, just fifteen miles from
downtown Atlanta, lies the world's largest mass of exposed
granite and the most imposing landmark in the old South,
Stone Mountain. Football-field-size reliefs of Civil War generals Robert E. Lee, Thomas "Stonewall" Jackson and Confederate president Jefferson Davis have been blasted into the side
of the gigantic rock that rises out of the leafy burbs like a Dix-
ieland version of Devil's Peak. We're getting an "unofficial"
tour from former Congresswoman Cynthia McKinney, who
lives not far away.

In 1915, she explains, a ceremony was held on top of the
mountain to commemorate the reestablishment of a struggling Confederate veterans association called the Ku Klux
Klan. The Klan soon enjoyed a revival, triggering a wave of
beatings, cross-burnings, and lynching that culminated in a
forty-thousand-hood march on Washington, D.C., in 1925.

Today, Stone Mountain bills itself as "Georgia's No. 1

Family Tourist Attraction," complete with a tram, a laser light show, and an authentic "Antebellum plantation and farmyard." The KKK connection isn't mentioned.

For this daughter of 1960s Atlanta, the rock has a different meaning. It's "one of the mountaintops" from which her hero Dr. Martin Luther King called to let freedom ring in his historic 1963 speech.*

"I have been through nothing compared to the trials of Dr. King," she tells us. "His life and his legacy keep me going."

Despite her soccer-mom looks and wide smile, McKinney is one of the most controversial American politicians in recent memory. Few elected officials have attracted as much outright ridicule or rallied as much grassroots support in the tumultuous post-9/11 era. Elected in 1992 as Georgia's first African American Congresswoman, she was always outspoken. She held Bill Clinton, the man Toni Morrison called the "first black president,"[1] to the fire on everything from welfare reform to drug laws, to what she saw was his indifference to human-rights abuses in Africa. But it wasn't until Bush was appointed to the presidency that she began to ruffle feathers in the nation's capital. McKinney held hearings about the Florida election debacle, and she was one of the most vocal advocates of investigations into Bush crony business dealings. After 9/11, when the rest of the political class blindly fell in line behind the commander in chief, McKinney didn't back down. In fact, she only got more aggressive, raising questions about everything from the Bush family connections to the Saudis, to the prior warnings the government received that might have prevented 9/11. She was one of the first elected officials to demand the creation of an independent 9/11 commission at a

---

*Cynthia McKinney is completing her Ph.D. dissertation at UC Berkeley on the assassination of Dr. Martin Luther King Jr.

time when the White House was doing everything in its power to thwart it.

"[W]e hold thorough public inquiries into rail disasters, plane crashes, and even natural disasters. Why then does the administration remain steadfast in its opposition to an investigation into the biggest terrorism attack upon our nation?" she asked.[2]

An independent commission was eventually formed—only because of the tireless efforts of some other single mothers, the four 9/11 widows from New Jersey. But by the time the commission finally held its dramatic public hearings in April 2004, McKinney was like them—a private citizen.

In August 2002, her decade-long run in Congress was terminated when a perfect storm of local race politics, Arab–Israeli politics, post-9/11 fear-mongering, media hysteria, and her own political missteps combined to knock her out of office. Her story is a classic "War on Terror" case study in what is safe and not safe for an American elected official in a time of national crisis. It's also a story of mass denial, in which a lazy and compliant news media will happily play the public executioner when someone starts asking the questions they should be asking themselves, as McKinney put it:

> *"One Atlanta city council member told me, when you become an elected official, you have a very special and unique opportunity to look inside the file cabinet," she said. "But you're not supposed to tell what's inside the file cabinet. I told what was inside the file cabinet, and that's what got me into trouble."*

Our Stone Mountain tour over, McKinney returns to her purple Pontiac Firehawk, a souped-up version of the Trans Am with enough horsepower for the quickest of getaways. As the former African American congresswoman for a district that was once a hotbed of KKK activity, McKinney takes few chances. She is often chaperoned, as she is today, by Jocko, her longtime friend and pistol-packing bodyguard who likes to quote his favorite bumper sticker: YOU CAN TAKE MY GUN, BULLETS FIRST.

She pumps up the jams on the Firehawk's booming sound system and revs the engine. "Keep close," she says with a playful grin. "Don't get too far behind."

She peels off, heading toward Cynthia McKinney Parkway, an unexceptional stretch of suburban road that leads to Stone Mountain. In August 2002, just days before her congressional defeat, local conservatives petitioned to have the road changed back to its previous name, Memorial Drive. It had been a sore spot to conservatives ever since the road, which was named in memory of fallen Confederate soldiers, was changed to honor "a black female progressive," as McKinney calls herself. The conservatives argued that they wanted to change the name back to Memorial, this time in memory of the victims of 9/11. Their petition failed, but the tensions linger.

The controversy over *Memorial* versus *McKinney* was in many ways a microcosm of the political battles that dogged her throughout her final year in office. For local Republicans, and even many Democrats, McKinney's outspoken criticism of the Bush administration's handling of 9/11 had made her a political embarrassment, a loose-lipped wild card who needed to be muzzled. But for many African Americans, especially her core constituents here in suburban Atlanta, McKinney would become a martyr, the hometown girl who had taken on the world's most powerful cabal of rich white men and didn't blink.

Three Strikes

When George Bush Jr.'s legal team successfully blocked a statewide recount in Florida, McKinney was outraged. Her neighboring congresswoman Corrine Brown (D-Fla.) was reporting that thousands of African American voters had trouble recording their vote on election day.

McKinney had also picked up on the reporting of Greg Palast, the BBC and *Guardian* newspaper reporter. In December 2000, Palast broke the story of how ChoicePoint, a data retrieval, storage, and analysis firm, was hired by the state of Florida to effectively scrub thousands of names, primarily of African Americans, from the voting rolls. After reading his articles and hearing of his BBC broadcasts, McKinney decided that she needed to take matters into her own hands.

It would prove to be a dangerous move. ChoicePoint, which was paid more than $2 million by the state of Florida, is a successful Atlanta-based corporation with strong ties to powerful Republicans. On April 17, 2001, McKinney held a public hearing in Atlanta on ChoicePoint's contract with Florida. In the hearing, ChoicePoint vice president James Lee all but confessed that direct orders from the state resulted in ChoicePoint subsidiary Database Technologies (DBT) knocking off thousands of qualified voters from the voter rolls. In Florida, convicted felons can't vote, but Lee testified that Florida ordered DBT to use only an 80 percent match when analyzing names of suspected felons, meaning John Smith might find himself a felon, and unable to vote, if a John Smyth had been convicted of a crime. Lee testified that DBT warned the state such a liberal standard might end up disenfranchising the innocent, and asked if they could cross-check additional databases, but Florida officials refused.

The result was "the list of voters DBT supplied to the state [to be used to delete felons] did include the names of people who were eligible to vote," Lee explained. "The state officials knew this would be the result."

The hearing appeared to be the smoking gun. A company official had admitted that the state had ordered them, against their best judgment, to knock off legitimate voters from the state's rolls. But the confession came and went, few national media outlets picked up the story, and nothing happened.*

The day before the ChoicePoint hearings in Atlanta, McKinney was in Washington conducting hearings on another highly connected corporation under fire. This time the company was Barrick Gold, a Canadian gold-mining company on whose board George Bush Sr. was paid a million dollars to sit shortly after he left the White House. In his last days in office, Bush Sr. had approved the sale to Barrick of a mining claim for ten thousand dollars by the U.S. government worth tens of millions. In 1996, human-rights activists claimed a mine owned by a Barrick subsidiary in Tanzania was bulldozed, burying about fifty miners alive. Barrick issued a strong denial of any wrongdoing on their part. Palast wrote about the allegations in an article for the London *Observer*. His primary source, a well-known Tanzanian lawyer who was calling for an investigation, was charged with sedition and arrested. McKinney demanded congressional hearings and started an international campaign to save the lawyer's life. Barrick sued Palast and the *Observer* in the UK courts, where draconian libel laws place the burden of proving truth on the defendant. In August 2001, the *Ob-*

---

*ChoicePoint later received a multimillion-dollar contract from the federal government to help gather information on everyday citizens as part of the USA Patriot Act. Former Rep. Bob Barr (R-Ga.) commented, "The government is now turning more and more to private industry to do its dirty work, to gather information on people, manipulate that information on people and, in so doing, circumvent the Privacy Act."[3]

server, in Palast's view caving in, apologized to Barrick, paid the company an undisclosed cash settlement, and removed the story from their Web site.

If ChoicePoint and Barrick were strikes one and two, then McKinney's comments in the wake of 9/11 would be the third. When September 11 hit, like every American, McKinney felt shock, fear, and a deep sadness. But unlike almost every American elected official, including some of the most liberal members of her own party, she didn't blindly rally behind the president. In fact, McKinney said, "I was consumed with trying to understand what it was; how something of this magnitude could have happened, why it happened, who did it; and why we didn't stop it? Why didn't we intercept those plans, wherever they emanated from, for that day?"

She continued, "We were given talking points [from the White House]. The talking points said that we were hit because we were free. That wasn't good enough for me."

McKinney noticed that the foreign press was painting a dramatically different picture about what happened on 9/11 than what the American people were getting. "I began to read from the *Scotsman, Sydney Morning Herald,* the *Independent,* the *Guardian,* the British newspapers, papers from around the world. I was able to find that in certain foreign press, they were printing more than the American press, and I found that disconcerting and odd," she remembers.

In particular, she noticed the disturbing references to numerous foreign-intelligence warnings that were allegedly delivered to the White House prior to 9/11 but were apparently ignored. For instance, the London *Telegraph* reported, "Israeli intelligence officials say that they warned their counterparts in the United States last month that large-scale terrorist attacks on highly visible targets on the American mainland were imminent." Similar reports came from Russia and Egypt.[4]

McKinney also began to openly question the Bush family's relationship to the Saudis and the impact it had on our anti-terror efforts.* Fifteen of the nineteen hijackers were Saudi (or at least were traveling with Saudi IDs), yet Saudi Arabia had been dubbed our main ally in the burgeoning global war on terror. What many didn't know was that the Bush family had connections to various prominent Saudis that went back decades. In fact, according to Bill White, a Texas businessman once close to the Bush family, in the 1970s, when George W. Bush was first setting out into business, one of his first financial backers was a man tied directly to bin Laden.

According to White, Salem bin Laden, older brother to Osama, entered into a trust agreement with a Bush business partner named Jim Bath. Bath acted as the bin Laden family's representative in North America, investing money in various business ventures. Bath was also the business representative of Khalid bin Mahfouz, a member of Saudi Arabia's most powerful banking family and owners of the National Commercial Bank, the principal bank of the Saudi royal family.[5a]

According to White, a Harvard business school graduate and a navy pilot, in 1978, Bath invested money from Salem bin Laden and bin Mahfouz directly into Arbusto, Bush's fledgling oil venture. White claims Bath told him that he pumped more than $1 million of the Saudis' money into the company, which soon received valuable drilling rights in the Gulf. Bath claims the money he invested was his alone.[5b]

Bin Mahfouz would later be indicted by the U.S. for fraud in the BCCI scandal. The U.S. Federal Reserve also alleged

---

*In November 2001, unnamed FBI and CIA agents told the BBC they were ordered "to 'back off' investigating the bin Ladens and Saudi royals, and that angered agents." Greg Palast, *BBC Newsnight*, November 7, 2001.

that he breached banking regulations. He denied any wrong-doing and on his Web site, www.binmahfouz.com, vehe-mently protests the allegations. The charges were dropped in 1993, but only after he agreed to pay $225 million, including $37 million in lieu of fines.[6] In October 2001, the U.S. Treasury accused a charity that bin Mahfouz had financed of being an al Qaeda front.[7a]

As Craig Unger details in his book *House of Bush, House of Saud*, the Saudi connections don't end there.* Bush Sr. enjoys an almost familial bond with Prince Bandar bin Sultan, who for twenty-five years has been the Saudi ambassador to the U.S. Often called the Arab Gatsby, he's famous for jetting the former president and his friends in his private airbus to hunt birds in Spain, and for joining the revelries at Washington's swankiest soirees. He even contributed over $1 million to the Bush presidential library.[8]

In April 2004, Bob Woodward made headlines with the release of his book, *Plan of Attack*, with claims that Bush Jr. showed Bandar the highly classified plan (marked NOT FOR FOREIGN EYES) to invade Iraq before it was presented to his own secretary of state Colin Powell. Woodward also claims Bandar promised President Bush he'd drop oil prices just in time for the 2004 election, all charges the administration and Bandar denied.

McKinney also wanted to know more about the secretive Carlyle Group, a superconnected private investment firm. The

---

*Unger also broke how 140 people—mostly Saudis—were whisked out of the U.S. on private jets immediately following 9/11. Passengers included nearly two dozen members of the bin Laden family, including Osama bin Laden's sister and a Saudi prince later identified during the interrogation of the alleged mastermind of the USS *Cole* attack as one of his main contacts.[7b]

group had heavy footing in defense contracts and deep con-nections to the Saudi royal family. A former Carlyle subsidiary, for instance, once trained Saudi troops to defend its oil wells. The company also had extensive ties to another political dy-nasty—the Bushes. In 1990, Carlyle tapped George W. Bush to briefly run another one of its subsidiaries, and later brought on George Bush Sr. as an "adviser." At one point, its board read like a rogue's gallery of international heavyweights, includ-ing former Philippine president Fidel Ramos, Frank "Spooky" Carlucci (the notorious former CIA dirty tricks man and secre-tary of state under Reagan), and James Baker, the Bush family consigliere who orchestrated the Florida recount battle and is now representing the Saudi government in a suit brought by 9/11 victims' families. On 9/11, Carlyle's board also included members of the bin Laden family, who run the hugely success-ful Saudi-based construction and investment group Osama worked for as a young man.*

If it wasn't a "conspiracy," the Bush–Saudi–bin Laden family connection was at the least downright creepy. To top it all off, on the morning of 9/11, George Bush Sr. was in a meeting for the Carlyle Group at the Ritz-Carlton Hotel in Washington, D.C., just a few miles from the Pentagon. Also in attendance—Carlyle partner Shafig bin Laden, one of Osama's brothers.

As Unger explained to us, "To many people, it was seen as ironic that the bin Ladens had actually been investors in the Carlyle Group, this huge private equity firm with the Bushes, and they were actually present at a Carlyle investment confer-

---

*Many question whether Osama has really cut his ties with the family. His sister-in-law told ABC's *Primetime Live* in October 2001, "I think Osama has a lot of backing from Saudi Arabia, from the family, money-wise." The *New York Times* re-ported Osama called one of his father's four wives on the eve of 9/11 to tell her something big was coming.

ence on September 11. In fact, as I see it, nothing could have been less ironic. Irony suggests something unexpected."

Charles Lewis, executive director of the Center for Public Integrity, was more blunt, saying:

> *Carlyle is as deeply wired into the current administration as they can possibly be. George [H. W.] Bush is getting money from private interests that have put business before the government, while his son is president. And, in a really peculiar way, George W. Bush could, someday, benefit financially from his own administration's decisions, through his father's investments. The average American doesn't know that. To me, that's a jaw-dropper.*[9]

The average American didn't know because there was a near media blackout of Carlyle's tentacles, even as Carlyle subsidiary United Defense, maker of the Bradley attack vehicle and the Crusader artillery system, won massive Pentagon contracts shortly after 9/11.

"This was a huge conflict of interest," Dan Briody, author of *Iron Triangle: Inside the Secret World of the Carlyle Group*, told us. "Carlyle is the eight-hundred-pound elephant in the living room that everyone tiptoes around and nobody wants to talk about."

McKinney was one of the only American politicians who did want to talk about it. She demanded Bush tell the American people "where the Bush family interests end, and America's foreign policy begins."[10]

As Briody explained, Americans were still mourning September 11. They were not willing to hear this kind of talk from an upstart congresswoman. He added, "it was political suicide."

Flashpoint

McKinney's downfall began in earnest on March 25, 2002, with an appearance on Pacifica Radio's *Flashpoints*, a lefty current affairs program produced out of Berkeley's uber-liberal KPFA. It was a familiar gig. Her outspoken views on the Florida debacle, and more recently the USA Patriot Act, had made McKinney a regular fixture on the progressive-radio circuit. Reading from a prepared op-ed, McKinney launched into her most pointed critique yet on the president and 9/11. Considering what would happen in the weeks to come as a direct result of what she would say next, the way she began was chillingly prescient:

> *Authorities tell us that the world changed on September 11. As a result, university professors must watch what they say in class or be turned in to the speech police. Elected officials must censor themselves or be censured by the media. Citizens now report behavior of suspicious-looking people to the police. Laws now exist that erode our civil liberties. Americans now accept these infringements as necessary to win America's New War.*

The op-ed ended with the following two sentences, thirty-six words that would all but bury her political career: "What did this administration know, and when did it know it about the events of September 11? Who else knew and why did they not warn the innocent people of New York who were needlessly murdered?"

It took two weeks to hit, but when the backlash came, it came in heavy. McKinney was accused of claiming Bush was in on a 9/11 conspiracy to kill innocent Americans so his buddies could turn a profit. The fiery congresswoman had danced a little too close to the flame. This was March 2002, but it might as well have been September 12.

The allegedly left-leaning National Public Radio reported that "[McKinney] suggested the Bush administration may have known in advance about the 9/11 attacks and allowed them to happen in order for people close to the president to profit." The *New York Times'* Lynette Clemetson picked up on the story, reporting, "Ms. McKinney suggest[ed] that President Bush might have known about the September 11 attacks but did nothing so his supporters could make money in a war."

McKinney's words were now in the "media mix master," and the results weren't pretty.[11]

"McKinney has made herself too easy a target for mockery," *Atlanta Journal-Constitution* editorial page editor Cynthia Tucker opined. "She no longer deserves serious analysis." *National Review Online* editor Jonah Goldberg, son of Lewinsky-gate maven Lucianne Goldberg, diagnosed her with "paranoid, America-hating, crypto-Marxist conspiratorial delusions." Unnamed Bush aides got in on the action, deriding McKinney's "ludicrous, baseless views." White House spokesman Ari Fleischer quipped, "All I can tell you is the congresswoman must be running for the hall of fame of the Grassy Knoll Society." Even Sen. Zell Miller, a fellow Democrat from Georgia, called her a "loony" and her comments "dangerous and irresponsible."[12]

McKinney, who had always been outspoken, was now a certified outcast. In a time when people were literally getting arrested in malls for wearing PEACE ON EARTH T-shirts, she was branded the worst thing a patriotic American could be in the post-9/11 era: "conspiracy theorist."

Soon McKinney-bashing became a story itself—the uppity black congresswoman who accused the president of being involved in a twisted plan to kill thousands of innocent Americans so his fat-cat buddies could make a buck. It was a ludicrous claim.

The only problem, of course, was that McKinney never said it. No one, it seemed, had bothered to read her full statement in context. If you read her op-ed in its entirety, it's clear she never said Bush knew specifically about the attacks, and that he didn't do anything so his friends could profit. They were two separate points that got grafted together.

Judge for yourself. Here's the last minute or so of McKinney's statement taken from a transcript on the *Flashpoints* Web site. It ends with the two sentences in question:

> *In February 2001, the United States Commission on National Security, including Newt Gingrich, recommended that the National Homeland Security Agency be established with a hefty price tag. Most people chuckled at the suggestion.*
>
> *After September 11, we have OK'd the targeting and profiling of certain groups of people in America while not addressing in any way the racial profiling and discrimination that existed prior to September 11. Mass arrests, detention without charge, military tribunals, and infringements on due process rights are now realities in America. Even more alarming are the calls in some circles to allow the use of torture and other brutal methods in pursuit of so-called "justice." Sadly, U.S. administration of justice will be conducted by an administration incapable of it. Interestingly, prominent officials explain to us that September 11 happened because we are free. And "they" hate us because we are free.*
>
> *Moreover, persons close to this administration are poised to make huge profits off America's new war. Former Presi-*

dent Bush sits on the board of the Carlyle Group. The Los
Angeles Times *reports that on a single day last month,
Carlyle earned $237 million selling shares in United De-
fense Industries, the Army's fifth-largest contractor. The
stock offering was well timed: Carlyle officials say they decided to take the company public only after the September
11 attacks. The stock sale cashed in on increased congressional support for hefty defense spending, including one of
United Defense's cornerstone weapon programs.*[13]

*Now is the time for our elected officials to be held ac-
countable. Now is the time for the media to be held accountable. Why aren't the hard questions being asked? We
know there were numerous warnings of the events to come
on September 11. Vladimir Putin, President of Russia,
delivered one such warning. Those engaged in unusual
stock trades immediately before September 11 knew enough
to make millions of dollars from United and American
Airlines, certain insurance and brokerage firms' stocks.
**What did this administration know, and when did it
know it about the events of September 11? Who else knew,
and why did they not warn the innocent people of New
York who were needlessly murdered?** [emphasis added]*

McKinney may not be everyone's idea of a leader. But after
reading and rereading this transcript, we still can't find the
part where she says that either (a) Bush had advance knowledge of 9/11 or (b) that he knew that bin Laden's boys were
coming and did nothing to stop it so his cronies could make a
buck. In fact, all she appears to be doing is asking a series of
"hard questions"—questions that America should want to
know about how we were left wide open for the most devastating attack on the American homeland since Pearl Harbor.

Ironically, the questions she was asking back in 2002 are essentially the same questions the members of the 9/11 Commission are asking administration officials in their investigation in 2004.

As *Iron Triangle* author Briody put it, "She asked the right thing at the wrong time."

The mechanics of how her questions became "conspiracy" fodder are fairly simple: Taken *out of context*, the final line, "Who else knew and why did they not warn the innocent people of New York who were needlessly murdered?" appears to refer to the subject in the previous sentence, "the administration," as in "Who else (other than the Bush administration) knew that 9/11 was coming? . . ." It's a seemingly damning indictment. But when you look at the entire last paragraph, it's clear that when McKinney asks, "Who else knew?" she's *not* referring to the administration, but to the two other aforementioned parties appearing to have "known" something about the impending terrorist attacks before it happened, namely, former KGB head Vladimir Putin and the mysterious traders involved in short selling right before the attacks.*[14]

None of the news outlets that ran "McKinney the Conspiracist" stories bothered to provide her comments in context, nor did they call McKinney for clarification.

For McKinney, the whole sorry affair had more to do with the media's own failings than what she had actually said or implied. "The media were complicit in distorting what I asked in order to take attention away from the substance of the issue," she told us. "And to this day, the substance of my question has not been responded to by the responsible media."

McKinney, it should be noted, didn't exactly help her own

CBS News reported on September 19, 2001: "The afternoon before the attack, alarm bells were sounding over unusual trading in the U.S. stock options market."

cause. Just weeks after 9/11, a Saudi Arabian Prince named Alwaleed bin Talal offered New York City mayor Rudolf Giuliani a gift of $10 million to help rebuild the city. But the prince had recently criticized U.S. foreign policy, and Giuliani bluntly rejected the check. McKinney wrote the prince a letter apologizing for the mayor's actions, and saying she could put it to good use in the black community. Politically, it was a disastrous move, especially considering her own criticism of the Bush family's Saudi connections.

"McKinney the kook" became the meme, and each time it was repeated, it morphed into a self-replicating virus rippling down from the Paper of Record to the farthest reaches of the right-wing Internet until McKinney had become an emblem of the Bush-hating, Arab-loving, irrational left-wing nut. The whole saga would almost be funny if the stakes weren't so high.

Ironically, just as McKinney-bashing was reaching its crescendo, in May 2002, something extraordinary happened: It was revealed that Bush had been warned of an impending "spectacular" al Qaeda attack on U.S. soil in an August CIA memo. This would be the first in a string of embarrassing revelations to come from various law enforcement and intelligence agencies.

Even the *Constitution-Journal*, the very paper that had recently called for McKinney to be taken away by men in white jackets for asking if there was intelligence that might have prevented 9/11, ran a headline that read: "Bush warned by US intelligence before 9/11 of possible bin Laden plot to hijack planes." The *New York Post*, the right-wing tabloid owned by Rupert Murdoch, put it more bluntly: BUSH KNEW. It was a shocking turn of events.

The floodgates appeared to have broken.

As we detail in chapter 3, a Minnesota-based FBI agent named Coleen Rowley released a memo dated May 21, 2002, which she had written to FBI director Robert Mueller. Prior to 9/11, Rowley had been tracking Zacarias Moussaoui, a suspicious Moroccan who spoke little English but was taking flight lessons in which he told his instructors he only wanted to learn how to fly a large commercial jetliner and he didn't want to learn how to land.[15] In Phoenix, a similar story broke. FBI agents there reported a similar shutdown of their investigations.

Even McKinney's Republican rivals couldn't ignore the intelligence blockbusters. Senate Intelligence Committee Vice Chairman Richard Shelby, a Republican from Alabama, said, "I believe, and others believe, if [information on threats] had been acted on properly, we may have had a different situation on September 11."

McKinney responded to the May 2002 revelations defiantly.

It now becomes clear why the Bush administration has been vigorously opposing congressional hearings. The Bush Administration has been engaged in a conspiracy of silence. Two weeks of public hearings and a dozen detailed reports make clear that predictions of an attack by al Qaeda had been communicated directly to the highest levels of the government.

In anything resembling a sane, just world, McKinney would have been issued an apology, a correction, some flowers, an *All Things Considered* coffee mug—something, anything, from the numerous news outlets, commentators, and elected officials who had maligned her. She got none of the above. In fact, "McKinney the terrorist-loving, conspiracist" story would only grow, and down in Georgia, a growing contingent of anti-McKinney forces smelled the blood in the water and had begun to mobilize.

Goodbyecynthia.com

Thanks to redistricting after the 2000 elections, McKinney's once-safe Fourth Congressional District, which runs from the suburbs of Dunwoody north of Atlanta down to DeKalb in the urban south, became vulnerable. While still majority (60 percent) Democratic, she lost a few key nearly all African American precincts to the newly created Thirteenth District and gained five solidly Republican precincts in return. She also experienced problems with a few heavily Jewish precincts who no longer wanted to be represented by McKinney, because of pro-Palestinian positions she had taken that year. This would be an ominous sign of things to come.

McKinney had always had problems with Jewish voters, mostly because of her father Billy. While Cynthia may be outspoken, she doesn't fight dirty. Billy is from the old school, a veteran of an era of Southern politics when blacks had to fight tooth and nail for every political advantage they could get. He was the one who got her into politics, and has always stayed closely involved in her battles. He has been part protector, part adviser, and, unfortunately, part albatross.

In 1986, Cynthia was living in Jamaica with her then-husband and their child when her father put her name on a ballot for state legislator. "He was having a political fight with one of his colleagues. So he put my name on the ballot. I got 20 percent. Not bad for not campaigning."

Shortly after, her marriage fell apart, she returned to Georgia and ran for real this time. She won. The year was 1988. Cynthia and Billy McKinney were the first father-daughter political team in Georgia state legislature history. McKinney was a quick study. After serving two terms, she was elected to the U.S. Congress. Billy was there at every step.

But there were problems. Despite the fact he once worked for a Jewish candidate, Billy was often linked to the Nation of Islam, and he was quoted making a series of blatantly anti-Semitic cracks. For many Jews and white liberals, he was a symbol of the kind of subtle and not-so-subtle anti-Semitism often attributed to Louis Farrakhan. For many, McKinney never did enough to distance herself from him.

So in 2001, when McKinney began bitterly criticizing Israeli prime minister Ariel Sharon's increasingly harsh policies toward the Palestinians, and the Israeli occupation in general, many right-wing Jewish groups began to take notice. She was the senior Democrat on the human-rights subcommittee of the International Relations Committee. The heavily funded American Israeli Public Affairs Committee (AIPAC) began working behind the scenes with Republican strategists to target candidates they deemed anti-Israel for elimination from public office.* It was a new, aggressive strategy, and it worked.

In the 2002 Democratic primary, McKinney was facing off against a relative unknown named Denise Majette, a moderate Democrat state judge. Most observers dismissed Majette's candidacy as a "quixotic quest." McKinney had easily defeated her 1996 primary challenger and general election opponents.

But Majette would get help from an unlikely source.

The unofficial campaign to unseat McKinney was spearheaded by a Republican entrepreneur named Mark Davis. Davis is part computer geek, part hunting enthusiast, but 100 percent "good old boy." He is also CEO of Data Productions

---

*"Jewish backing for challengers of incumbents in Democratic primaries made national news in 2002, when Jewish support for Denise Majette in Georgia and Artur Davis in Alabama helped unseat U.S. Reps. Cynthia McKinney and Earl Hilliard respectively." Matthew E. Berger, "In 2004, U.S. Jewish fund raising shifts to supporting—not unseating—incumbents," *JTA—Global Jewish News*, February 16, 2004.

Inc., Georgia's leading political direct marketing printing company.

Data Productions is located in a sterile office park just off Highway 85 in Duluth, Georgia. The only sign of color there is Davis's brand-new, tricked-out Hummer H2 sitting in the sun-drenched parking lot. It's dark red with a raised suspension. And, like all Hummers, it gets nine miles to the gallon, on a good day. "I'm one of the few people who bought these that actually uses it for what it was made for—to get you out of the swamp," Davis boasts, the monster truck towering over him.

Davis's office is nearly empty, save for the stuffed head of a wild boar he hasn't got around to mounting, a computer that hums like an airplane engine, and the instruction manuals for Map Info, his secret weapon. Map Info is a computer program that allows Davis to pinpoint with laserlike accuracy vast amounts of demographic information on every congressional district in Georgia. Using the program, he was able to lay the groundwork for what would become one of the most successful and devious electoral strategies in the post–Voting Rights Act era.

On first meeting, Davis appears far from a political zealot. He speaks in a carefully parsed monotone. Taking down Cynthia McKinney, he says, was something that he did "pro bono" as a service to the community and the nation. For Davis, McKinney was a danger to the republic. There was a war on, and she needed to be removed. He had the connections and resources to get it done.

In early 2002, Davis had come up with the plan. After Georgia's redistricting in August 2001, Davis claimed his company had one of the only accurate voter registration databases in the state. He crunched the numbers, cutting them and recutting them, trying to figure out a way to beat McKinney.

Then he remembered a lesson from the past: "I recalled the way that Republicans used to exert political influence when we were an extreme minority and that was through 'crossover voting.'"

In Georgia, voters of any political affiliation can vote in any primary. Davis's plan was to convince DeKalb County Republicans to "crossover" and vote in the Democratic primary for Majette. "Asking Republican voters to leave our primary and vote in the Democrat primary for a black female Democrat— that's a tall order, and honestly," he recalled, "I was not certain how that would be received, even under the circumstances."

Davis approached his number one customer, Georgia's Republican Party, with the idea. According to Davis, the local GOP bigwigs were more than happy to give their blessings— but not their direct support. That would have been illegal. While voters are free to take any ballot they want in a Georgia primary election, it is against the law for the parties themselves to officially fund or endorse a "crossover campaign."

The legacy of crossovers goes back to the post-Reconstruction era, when whites used them to manipulate primaries in black districts. Under the Voting Rights Act of 1964, party-sponsored crossovers were made illegal.

Davis technically is not a Republican Party official, though the distinction seems almost semantic. He speaks of himself and the Republican Party in the royal *we,* but is careful never to say he was working directly for anyone but himself. Despite funding that poured in from major Republican backers, and the fact that Davis's "crossover" headquarters was located in the same office park, just a few doors down from the DeKalb County Republican Party, Davis portrays what he did as a "grassroots" campaign, independent of the party apparatus:

I like to compare it to knocking the top off a radiator. If there is no steam built up, nothing is going to happen. But if there is steam built up, it's obviously gonna gush. And that's basically all that happened here. We were able to get out a direct-mail campaign that was humorous and funny and the message basically was that there was an organized effort at promoting a Republican crossover.

Denise Majette, a relatively low-profile state judge who had previously voted as a Republican, was the perfect opponent: conservative enough to receive Republican backing and African American and female enough to compete head on with McKinney for black Democrat votes. But despite her mild-mannered appearance—she could have passed for McKinney's more "corporate" sister—Majette wasn't afraid to take the gloves off.

In a series of raucous debates, one held in an Atlanta shopping center, the atmosphere was often more of a schoolyard spat than a political debate. Majette did not shy away from questioning McKinney's patriotism.*

I'm asking you to question why my opponent has continued to vote against appropriations for military and intelligence support. If she is so concerned whether or not we can meet the challenges here in this country and across the world. If you want to continue to have the liberties that you have you are going to have to make a sacrifice just like my parents sacrificed, your parents sacrificed, other

---

*In another contentious Georgia race, then-Sen. Max Cleland (D), who lost three limbs in Vietnam, was also portrayed as unpatriotic by his challenger for opposition to the USA Patriot Act. Cleland lost.

*people's parents and grandparents sacrificed. And if you
don't think it's worth it, then you need to move somewhere else.*

Davis and a personal injury attorney named Bubba Head
launched goodbyecynthia.com, a mean-spirited Web site full
of off-color jokes and unflattering photos. Their catchphrase
was "ABC"—Anybody but Cynthia. Most of the material
on the site was simply reprinted articles from the *Atlanta
Journal-Constitution.*

The *Atlanta Journal-Constitution* had always been known
as Georgia's "left-leaning" paper. (It supported affirmative action, for instance, among other progressive causes.) But in the
spring of 2002, the paper turned on McKinney, launching a
series of articles that did more damage to her political reputation than anything Davis and his cohorts could have dreamed
of. It was a prime example of how local reporters, following
the lead of national media, found themselves becoming the
mouthpiece for a powerful nexus of political operatives.

The negative coverage was epitomized by an article by reporter Bill Torpy, headlined MCKINNEY DONORS PROBED FOR
TERROR TIES.[16]

Torpy quoted Steven Emerson, whom he identified as running an unnamed "private counterterrorist institute in Washington," as saying McKinney's contributors were "the A-list
of militant Islamic front groups." Torpy's article also quoted
the Atlanta-based Southeastern Legal Foundation (SLF), one
of the many right-wing organizations that by this time had
taken an active interest in McKinney's campaign. In April
2002, the SLF had accused McKinney of accepting campaign
contributions from what they referred to as "terrorist-
sympathetic organizations," including the American Muslim
Council and the Council on American/Islamic Relations. Ac-

cording to the SLF, 21 percent of McKinney's individual contributors who gave more than $101 in 2001 were "identifiably Arab or Middle Eastern–connected."

Torpy's article listed several prominent Arab American figures who contributed to McKinney's campaign, including Abdurahman Alamoudi, founder of the American Muslim Council. What the article failed to mention was that several of the figures in McKinney's donor list also had political connections with other politicians, notably President George W. Bush. The American Muslim Council endorsed Bush for president, for example, and Alamoudi contributed to Bush's campaign in 2000 (though the contributions were later returned). Alamoudi was invited by the White House to appear at the National Cathedral memorial for 9/11 victims on September 14, 2001.

In fact, as author Unger details in *House of Bush, House of Saud*, the Bush campaign carefully courted the Arab vote. Bush happily accepted millions of dollars in donations, and many say it was the Muslim vote that pushed him over the edge in several swing states including Florida, where 88 percent of Muslims voted for Bush.

An investigation of FEC records by *Southern Exposure* magazine revealed that among the names on McKinney's list of contributors was Sharif Abdur-Rahim—a star basketball player for the Atlanta Hawks, an African American who grew up in Georgia.[17]

But the damage was done. To the public, "McKinney the terrorist lover" had now been documented. And her opponent, Majette, had no problem with using the *Constitution-Journal* ammo in a bitter televised debate, saying, "McKinney had taken campaign contributions from Arab terrorists on September 11."

Even Davis conceded to us that the *ACJ*'s coverage of McKinney had been a boon for his side.

They are known to be a liberal paper, or at least the conser-
vatives tend to view them that way. But in terms of Mc-
Kinney, they really were not very generous to her at all, and
this probably comes from this long history she had of mak-
ing inflammatory-type comments. But what I did notice
was that the Majette campaign was pretty much treated
with kid gloves. I would say their coverage was pretty re-
flective of the sentiment in the community. At the same
time, I could see someone making the argument from a
scholarly perspective that it might not have been quite as
even-handed as it should have been.

In the end, Majette ultimately raised more than twice as
much money as McKinney—more than $1.1 million, an enor-
mous sum for a congressional primary race. Much of Majette's
funding came late in the campaign from the pro-Israel political
action committees (PACs) that had targeted her and Earl
Hillard, another African American and a ten-year incumbent
for defeat. Hilliard, who like McKinney had voted against a
House resolution that endorsed Israel's conduct in its own
"War on Terrorism," was beaten by Artur Davis, who received
80 percent of his funding from out-of-state pro-Israel backers.

The late insurgence of cash allowed Majette, a first-time
candidate, the rare opportunity to outspend an incumbent opponent in the home stretch of the race. This amounted to
nearly twenty dollars for every vote she received.

Billy McKinney did little to help his daughter's cause. On
the eve of the primary election, a television reporter asked him
why the race with Majette was so tight. He responded by
spelling out a word: *"J-e-w-s."*

On the day of the primary election, Billy McKinney's comment received massive coverage. Reports also leaked out that
Farrakhan was in DeKalb County to stump in McKinney's be-

half. Media swarmed the campaign headquarters wanting to know if she planned to appear with Farrakhan. After some deliberation, it was announced that Farrakhan had come at his own behest, and that McKinney would not be appearing with him.

"There was no move this time by Cynthia to distance herself from her father's comment, nor has she done so since. And her association with Farrakhan, whether real or perceived, remains an open wound," says local civil-rights activist and onetime McKinney supporter Buddy Grizzard.

The bulk of the civil-rights establishment backed McKinney, but with little enthusiasm and to little effect. McKinney got trounced. Majette beat McKinney by 19,554 votes. The race would have been close it if there hadn't been a huge turnout in white, upper-middle-class precincts, where Majette won by margins approaching 30–1.

The following day, news outlets reported that the crossover had buried her. On CNN.com, the headline read: "Crossover voters were key in Georgia races: Colorful, controversial incumbents defeated."

"Crossover voting was a huge factor in the Fourth District," Merle Black, a professor of political science at Emory University in Atlanta told CNN. "As many as twenty thousand voters. There was overwhelming participation in the Democratic primary in north DeKalb, a lot of which is strong Republican territory, and there was very little activity in the Republican primary. Massive amounts of Republicans were voting in the Democratic primary, because that's their only opportunity to vote McKinney out of office."

In her concession speech, McKinney summed it up, saying, "Republicans wanted to beat me more than the Democrats wanted to keep me."

For Davis and his people, it was the political victory of their lives. "It was a party atmosphere, people were high-fiving each other as they came out of the polls."

The next morning Davis sent out an e-mail to their mailing list that read, "The kitchen is open at goodbyecynthia.com. This morning we will be serving crow."

But many in McKinney's camp called what had happened in DeKalb County, Florida 2000 all over again—a heavily orchestrated attempt to deny African Americans the right to vote for the candidate of their choice. Five African American voters from the Fourth District subsequently filed a lawsuit charging that the crossover had been orchestrated by the highest levels of the Republican Party.

The *Constitution-Journal* kept up its negative coverage even after the election, downplaying the significance of the crossover effect. They even did their own analysis of the election data in which they concluded that the GOP crossover in the McKinney–Majette primary was only 3 percent, or between 3,000 and 3,500 Republicans.

When we asked *ACJ* editor Ben Smith about his paper's coverage of the race in an interview at the paper's downtown Atlanta headquarters, he denied that he or his organization had an anti-McKinney agenda. "I personally have no dog in this fight, and I don't think this newspaper has a dog in this fight. I don't think that's true at all," said Smith. "I think that the argument seems to be filled with a lot of hyperbole, and we were trying to find a way to stay clear through all the hyperbole and get to what was factual. The argument presented by the McKinney campaign was that tens of thousands of hard-core Republicans crossed over in a malicious effort orchestrated by top Republican officials to defeat McKinney. Our reporting shows that that's simply not true."

Mark Davis does not agree and is proud to claim that the crossover wasn't just a factor, it was *the* factor in kicking McKinney out of office, and he's got the numbers to prove it: The *ACJ* analysis was "ridiculous," Davis told us, as if he were defending a family member's honor. "The numbers to me are very clear. There were somewhere between minimum low twenty thousand, maximum thirty-five thousand or forty thousand Republicans in that primary. Only six thousand or so people voted in the Republican primary in 2002. Turnout in the Republican primary statewide was up 52 percent. But in DeKalb County, it was down 75 percent.

Other vote counts only further his argument, Davis explained:

> There were about 125,000 votes cast in DeKalb County in the Democrat primary, but the Democrat nominee for governor, Roy Barnes, running unopposed, only got about ninety-five thousand votes. So why was he missing thirty thousand votes? Well, they were Republicans. They were willing to go vote for Denise Majette but they weren't going to vote for Roy Barnes. So it's pretty ludicrous to claim that there were so few Republicans.

Since our original interview with the *Journal-Constitution*, in which we challenged their analysis of the McKinney and Davis camps, Ben Smith seemed to soften his stance, acknowledging, "The effect of the crossover in the 2002 Democratic Primary has been widely debated." He has also published the crossover numbers claimed by McKinney's camp (45,000) and Mark Davis (at least 25,000), both of which are significantly higher than the margin of victory.

Comeback Kid

In some ways, what happened to McKinney in 2002 is eerily similar to what happened in Florida in 2000. In both cases the Republican Party benefited by the services of Republican-connected corporations who had a particularly valuable asset, the voter database. By strategically calculating the necessary margin of victory and utilizing the data to their advantage, Republicans were able to outsmart the Democrats in each race. Both victories for the Republicans also came at the expense of one particular group, namely, black voters.

But the real lesson of McKinney's defeat may be that in America there are certain things that are just not safe to say, particularly by the most politically vulnerable. If you touch certain issues (the president's handling of 9/11, major corporations' political ties, Israel), you'll find yourself in the "media mix master"—and a national pariah.

Returning home on a cross-country flight from one of her forty-plus speaking engagements in late 2003, McKinney is still going like the Energizer bunny. Dressed in a yellow sweatsuit and tennis shoes, she answers our questions while mastering a new Palm PDA video game. She explains she's not bitter. It's hard not to believe her. Her broad smile and sweet Southern charm have not been dampened by her fall from grace.

"What I think I've learned is that I have a unique set of skills that can help to inform people that desperately want to know why our government acts in a certain way," she says. "People increasingly feel that there is something palpably, tangibly wrong with what's happening today in our country, and I can tell them not only what I saw inside the file cabinet, but I can also tell them who's putting it there."

Several months later, in April 2004, something interesting happened. The 9/11 Commission finally began to ask the White House hard questions—some of the same questions McKinney had been asking all along. The result was major blow to the Bush administration's repeated deceptions about prior warnings it had received. The *New York Times* summarized the intelligence revelations with a bold page-one headline: 9/11 FILES SHOW WARNINGS WERE URGENT AND PERSISTENT.

That same week, McKinney's old foe, Denise Majette, shocked Georgia's political establishment by announcing she was seeking a seat in the Senate. It was a bold move for a one-term African American congresswoman. Many political observers were perplexed by the decision. No one gave her a shot at winning. *But* many concluded that Majette simply didn't want to face a tanned, rested, and largely redeemed McKinney. In addition, Mark Davis publicly announced he wasn't going to back a crossover this time; there were too many Republican candidates in DeKalb who needed their supporters to take the Republican ballot. Majette would have been on her own.

For McKinney, it meant a new beginning. She immediately announced she was seeking her old seat.

Even the *Journal-Constitution* seemed to welcome McKinney's presence back in the local political mix, taking a much kinder and gentler tone than its previous coverage. But perhaps most tellingly, the national media seemed to pick up right where it left off. An Associated Press article that ran across the nation, including the *New York Times*, repeated the same distortions about her 2002 *Flashpoints* comments: "McKinney received national attention for her bold comments and conspiracy theories, particularly after the terrorism of September 11, 2001. She claimed the Bush administration did nothing to stop the attacks because the president's friends stood to profit."

McKinney told us, quoting one of her past campaign advertisements, "Here they go again, saying things about Cynthia that just aren't true."

5

The Anti-Imperial Imperialists

Is America an Empire in Denial?

■ ■ ■

We do not intend to free, but to subjugate the people of the Philippines. We have gone there to conquer, not to redeem.
—MARK TWAIN, "AN ANTI-IMPERIALIST,"
NEW YORK HERALD, 1900

Abu Hishma, Iraq

THE CROWD of about seventy-five gathered in protest outside the Abu Hishma town council building is angry and getting angrier by the minute.

We're smack in the heart of the Sunni Triangle, in an area controlled by Lieutenant Colonel Nate Sassaman, the square-jawed former West Point quarterback who is one of the most controversial commanders in the American occupation force.* After a series of attacks on his troops, Lt. Col. Sassaman rounded up local men in raids that inevitably snagged innocent civilians, some of whom were injured. After lengthy interroga-

---

*Although Lt. Col. Sassaman defended his actions as necessary to protect his men, locals complained that he used indiscriminate tactics—what some might describe as "collective punishment"—that were unfairly harming innocent civilians. His men had recently bulldozed a date palm orchard after insurgents used it as cover to fire on passing convoys. The orchard's owner told us the hundred-year-old trees had sustained an entire village.

tions, most were released. But the townspeople are upset, and they want the lieutenant colonel, and the local sheiks he has chosen to run the town council, to know it.

"We are poor people, we don't have any weapons," a man tells us. "They hit me on the mouth using the bottom of their heavy machine guns." To prove his point, he pries open his bloody, swollen lips.

Another man shows us a prisoner ID number scrawled in thick black ink across the back of his white robe. It reads, MC 2354162735.

"The number on this man's back, is this the freedom that they talk about?" asks his friend. "It's hypocrisy!"

Soon the crowd is chanting:

La ilaha illa Allah, America adew allah!
La ilaha illa Allah, America adew allah!

"There is no God but Allah, America is the enemy of
    Allah!
There is no God but Allah, America is the enemy of
    Allah!"

Inside the town council building, it's not going well either. Lt. Col. Sassaman is trying to explain his plans for the town during Ramadan, the upcoming monthlong Muslim holiday, to a room full of grim-faced sheiks. "I will be fasting—I hope you will be, too," he says, in an awkward attempt to show his solidarity. It doesn't work. The sheiks are growing impatient and want to discuss the recent raids.

"I'm to be humiliated, tortured, and then found to be innocent?" a sheik asks, exasperated. "In front of my wife, my sister, and my family?"

"Is this democracy?" another sheik interjects.

A soldier answers, "Democracy is when you hit us, we hit you."

The room explodes in anger. Lt. Col. Sassaman quickly adjourns the meeting, and he and his troops make a hasty exit.*

This was a scene that probably played out hundreds of times across Iraq during the first year of America's ill-conceived, ill-executed occupation—an American commander trained to kill, trying to play the stern but benevolent "nation-builder," and failing miserably.

We toured Iraq six months after the fall of Baghdad and six months before the bitter frustration in towns like Abu Hishma erupted into a nationwide revolt that united Shiite and Sunni Iraqis against the common foreign foe in April 2004. It was a spectacular failure for the neocon dream of a "free," "democratic," and, most important, "America-friendly" Iraq. But it should have come as no surprise. At least, not to those who understand the legacy of imperial interventions.

As an Egyptian businessman in Iraq reminded us, "It was the Americans who said, 'There's no such thing as a free lunch.'"

Like any successful capitalist, America doesn't act for nothing. Liberation comes with a price tag, and a leash. And for many Iraqis, that leash became too tight. The rhetoric of freedom had finally caught up with the reality on the ground. The chasm between word and deed had become too great.

When U.S. troops marched triumphantly into Baghdad, Americans cheered the made-for-TV moment as if the Berlin wall were coming down. But when the rest of the world watched the Stars and Bars draped over Hussein's head, they shuddered and asked, Is America the new global empire?

*Three months later, Lt. Col. Sassaman ringed Abu Hishma with razor wire and required all residents to be issued ID cards, telling the *New York Times* (December 7, 2003), "With a heavy dose of fear and violence, and a lot of money for projects, I think we can convince these people that we are here to help them."

It's a question most Americans—our news media included—
have appeared unwilling, or unable, to face, because they seem
to understand that it's another way of asking, Does America's
foreign policy live up to the democratic ideals we hold so dear,
or are we no different from any other of history's great con-
querors, from Genghis Khan to Queen Elizabeth, greedily
seeking out new markets, securing trade routes, and seizing
other peoples' natural resources to satisfy our ever-expanding
need to consume?

Trojan Horse

George Bush's campaign for the 2000 presidential election
may have been inarticulate, but it was on message. While Al
Gore seemed to flutter back and forth between positions on
abortion, capital punishment, and gun control, Bush had his
script down: America is no imperial wannabe.

In the first presidential debate, Bush couldn't have laid out
the difference between himself and his opponent on foreign policy issues more clearly, "He believes in nation-building. I would
be very careful about using our troops as nation-builders."

In the second debate, the newly dubbed "compassionate
conservative" candidate stuck with what had become a popular theme. "We've got to be humble," Bush announced in his
best West Texan drawl. "If we're an arrogant nation, [other
countries] will resent us." He used the debacle in Somalia,
which "started off as a humanitarian mission and . . . changed
into a nation-building mission," to make the case against Clinton's ill-defined foreign adventures. Bush scolded, "That's
where the mission went wrong. The mission was changed. And
as a result, our nation paid a price. I don't think our troops
ought to be used for what's called nation-building."[1]

At the same time, the governor was playing the isolationist card to an unwitting public, behind the scenes another, diametrically opposed, policy was being crafted by the men who would become his key foreign policy gurus. In a smoke-free conference room somewhere in the nation's capital, a posse of Diet Coke–swilling chicken hawks were busy laying out a robust expansionist doctrine they believed was necessary to guarantee America's political and economic dominance into the twenty-first century.

The Project for the New American Century (PNAC) was founded in 1997 by a group of far-right radicals disillusioned with the weakened Republican Party who found shelter in the so-called neoconservative ideas of Leo Strauss and Albert Wohlstetter.* Strauss, a political philosopher, championed the supremacy of the American democratic model, and the validity of "good" states to impress their values upon "bad" ones. Wohlstetter, a mathematician and military strategist, offered a more pragmatic approach to world domination through limited nuclear and tactical battlefronts and was the inspiration behind Ronald Reagan's Star Wars initiative. The one trait they shared was a martyrish individualism and an unshakeable belief that the ends always could justify the means.

Think Machiavelli meets Dr. Strangelove meets Holden Caulfield.

Since there were no direct links between the two thinkers, it was in their "students" that neoconservatism would take form. For aggressive technocrats like Richard Perle, Paul Wolfowitz, and Charles Fairbanks, who fantasized themselves modern-day philosopher kings pacing the banks of the Potomac,

---

*According to *Adbusters* magazine, Wohlstetter taught PNAC cofounders Richard Perle and Paul Wolfowitz, the future Iraq War architect. Wolfowitz also studied under Strauss.

neoconservatism was the ultimate tree of knowledge. And the apples were ripe for picking.

As Irving Kristol, the so-called godfather of American neoconservatism wrote in *The Weekly Standard,* the "historical task and political purpose of neoconservatism [was] to convert the Republican Party, and American conservatism in general, against their respective wills, into a new kind of conservative politics suitable to governing a modern democracy."[2] After eight years of Clintonian high jinks, the GOP was rabidly determined to block another Democrat administration. And without any other clearly defined sociopolitical philosophy to compete against it, the neocon movement drew in some of the party's more powerful operatives, including Dick Cheney, Donald Rumsfeld, and Elliot Abrams.

Before PNAC, neoconservatism was the plaything of rightwing intellectuals, little more than a blackboard fantasy game for political philosophers. But with George W. Bush's campaign for president, the disciples of Strauss and Wohlstetter found themselves with the possibility of rolling through the White House doors in the bowels of a perfect Trojan horse.

Published in September 2000, PNAC's now-infamous white paper, "Rebuilding America's Defenses" (RAD), laid the framework for a militarized expansionism that was the antithesis of Bush's campaign platform. Declaring that, "America should seek to preserve and extend its position of global leadership by maintaining the preeminence of U.S. military forces," the paper went on to explain:

> [The U.S.] has an unprecedented strategic opportunity. It faces no immediate great-power challenge; it is blessed with wealthy, powerful and democratic allies in every part of the world; it is in the midst of the longest economic expansion in its history; and its political and economic prin-

ciples are almost universally embraced. At no time in history has the international security order been as conducive to American interests and ideals.

If nothing else, the neocons possess a grandiose bluntness that separated them from their political frontmen. Reading through the RAD report, it's clear they have no apprehension about saying things that most politicians operating in a democracy could never even contemplate. The report listed four core missions for which U.S. forces had to be prepared, and included:

- Fight and decisively win multiple, simultaneous major theater wars.
- Perform the "constabulary" duties associated with shaping the security environment in critical regions.

For them, the U.S. role of global peacekeeper implied "a permanent allocation of U.S. armed forces," as well as "American political leadership rather than that of the United Nations." It had all the markers of what many so-called conspiracy theorists had for nearly a decade loosely referred to as the "New World Order"*—a global, pseudofascist Pax Americana that would usher in a new era of trampled civil liberties and Big Brother–like control.

If there were any doubts about the power of PNAC, of which several members had assumed key positions† in the new

---

*To add a little more fuel to the conspiracists' fire, the report then went on to say that "the process of transformation, even if it brings revolutionary change, is likely to be a long one, absent some catastrophic and catalyzing event—like a new Pearl Harbor."

†PNAC-affiliated officials include Vice President Dick Cheney, Secretary of Defense Donald Rumsfeld, Deputy Secretary of Defense Paul Wolfowitz, and Undersecretary of Defense for Policy Douglas J. Feith.

administration, they were dashed by a careful reading of Bush's "National Security Strategy of the United States of America." Published in September 2002, the manifesto, which also became known as the "Bush doctrine," was a paraphrased patchwork of PNAC directives, "based on a distinctly American internationalism that reflects the union of our values and our national interests."

With its militant pledge to protect the American homeland, and at the same time "destroy terrorist organizations of global reach and attack their leadership," it was easy to view the document as a necessary and, indeed, welcome reaction to the 9/11 attacks. But critics argued there was a more insidious subtext, that the administration was cynically manipulating the public's fear of the elusive al Qaeda to justify a new policy of preemptive war against any target it pleased. The directive's warning seemed almost purposefully vague: "America will act against emerging threats before they are fully formed."*

Despite an underwhelming lack of evidence proving the affirmative, and nearly worldwide opposition, the administration declared Saddam Hussein's Iraq the first "threat" worthy of elimination. As Todd Gitlin wrote in *Mother Jones*, the administration "chose this moment to put down in black and white its grand strategy—to doctrinize, as it were, its impulse to act alone with the instruments of war."[3] In other words, America would unilaterally be scrapping the international rule of law, something that historically had been done by only two classes of states: empires and rogue nations. Perhaps it is time that we attempt to categorize the United States as either one or the other.

---

*The document went on to read, "History will judge harshly those who saw this coming danger but failed to act. In the new world we have entered, the only path to peace and security is the path of action."

Through the Looking Glass

Felipe Fernandez-Armesto is a historian's historian. He's the author of more than twenty-five books, essays, and collaborative works, including the critically acclaimed *Millennium,* an 816-page odyssey through the last thousand years of human existence written from the perspective of someone looking at the earth from an "imaginary distance." With a playful intellect that is not afraid to question the (self-anointed) primacy of European cultures, the Oxford professor covers the span of ten centuries and each major civilization that left its imperial stamp on the world. It's safe to say, Felipe Fernandez-Armesto knows an empire when he sees it.

Sitting in his book-lined London study, he explains to us that, historically, America has displayed all the traits of history's greatest empires: "territorial expansion by conquest, and the continuing subjugation of people and territory after conquest by force." What's fascinating today, he explains, "is that it's probably the most imperial and the most anti-imperial country that has ever been in the world. At least at a rhetorical level."

In other words, the question of whether or not America is an empire, as far as Fernandez-Armesto is concerned, is redundant. The fact that the U.S. could invade a country on the other side of the world, set up a puppet regime, let loose men like Lt. Col. Sassaman on the local population, pound its cities with five-hundred-pound bombs, and begin construction on fourteen permanent military bases on its sovereign soil,[4] and not see even the slightest contradiction between the rhetoric of "freedom" and "democracy" and the imperial tinge of those actions, he argues, requires a staggering level of self-deception and denial.

Psychologist Leon Festinger called it "cognitive dissonance,"[5] the tendency of the mind to exclude information or beliefs that are inconsistent with our worldview. In this case, the image Americans have of themselves is as the ultimate purveyor of goodwill and self-sacrifice.

Not everyone is living under the blanket of illusion. Ironically, those closest to power often have less allegiance to the myth, or maybe just less to hide from themselves. In an interview with British journalist Graham Turner, Tom Foley, Speaker of the House of Representatives for six years and now chairman of the Trilateral Commission, was uncharacteristically candid on the eve of the Iraq war:

> *Our belief is that we are not self-interested. For example, our perception is that we didn't go to war against Iraq to dominate the oil market, and we're very offended if anyone suggests such a thing. Yet we advance the same charge against the Russians and the French. We say they're only interested in getting contracts there. We always excuse ourselves from self-interested motives.*[6]

When the reporter suggested, "Americans had been thoroughly brainwashed with a belief in their own virtues," Foley replied, "There is a lot in that."

It's no coincidence that Foley's interviewer was not a fellow American. In the lead-up to the Iraq war, the debate over America's foreign policy was probably the single most discussed subject in the international media. Nearly the entire world stood against the Bush administration's plans for invasion. In some countries, like Turkey, and in much of Western Europe, opposition was well over 90 percent. Yet most Americans were blissfully unaware of how isolated they had become. According to a spring 2004 study by the Program on

International Policy Attitudes, 59 percent of Americans polled thought most people around the world *supported* Bush's war on Iraq. One-fourth actually thought the majority of the world stood with the U.S., and nearly 40 percent thought that the ratio of pro- to antiwar views was about even. It's not hard to pinpoint why they were so deluded. Take the cover of the January 20, 2003, European edition of *Time* magazine. It featured a burning American flag and the headline: BLAMING AMERICA: WITH WAR IN IRAQ LOOMING, ANTI-U.S. SENTIMENT IS SPREADING ACROSS EUROPE. By contrast, on the cover of *Time*'s domestic edition, with a circulation of over 4 million, was a photo of an elegant model in a leotard doing yoga, under the text: HOW YOUR MIND CAN HEAL YOUR BODY.[7]

If the American media couldn't face the facts, it would be British historians like Felipe Fernandez-Armesto and his counterpart in the right, Niall Ferguson, who would have to do it for them. Ferguson rose to national celebrity after the publication of *Empire*, his definitive study of the British imperial dynasty, though his notoriety came not from the way he described British legacy, but the American one. Writing in *Newsweek International*, Ferguson stated what would become his mantra: "The United States is now an Empire in all but name—the first case in history of an Empire in denial."[8] Ferguson argues that America has so widened the gap between itself and the rest of the world through economic power, military technology, cultural influence, and the sheer breadth of its global troop deployment that it makes the British Empire look like a "half-baked thing."

In a public debate that pitted the historian against neocon writer and PNAC cofounder Robert Kagan, Ferguson reduced the argument to a psychological block that affects the collective American psyche saying,

> *It's understandable that Americans should feel at best ambivalent, if not downright hostile towards the word* empire. *Their creation myth, the very essence of that strange state religion in which the United States' political culture is founded is that of an anti-imperial, rebellious colony that fought against an evil empire for its own independence. And it's therefore an assumption that I think most Americans share that having once thrown off an imperial yoke, it would be inconceivable that the United States itself should become an empire.*[9]

As another Oxford historian, Ferguson's incontestable credentials made it difficult for American neocons to refute his claims on "empirical" terms. So they resorted to wordplay. Kagan responded, "I won't call it *empire* because I don't believe it is an empire, but the most successful global hegemon, the most successful global power in history."

One of the most adamant protagonists of the Iraq war, Secretary of Defense Donald Rumsfeld, was also one of the most public disavowers of the "America as Empire" meme. At a press conference in Doha, Qatar, in late April 2003, a reporter from the Arab television news network al-Jazeera asked Rumsfeld if America was intent on "empire building." The secretary lashed out, "We don't seek empire. We're not imperialistic. We never have been. I can't imagine why you'd even ask the question."[10]

Bush's "axis of evil" speechwriter, David Frum, offered a less defiant, more paternalistic response when a Canadian Broadcasting Corporation reporter posed a similar question, "This isn't imperialism. This is the adolescence of the human race."

Vice President Dick Cheney drew the ire of the anti-imperial crowd with, of all things, his 2003 Christmas card. Quoting Benjamin Franklin, it read, "And if a sparrow cannot fall to the ground without His notice, is it probable that an empire can arise without His aid?"[11]

For many, this reference to God and empire simply proved how pervasive Christian fundamentalist ideology was within the White House—one that reeked with archaic themes of manifest destiny and, it would seem, the divine right of kings. To the cynical observer, Cheney's card, whose text spread virally across the Net, had the feel of a taunt. A well-positioned bit of psychological warfare, deliberately created to simultaneously confuse his critics and enrage the Muslim world. For the rest, it was yet another example of the administration's latent flirtation with the notion of empire . . . and with the role of imperial architect.

When questioned about the intended meaning of the quote, Cheney played coy, saying that since his wife had chosen the words, "She would have to explain why it was on the Christmas card." But he did not waste the opportunity to parrot the administration's imperial repudiation, telling an audience at the 2004 World Economic Forum in Davos, Switzerland, "It did not refer, or should not be taken as some kind of indication, that the United States today sees itself as an empire. . . . If we were a true empire, we would currently preside over a much greater piece of the earth's surface than we do. That is not the way we operate."[12]

In his trademark taciturn way, Cheney could not have offered a more deceptive appraisal of the new-millennial imperial system.

The architects of U.S. foreign policy will never characterize those policies as imperialist, no matter how much men like Lt. Col. Sassaman appear to be doing the dirty work of empire, or established (rightist) historians like Ferguson point out the obvious historical parallels. They will tailor their definition of empire to ensure that America does not qualify. In an era of shrinking resources and increasingly hostility between Western governments (and their corporate tentacles) and the rest of the world, the last thing they will do is confess to their expansionist designs.

Legacy of Lies

Felipe Fernandez-Armesto is smiling mischievously. Halfway through our interview, we've turned to the question of how self-delusion and denial keep American citizens from the truth of their predatory role in the world.

"Life is unsustainable without lubrication by lies. Who can put his hand on his heart and say that everything that he's ever told his wife or his children has been crudely truthful? The truth is often hurtful; it very often directly inspires violence. We always need to protect ourselves from the ill effects of the truth."

Echoing Daniel Goleman's belief in the transference of character attributes from person to state, Fernandez-Armesto continues: "What's true in ordinary individual and family and community life is also true of bigger communities and bigger collectives that we call nations and countries and states. History is motivated, moved along, far less by the facts which really happened, than by the false constructions people put on them. The Iraqi conflict is a very good example."

When Saddam Hussein was captured in December 2003 under suspicious circumstances (Kurdish officials having told foreign reporters that they had captured him first),[13] the prospect of a public trial raised the possibility, and the hope, that the full story of Hussein's relationship with the United States, from client to enemy, would be revealed. In the previous year, numerous juicy details about Hussein's dubious relationship with the U.S. had been made public, from secret pipeline deals to CIA hit squads, but most Americans still knew little or nothing about them. With astounding discipline, the corporate media maintained a virtual blackout of any information that demonstrated just how much of a Frankenstein's monster was found down that spider hole.

The sordid saga begins in 1963. The Beatles released their first album in America. Martin Luther King Jr. gave his "I Have a Dream" speech. President John F. Kennedy traveled to Berlin and told the assembled masses he's "a jelly doughnut."* The Cold War was heating up, and the battle for global dominance was moving ahead at a steady clip. In Vietnam, U.S. "advisers" were flooding into the country to fight alongside the inept South Vietnamese army. Kennedy and a White House full of Cold Warriors were ready to play hardball with any leader who threatened American interests. So when Abdel Karim Kassem, Iraq's populist Shiite leader, who had taken power in 1958, began to threaten U.S. and British influence, alarm bells went off. Kassem began to arm and, most ominously, challenge the Iraq Petroleum Company, a consortium of British Petroleum, Shell, Mobil, and Standard Oil that had a total monopoly of Iraq oil production. He soon made the CIA short list for liquidation.

Kennedy turned to the newly formed Ba'ath Party, a staunchly anticommunist, secular political front, to remove the populist Kassem. The CIA's black ops men went to work. They set up a young officer from Tikrit named Saddam Hussein with an apartment on Baghdad's Al Rashid Street, conveniently located across the street from Kassem's offices. Hussein's CIA

---

*During Kennedy's address to the West Germans, he proudly declared, "Ich bin ein Berliner," or, "I am a jelly doughnut." He meant to say "Ich bin Berliner," meaning, "I am a citizen of Berlin."

handler was an Iraqi dentist working for CIA and Egyptian intelligence, according to a UPI report.[14]

First they sent Kassem a poisoned handkerchief, but the plot failed. Then, on October 7, 1959, a CIA-organized hit squad, which included the twenty-two-year-old Hussein, made a more direct attempt on Kassem's life. The operation was a complete failure. One former CIA official told UPI in 2003 that Hussein lost his nerve and began firing too soon, killing Kassem's driver and only wounding Kassem in the shoulder and arm. Adel Darwish, Middle East expert and author of *Unholy Babylon*, told UPI that one of the assassins brought the wrong caliber bullets for his gun and another had a hand grenade that got stuck in the lining of his coat.

"It bordered on farce," a former senior U.S. intelligence official told UPI of the clownish, botched assassination attempt. Kassem, hiding on the floor of his car, escaped death, and Hussein, who was hit in the leg by friendly fire, escaped to Tikrit, thanks to CIA and Egyptian intelligence agents, several U.S. government officials told UPI.

On February 8, 1963, CIA-backed plotters tried again. This time, the Ba'athists succeeded. Kassem was arrested, brought to trial, then summarily executed. Images of his dead body were then broadcast on Iraqi television.

Kassem became a martyr for Iraq's Shiite majority. His assassination set off a bloody five years of coups and countercoups, in which various Ba'athist factions vied for power. In 1968, a final coup installed Gen. Ahmad Hassan al-Baqir as president and a still fresh-faced Hussein as head of security. Declassified British biographic sketches from that era describe Saddam Hussein's "engaging smile." They write Hussein is "a formidable, single-minded and hard-headed member of the Ba'athist hierarchy, but one with whom, if only one could see more of him, it would be possible to do business."[15] He turned out to be a jolly good chap indeed. As Roger Morris, a former senior staff officer for the National Security Council, attested in a *New York Times* op-ed in 2003, with Kassem gone, suddenly "Western corporations like Mobil, Bechtel and British Petroleum were doing business with Baghdad."

The 1967 Six Day War between Israel and almost the entire Arab world created a rift in U.S.–Iraq relations. But in 1978, when an Islamic revolution overthrew another U.S.-installed dictator, the Shah Reza Pahlavi, and angry Iranians took fifty-four embassy staff members hostage, Iraq was once again on the American radar as a potential ally. Later that year, Iraqi president Al-Baqir resigned, and his deputy, Saddam Hussein, was installed as the new leader of Iraq. He lost no time getting to work, holding a televised assembly of Ba'ath Party leaders in which suspected enemies were hauled off to be executed.

In 1980, Hussein invaded Iran, kicking off one of the decade's bloodiest conflicts. The war raged for eight years and took an estimated 1.5 million lives. It also put Hussein squarely back in Washington's good graces. He was taking on one of America's thorniest foes, the Grand Ayatollah Khomeini.

In 1982, Ronald Regan returned the favor by taking Iraq off the list of nations that sponsor terrorism.* In November 1983, U.S. secretary of state George Shultz received an intelligence report describing how Hussein's troops were resorting to "almost daily use of CW [chemical weapons]" against the Iranians. With a larger population, Iran had the advantage, and Hussein was using everything at his disposal to counter the Islamic republic's onslaught. Undeterred by Hussein's use

---

*Despite the fact it was widely known Hussein was harboring Abu Nidal, one of the world's most notorious terrorists-for-hire.

of weapons of mass destruction, Reagan signed a secret order instructing his charges to do "whatever was necessary and legal" to prevent Iraq from losing the war. A month later, the president dispatched a special envoy to Baghdad on a secret mission. The envoy wasn't a diplomat or a member of Reagan's cabinet—he was a private citizen, and the CEO of a Fortune 500 company.

On December 20, 1983, the envoy met with Saddam Hussein. He was not there to lecture the dictator about his use of weapons of mass destruction or the fine print of the Geneva Conventions. He was there to talk business.

According to a recently declassified State Department report of the conversation, the envoy informed the Iraqi leader that Washington was ready for a resumption of full diplomatic relations and that they would regard "any major reversal of Iraq's fortunes as a strategic defeat for the West." The envoy even threw in a pair of golden cowboy spurs to show the dictator he was serious.[16] Iraqi leaders later described themselves as "extremely pleased" with the visit.

That envoy was Donald H. Rumsfeld, then the CEO of pharmaceutical giant Searle. The meeting was considered by some the trigger that ushered in a new era of U.S.–Iraq relations. In the years that followed, the United States supplied Hussein with shipments of dual-use munitions, supercomputers, and some of the very same chemical and biological agents, including anthrax, that Colin Powell would emphasize with such gravity in his presentation to the United Nations Security Council nearly twenty years later, making the case for America to invade Iraq.

But the real reason Rumsfeld was there was even more illuminating. Examining recently released government and corporate sources in the spring of 2003, researchers Jim Vallette, Steve Kretzmann, and Daphne Wysham discovered that Rumsfeld, under direct instructions from the White House, was there to convince Saddam Hussein to approve a highly lucrative, and highly secret, oil pipeline from Iraq to Jordan.

In their report, "Crude Vision," the researchers document how a close-knit group of high-ranking U.S. officials (including Rumsfeld, Attorney General Edwin Meese, and then–Secretary of State George Shultz*) worked in secrecy for two years attempting to secure the billion-dollar pipeline scheme for Bechtel, the same corporation that in 2003 would receive hundreds of millions of dollars of U.S. taxpayer money to reconstruct Iraq.

The pipeline would have carried millions of barrels of Iraqi crude oil a day through Jordan to the Red Sea port of Aqaba.

But there was a catch. Hussein demanded written assurance from the Israeli government that it would not instigate "unprovoked aggression" toward the pipeline. Israel's 1981 air strike on his nuclear plant at Osirak had left him a little gun-shy, so according to the Vallette report Rumsfeld sent a middleman to offer Shimon Peres's Labour Party a $500 million payment for the guarantee. The scandal broke in Israel and almost brought down the Peres government.

But it wasn't until the spring of 2003, when Vallette's team uncovered the documents, that the story was reported here in the U.S. Vallette appeared on NPR, and the *New York Times*' Bob Herbert noted his findings in one of his columns, but the story remained absent from the national debate about the war. It was as if it didn't happen. As Vallette told us,

The men who courted Saddam while he gassed Iranians are now waging war against him, ostensibly because he holds these same weapons of mass destruction. To a man, they now deny that oil has anything to do with the conflict.

*Shultz's job before entering the Reagan administration: CEO of Bechtel.

Yet during the Reagan Administration, and in the years leading up to the present conflict, these men shaped and implemented a strategy that had everything to do with securing Iraqi oil exports.

The Aqaba pipeline deal, although ultimately a failure, was just one instance of American cooperation with Hussein. Throughout the 1980s, successful deals included sending technology to the Salah al-Din military factory which helped manufacture, among other things, radar that Iraq used to shoot down U.S. bombers during the first Gulf War. The Pennsylvania-based International Signal and Control company manufactured fuses for artillery that was produced in South Africa and then sent to Iraq with the full knowledge of U.S. intelligence.[17] Even top U.S. Defense Department labs, including Lawrence Livermore, Los Alamos, and Sandia National Laboratories, supplied Iraq with WMD technology.[18]

In 1988, the most infamous incident in U.S.–Iraq relations occurred. While Hussein was enjoying the height of U.S. largesse, a major battle erupted in the northern Iraq city of Halabjah. After the invading Iranians gassed the city with cyanide, Hussein drove the Iranians out with a particularly lethal form of mustard gas, killing at least 3,200 Kurdish civilians in the process.

As images of chemically frozen Kurdish corpses were beamed around the world, evoking horrible memories of World War I,* the international community erupted in outrage. In Washington, a bipartisan effort swept through Congress to pass the 1988 Prevention of Genocide Act, a law

---

*Winston Churchill was actually the first leader to gas the Kurds, saying, "I do not understand this sqeamishness about the use of gas. I am strongly in favour of using poison gas against uncivilised tribes." Geoff Simons, *Iraq: From Sumer to Sudan*, St. Martin's Press, 1994, 179–81.

specifically targeting Iraq for strict sanctions and the Kurdish people for humanitarian aid. It would have imposed the harshest American economic sanctions against any country in twenty years.[19] The law stated in part that "Iraq's use of chemical weapons is a gross violation of international law; and Iraqi's campaign against the Kurdish people appears to constitute an act of genocide, a crime abhorred by civilized people everywhere and banned under international law."

But Senate and House leaders argued over the fine print and failed to pass the bill before Congress adjourned for the session. This suited Ronald Reagan, who had sent National Security Adviser Colin Powell to Capitol Hill to oppose the bill, even threatening to use his veto.[20] Hussein was off the hook, and aid to Iraq subsequently jumped from $500 million to $1 billion a year.[21]

In October 1989, newly elected president George H. W. Bush, with Dick Cheney as his secretary of defense, issued a national security directive, declaring "normal relations between the United States and Iraq would serve our longer-term interests and promote stability in both the Gulf and the Middle East." Two years and an invasion of an ally later, Bush I would announce, "We're dealing with Hitler revisited, a totalitarianism and brutality that is naked and unprecedented in modern times."

In all, the secret arms and technology sales made to Iraq before, during, and after it was widely known that Hussein was using chemical weapons on Iran and his own people made the Iran-Contra affair look like child's play. As *Nightline*'s Ted Koppel reported in a September 1991 broadcast:

> *[D]uring much of the 1980s and into the 1990s, [Iraq] was able to acquire sophisticated U.S. technology, intelligence material, ingredients, acquiescence, and sometimes*

*even the assistance of the U.S. government. . . . The sheer
quantity of the technology, weapons and money that were
transferred to Iraq over roughly the same period dwarfs
anything that went to Iran.*

On October 15, 2003, while Hussein was still in his hole,
Colin Powell, now Bush Jr.'s secretary of state and lead pitch-
man for Operation Iraqi Freedom's traveling road show, jour-
neyed to Halabjah to memorialize the gas attacks. His speech
that day, which had all the emotional triggers of a sermon, was
characterized by the mainstream media as typical of Powell the
Moderate's human touch.

The speech, which you can find prominently displayed on
the Coalition Provisional Authority's Web site, lays it on thick.
There's no mention of the role the U.S. played in arming the
man responsible for the Halabjah attacks, or of the role General Powell himself played in making sure Saddam Hussein remained in power after the atrocities. But read it closely. You
can almost hear the guilt seeping through:

*This is a special place and I should say something special to
you.*
But what can I say to you?
*I cannot tell you that choking mothers died holding their
choking babies.*
You know that.
*I cannot tell you that Saddam Hussein was a murderous
tyrant.*
You know that.
I cannot tell you that the world should have acted sooner.
You know that.
*I cannot tell you of the suffering of those who were poisoned
but lived.*

You know that.
What I can tell you is that what happened here in 1988 is
not going to happen again.

Weak Wills Need Not Apply

America's foreign policy has never been for the weak-willed. America's first imperial adventure set the model for decades to come. In 1899, U.S. forces went to war against Spain, with what by now should be a familiar promise to the peoples of Cuba, Puerto Rico, and the Philippines: We've come to "liberate" you from your oppressors. Fueled by the new "yellow journalism" of media mogul William Randolph Hearst, who famously told his correspondent in Cuba, "You furnish the pictures—I'll furnish the war," U.S. war ships headed to the Caribbean and the far-off Pacific archipelago. After defeating Spanish troops, President William McKinley declared U.S. forces needed to stay in the Philippines in order to "uplift and civilize and Christianize them, and by God's grace do the very best we could by them, as for our fellow men for whom Christ also died."*

As historian Howard Zinn writes in his *People's History of the United States*, apparently "the Filipinos did not get the same message from God" and fought back. The ensuing guerrilla war was brutal and long. Over the three years it took to crush the insurgency, the Americans dispatched over seventy thousand troops—four times the amount needed to defeat the Spanish. As Zinn recounts, instead of deterring Americans from future adventures, the experience stirred the imperial

*Gore Vidal wrote in his book *The American Presidency*: "When reminded that Filipinos were already Roman Catholic, the president responded, 'Exactly.'"

dreams of a capitalist class hungry for new markets. In 1900, Sen. Albert Beveridge put it bluntly:

> *Mr. President, the times call for candor. The Philippines are ours forever. . . . And just beyond the Philippines are China's illimitable markets. We will not retreat from either. . . . We will not renounce our part in the mission of our race, trustee, under God, of the civilization of the world. . . . The Pacific is our ocean. . . . Where shall we turn for consumers of our surplus. Geography answers the question. China is our natural customer. . . . The Philippines give us a base at the door of all the East.*

The occupation was not without its opponents. For many Americans, the Philippine annexation represented a dangerous precedent, a step backward toward the colonial cruelty of our European rivals. Mark Twain, America's first celebrity antiwar activist, wrote, "What we wanted, in the interest of Progress and Civilization, was the Archipelago, unencumbered by patriots struggling for independence." He suggested we replace the stars and stripes in our flag with "the skull and crossbones."

An Anti-Imperialist League was formed that "carried out a long campaign to educate the public about the horrors of the Philippine war and the evils of imperialism," writes Zinn. They published letters from soldiers depicting scenes of collective punishment that make Vietnam's My Lai massacre seem tame in comparison. In one account, a U.S. officer wrote, "Caloocan was supposed to contain 17,000 inhabitants. The Twentieth Kansas swept through it, and now Caloocan contains not one living native."

Fallujah may not be another Caloocan, but the connection between the Philippines and Iraq is not lost on today's anti-imperial activists. Nor, apparently, are the lessons of that conflict forgotten by the American elites, though for entirely different reasons.

In an interview with the conservative *National Journal*, retired Gen. Jay Garner (who headed the Coalition Provisional Authority until he proposed holding early elections and was promptly replaced), described Iraq's geostrategic importance. Garner explained, "Look back on the Philippines around the turn of the 20th century, they were a coaling station for the Navy, and that allowed us to keep a great presence in the Pacific. That's what Iraq is for the next few decades: our coaling station that gives us great presence in the Middle East . . . I hope [we're] there a long time."[22]

According to many experts, the "coaling station" the U.S. needed to replace was Saudi Arabia. The source of as much as 10 percent of America's daily oil supply* and the longtime hub of America's military presence in the Middle East was increasingly becoming unstable. As former CIA operative Robert Baer writes in his book *Sleeping with the Enemy*, "Saudi Arabia is more and more an irrational state—a place that spawns global terrorism even as it succumbs to an ancient and deeply seated isolationism, a kingdom led by a royal family that can't get out of the way of its own greed." He asks, "Is this the fulcrum we want the global economy to balance on?"

Economist Jeffrey Sachs calls the Saudi Arabia–Iraq War connection the "ricochet effect." Sitting in his Columbia University office below photos of him with Clinton, Mandela, and the pope, he echoes the CIA officer's analysis: The U.S. knew it needed to get out of Saudi Arabia and find a more reliable base of operations. With proven oil reserves second only to

---

*Saudi Arabia sits on 25 percent of the world's known oil reserves.

Saudi Arabia's, and a strategic location straddling Iran to east, Jordan and Israel to the west, and Turkey's Mediterranean trade routes to the north, Iraq was the logical move.

"Nobody in the world believes that the U.S. is in this war for anything other than oil," Sachs explained to us. "The view that 'this is not about oil' is a purely American perception not held in any other part in the world. Why we would spend $100 billion dollars for the removal of this particular dictator rather than spending billions on many other miserable governments around the world—that would be a huge question mark if indeed oil had nothing to do with this."

In fact, Iraq may just be the beginning of a geostrategic shift away from the Gulf and to the north to more stable sources of Hummer juice.

On the twentieth anniversary to the week of his secret 1983 trip to Baghdad, Secretary of Defense Donald Rumsfeld was quietly whisked off to Turkmenistan, a former Soviet Republic nestled in the Kopetdag Mountains north of Afghanistan. Like his 1983 jaunt, the seemingly sensitive diplomatic mission got sparse media attention. Turkmenistan is a key ally in the war on terror, and strategically crucial for securing the vast Caspian oil reserves that lie to the east of its borders. It also happens to be run like a "private Disney World" by a megalomaniacal former Communist Party boss. His real name is Saparmurat Niyazov, but if you're a Turkmen, by decree, you must call him "Serdar Turkmenbashy"—which means "Great Leader of all Turkmen." He's a squat, bullish man whose cult of personality rivals only North Korea's Kim Ill Sung for audacity. In terms of sheer strangeness, he makes Hussein look like Orin Hatch.

In the middle of the Turkmen capitol, there's a giant golden Turkmenbashy statue that rotates so it always faces the sun. Turkmenbashy's mug is on the airplane that brings you to the main port city, named Turkmenbashy. Turkmenbashy personally decides who enters the country and who is able to get a visa to leave. Turkmenbashy even issued a new calendar, in which he changed January to "Turkmenbashy," and renamed April after his mother.[23]

He has even written a sort of national self-help book "to eliminate all shortcomings, to raise the spirit of the Turknen"—think Mao's *Little Red Book* meets the Koran meets Dr. Phil. According to a *60 Minutes* report, "half the country lives in poverty, and Turkmenistan has the highest infant mortality rate in the region and the lowest life expectancy." There's no press freedom, since Turkmenbashy controls the newspapers and television. Citizens cannot listen to car radios or smoke in the street. Opera and ballet performances are banned. Turkmenbashy often destroys churches.

The Carnegie Endowment's Central Asia expert Martha Brill Olcott writes:

> *Looking at the political trials and arrests of family members of alleged traitors that we see going on in Turkmenistan, it's impossible not to think back to the period of Stalin's trials—so much of it seems scripted from the same school of political theater. In the 1950s and 60s, when we learned the scale of what had gone on in the Soviet Union during the 1930s and 40s, all over in the West the question was: "Why didn't people do anything?"*[24a]

Turkmenistan is not the region's only human-rights catastrophe. In fact, to the north and west of Iraq and Iran, two spokes of the axis of evil, lay a cluster of American-friendly despots—each the lord of his own brutal domain.

Human Rights Watch estimates that in Uzbekistan between seven thousand and ten thousand people, including minors, are being held in prison for their political or religious beliefs. The country's president, Islam Karimov, is a neo-Stalinist autocrat who makes old Turkmenbashy look almost quaint. According to news reports, Karimov regularly arrests anyone wearing an Islamic beard, and torture is widespread—he's been known, on occasion, to boil dissidents alive.[24b]

In Azerbaijan, the situation is just as bleak. A January 2004 Human Rights Watch report, titled "Crushing Dissent: Repression Violence and Azerbaijan's Elections," details hundreds of arbitrary arrests, widespread beatings and torture, and politically motivated firings of opposition activists and supporters following the country's October 15 presidential elections, which most Western observers considered a fraud.

On the eve of the Iraq war, 85 percent of Americans couldn't find the country we were invading on a map.[25] It's hard to imagine them doing much better locating Turkmenistan, Uzbekistan, and Azerbaijan. With approximately 39 million people and some of the lowest standards of living in the former Soviet Union, they are insignificant trading partners. But they have one thing in common that renders them infinitely strategic for America: oil. Turkmenistan, Uzbekistan, and Azerbaijan all lie to the east of the world's largest lake, the Caspian Sea. Its vast oil reserves are estimated to compare only to those of the Middle East.

So when Rumsfeld popped into Turkemistan for a visit in 2003, he wasn't there to lecture the Great Leader on the finer points of the international charter on human rights; he was there, as he had been in Baghdad back in 1983, to talk business. The country sits on an estimated 1.4 billion barrels of oil reserves, and near several of the battlefronts in the war on terror. During his visit, Rumsfeld publicly thanked Turkmenbashy for his cooperation with the U.S., and later, Gen. Tommy R. Franks met with him to offer to "expand military cooperation with Turkmenistan, including having the U.S. train and equip Niyazov's army and police." This, for a man Central Asia expert Olcott soberly compared to Josef Stalin.

Shortly after Rumsfeld left Turkmenistan, he personally congratulated the new leader of Azerbaijan, Ilham Aliev, on his electoral victory there. Uzbekistan's Karimov can count himself one of America's newfound allies as well, despite the State Department's own declaration that "Uzbekistan is an authoritarian state with a very poor human rights record,"[26] The Bush administration gave Karimov an $80 million aid package in 2002, including a staggering 1,800 percent increase in military aid over the previous year. Bush declared the country one of the "foremost partners in the fight against terrorism."*

Since transporting the black gold from the landlocked Caspian Sea to a deepwater port is a major hurdle, whoever controls the pipelines controls the oil. The main corporate–military collaboration for the Caspian region is a 1,091-mile pipeline project, years in development, that begins at Baku, Azerbaijan, traverses Georgia, and runs southwest across Turkish Kurdistan to the Mediterranean, all the while avoiding Russia and Iran. The Baku–Ceyhan pipeline project has received significant military support under both Clinton and Bush, with hundreds of National Guard troops dispatched to train their Central Asian counterparts. In 2002, U.S. energy secretary Spencer Abraham went to Azerbaijan to officiate at the pipeline's groundbreaking ceremony.

The despots' flagrantly antidemocratic practices are habitu-

*By early March 2004, the human-rights abuses got so bad, the U.S. considered holding off $100 million in aid. But when forty-one Uzbeks were killed in Islamic terrorist attacks on March 29, Karimov was back in the running for the cash. The *Guardian* headline ran, "Suicide bombings in Uzbekistan may have saved its US aid package."

ally overlooked by the administration and American-based multinational oil companies, as the U.S. military set up shop to secure the Caspian oil—without which many experts believe our entire petroleum-based economy may be in peril.

"Peak oil"—the moment that world oil production hits its zenith and, as population and demand continue to increase, initiates a new period of global oil scarcity*—is commonly projected to come by 2037. That calculation has been criticized for underestimating the impact of the enormous increases in the demand for oil as markets like China continue to rapidly expand. Colin Campbell, an Oxford-educated petroleum geologist who has worked for Texaco, British Petroleum, and Amoco, argues that the tipping point could come as early as 2010. The basic facts are these: The entire world now both produces and consumes some 75 million barrels of oil a day. By 2015, or a decade away, demand is expected to increase by more than two-thirds, or by another 60 million barrels a day. Even Bush has acknowledged that there's a crisis looming, saying, "It's becoming very clear that demand is outstripping supply."[27]

Which isn't to say that the crisis is only being realized now. As far back as the 1940s, the key framers of American Cold War foreign policy held few illusions about the gap between the rhetoric of democracy and the realities of a rapidly expanding consumer economy. George Kennan, head of the U.S. State Department Policy Planning Staff, is credited with forming much of America's postwar geopolitical strategy. In

*In April 2004, the oil industry was rocked by a scandal as Royal Dutch/Shell downgraded its proven oil reserve by 20 percent. The *Jane's Report* wrote, "As the world's natural resources shrink and global warming changes the environment, competition for unimpeded access to them has intensified and will continue to do so. About four-fifths of the world's known oil reserves lie in politically unstable or contested regions."

this statement from 1948, Kennan offers a chilling look into how America's most elite leaders really saw the world:

> We have 50 percent of the world's wealth, but only 6.3 percent of its population. In this situation, our real job in the coming period is to devise a pattern of relationships which permit us to maintain this position of disparity. We need not deceive ourselves that we can afford today the luxury of altruism and world-benefaction. . . . We should cease to talk about vague and unreal objectives such as human rights, the raising of the living standards, and democratization. The day is not far off when we are going to have to deal in straight power concepts. The less we are then hampered by idealistic slogans, the better.

Yet fifty years later, what do we have other than idealistic slogans? How many Americans would back a war called "Operation Coaling Station"?

Sergeant Hollis's War

It wasn't until our next to last night in Iraq that we'd find someone who could truly understood just how little America's objectives had changed since Kennan's time.

After three intense days embedded with the U.S. Army in an area north of Baghdad, we are placed on a dangerous "presence patrol" that takes us into Samarra, a hotbed of anti-American violence. That night, after surviving the exercise without incident, we start talking to Sergeant Robert Hollis, a thirty-five-year-old tank commander. Standing in front of a poster of Britney Spears posing with NFL football players, he begins deconstructing the historical parallels between the Second Punic War and the battle he's been fighting.

"The Romans took the fight to them," he explains. "That's what we're doing here. They wouldn't field a credible army on the field of battle, so we came into their homeland."

Sgt. Hollis is something of legend in his division, as a fast-talking, hip-hop autodidact from Alabama who spouts off about the Romans any chance he can get. The other guys don't seem to know whether what he's talking about is pure bull, or pure genius. Either way, he cracks them up. Tonight, he's getting serious, and some start listening in.

"The reality is even the Roman Empire had to fight to secure its way of life," he says. "When America says liberation, we mean capitalism. It's about globalization. It's about expansion of markets. We have to stabilize new and emerging markets in order to secure resources."

As he talks, a group of plainclothes Special Forces operatives lock and load their weapons and check their radio headsets.

He continues, "Can you tell mothers and brothers and sisters that your sons and daughters are dying for capital goods? No, you cannot. You have to make sure you tell them you are fighting for moral, ethical reasons."

Then Sgt. Hollis offers a final bleak yet depressingly accurate assessment of the operation's prospect for success.

"Will we win the hearts and minds of people? Maybe not in this generation. But you have to think in the long term. Maybe not in fifty years, maybe not in one hundred years. There's no hate. The problem is one side must win; one side must lose. The war must be won in Afghanistan, and it must be won here to improve our way of life."

The problem is not will we win, but what we will become when we do.

6

Silver Bullet
or Dirty Bomb?

Is America Fighting a
Nuclear War in Iraq?

■ ■ ■

*DU is a low-level radioactive waste, and, therefore, must be
disposed in a licensed repository.*
—Army Environmental Policy Institute, 1995

Baghdad, Iraq

THE AUWEIRJ TANK GRAVEYARD is a ruinous mess of twisted
steel on the outskirts of Baghdad near the city's southern gate.

Locals call it the "tank graveyard," but there is a menagerie
of other vehicles here. In addition to the destroyed Russian-
made T-72 tanks, there are artillery batteries, troop carriers,
trucks—even double-decker buses imported from the UK and
big American cars like Chryslers and Buicks, popular in the
Middle East for their superior air-conditioning. The only thing
they all have in common is having been on the receiving end of
Operation Rapid Dominance, the American-led invasion force
that tore its way from the Kuwait border into the heart of Baghdad over the course of three weeks in March and April 2003.

The rusty shambles are a testament to just what a turkey
shoot the campaign actually was. Some of the vehicles only
have small, neat impact holes, but their insides are blackened

to a crisp. Others are scorched, bent, and twisted into unidentifiable carcasses.

Although it's an overused cliché when describing any war-ravaged country, the sea of destruction here lives up to even Hollywood's most exaggerated "postapocalyptic" images.

All traces of human carnage are gone, and it's hard to fathom the final, horrific moments of the thousands of people who occupied these vehicles. In the early-morning sun, the graveyard is strangely beautiful. With the soft rumble of rush-hour traffic streaming by in the background, it's actually quite peaceful.

We have come here to test for traces of depleted uranium, or DU, the controversial radioactive metal that the United States military first used in combat in its ammunition during the 1991 Gulf War. The use of DU by the U.S. military is one of those dirty little secrets that isn't actually little, nor is it technically a secret. Yet few Americans are aware that for more than a decade—first in Desert Storm, then in the Balkans, and again in Iraq—the U.S. has bombarded our enemies with thousands of tons of munitions tipped with a radioactive metal more closely associated with the atomic age than with conventional warfare. The question is, Why has the mainstream American media paid so little attention to this literally radioactive issue?

The Silver Bullet

Depleted uranium is the waste by-product of nuclear power reactors. The U.S. government is currently sitting on 1.1 billion pounds of the stuff. Most of it is buried underground in sealed bunkers—which seemed like a good idea since it has a half-life of 4.5 billion years.

In the 1970s, Cold War military researchers made a convenient discovery. DU is almost twice as hard as lead, which makes it a "killer app" for use in armor-penetrating shells. Munitions with DU tips actually sharpen on impact, slicing right through steel like butter. They then explode into an ultra-hot vapor, incinerating any living thing unlucky to be close by, spraying a fine radioactive dust and sending tiny glowing metal fragments throughout the immediate vicinity. Vehicles armored with DU, like America's premier battle tank the M1A1 Abrams, are nearly impenetrable to non-DU shells.

Early in the development of DU, even Republicans had political misgivings. In 1978, then-Senator Bob Dole (R-Kan.) said, "They seem to have chosen this material for bullets because uranium metal is dense and because DU is cheap. Needless to say, I find this proposal shocking." The military had been using tungsten, which performed adequately, with none of the toxic or radioactive downside. But DU was better and cheaper. So the Pentagon moved forward with an ingenious, if precarious, "recycling" program. America's atomic garbage was sold at pennies on the dollar to defense contractors eager to manufacture the military's next generation of superammo.

In some ways, DU is so good, it's unfair—Oakland Raiders playing a peewee football team without pads unfair. If the tank graveyard at Auweirj is proof of anything, it's that in war, there is no such thing as good sportsmanship.

In the first Gulf War, the media focused overwhelmingly on new technologies like the Patriot missile and the much-hyped "smart bombs." These weapons provided news networks with instant, bloodless, video game–like images to beam back to viewers safely ensconced in their living rooms. But the reality was America's rout of Iraqi forces was largely thanks to overwhelming air and ground firepower that killed the old-fashioned way: by dropping as many "dumb" bombs and shooting as many large-caliber bullets as we could.

Of the 88,000 tons of bombs dropped, only 7 percent were guided. According to the Pentagon, U.S. forces used 320 tons of DU. Eighty percent of it came from the A-10 "tank-killer" plane, whose seven-barreled 30 mm Gatling machine guns saturated with bullets hundreds of square feet in seconds.

The results were dramatic. Iraq went into the war with 4,280 tanks. When the dust settled, it had 580. Pentagon officials later said Iraqi shells literally "bounced off" the DU-enforced armor of U.S. tanks.[1] The final body count was even more shocking. In fact, the Gulf War (if you can even call it a war) was probably the most lopsided conflict in modern history. By some estimates, over 100,000 Iraqi soldiers and up to 35,000 civilians were killed. American losses amounted to 148 combat deaths and 145 noncombat deaths.*

While some experts debate just how much of a role DU rounds played in those astounding results, as far as the military brass was concerned, DU "radioactive kinetic penetrators" made a stellar debut in Desert Storm—and the Pentagon was not going to give up a cheap, highly lethal weapon without a fight.

Activists argue those successes didn't come without a price. A growing number of scientists and veterans claim the Pentagon's use of DU is a way of what they call "backloading" causalities. Armed with superbullets and armor, on the battlefield, DU gives our soldiers the tactical advantage. But the scenario masks a darker truth: the very weapon that is saving lives in the heat of battle may be slowly killing the warriors when they return home, conveniently away from the news media and outside the official battlefield body count.

Tens of thousands of Gulf War veterans are suffering from

---

*It gets even more ridiculous when you consider that out of the 148 Americans killed in combat, 35 of those were from "friendly-fire" incidents. In other words, more Americans died in Humvee accidents and other mishaps than were actually killed by Iraqi soldiers.

what have come to be known as "Gulf War Illnesses," an umbrella term that refers to a composite of ailments that include chronic fatigue, rashes, severe headaches, respiratory illness, memory loss, even cancer and birth defects in children. The Pentagon originally tried to claim the symptoms were from "stress." But it has since acknowledged that the illnesses are real.

According to Veterans Administration (VA) figures obtained by GNN, as of November 2003, 9,429 veterans who served in the Gulf War have since died, and 174,768 are listed as injured or sick. Even more alarming, the VA lists 221,020 vets—almost 40 percent of General Schwarzkopf's army—as having filed claims for medical care, compensation, and pension benefits as a result of their service in the Gulf War. Just how many of those are suffering from a "Gulf War Illness" the VA won't say. But by contrast, only 9 percent of World War II and Vietnam veterans filed similar claims.[2]

Just what is making the soldiers sick is still unknown, and that mystery is the subject of heated debate. Many point to DU, but acknowledge it is just one hazard in a toxic stew of battlefield contaminants soldiers were exposed to in the first Gulf War, including burning oil fields, fallout from destroyed Iraqi chemical weapons facilities, desert parasites, faulty vaccines, controversial malaria pills, even an industrial-strength bug repellent. Most doctors who have treated Gulf War Illnesses believe a combination of the above is to blame. But anti-DU activists point out that many of classic "Gulf War Illness" symptoms were also seen in foreign soldiers serving the Balkans, where none of the Gulf War–specific factors were present. DU, they argue, was the only constant.*

---

*In 2002, UN experts found radioactive hot spots in Bosnia they believe were a result of NATO air strikes using DU bombs in 1995.[3]

During the 2003 Iraq invasion, experts initially estimated coalition forces used between 1,100 to 2,200 tons of DU—three times what was used in the first Gulf War. In March 2004, the Pentagon released much lower numbers.* But in 1991, most of the DU rounds were fired in the open desert. This time around, the war was, and continues to be, fought in heavily populated areas where millions of Iraqi civilians and hundreds of thousands of American soldiers, civilian administrators, their coalition allies, and personnel from the news media, international NGOs, and private reconstruction firms currently eat, breathe, and sleep.

That's what has so many people worried.

Radioactive Playground

Raed Jarrar is a twenty-six-year-old Palestinian-Iraqi architect best known to the world as one-half of the now-famous "Baghdad Blogger" team. In the lead-up to the American invasion, his best friend Salam started a Web diary, or blog, under the pseudonym Salam Pax. For months it was the only uncensored reporting coming out of Baghdad. International acclaim, even a book deal followed.† After Baghdad fell, Jarrar started his own NGO, calling it Emarr ("reconstruction"). The organization reflected his mantra: "Democracy cannot come from the outside." Emarr completed more than a hundred small reconstruction projects, like fixing up local schools

*According to Department of Defense health official Michael Kilpatrick, only 120 to 130 tons were used.[4]

†Raed began writing for the blog after the regime fell, and in 2004 started his own called "Raed in the Middle." See http://raedinthemiddle.blogspot.com.

for five hundred dollars and building small bridges for ninety dollars—work that American contractors like Bechtel would bill for thousands.

For Jarrar, DU is a metaphor for everything that is wrong with the way the U.S. has gone about "liberating" Iraq.

"At the same time that the American administration tries to convince Americans and the rest of the people of the world that they just wanted to help the world get rid of Iraq's chemical and atomic weapons," Jarrar told us, "we find the same administration using radioactive weapons in the middle of cities and not putting any effort to clean and remove the Iraqi tanks and weapons hit by DU after the war stopped."

Whole neighborhoods in Iraq are littered with spent shells. Iraqi tanks and other armored vehicles destroyed by American forces still sit where they were hit—in the middle of narrow residential streets and in fields where animals graze.

"The children were playing on them like a playground," he says.

Jarrar began to photograph the evidence with his digital camera, alerting local elders of the danger radioactive contamination poses to their communities. We brought Jarrar a professional Geiger counter to help him pinpoint the hottest spots. With instructions from a reputable California lab, we hope to take radiation readings against background levels. The Geiger counter provides an easy-to-read digital screen and an audio alarm that sounds as radiation levels, measured in counts per minutes (CPMs), increase.

The first place we're starting is the Auweirj graveyard. As Jarrar moves through the destruction, the ominous ticking of the Geiger counter adds to the otherworldly, science-fiction-like scene. Soon men begin to appear like apparitions from the shadows of the debris, and we realize that this is not just a graveyard. It's a work site for scores of scrap-metal scavengers. Armed with blowtorches, some driving flatbed tractors to haul away their booty, they methodically dismantle the free metal. For them, the graveyard is a jackpot, an almost endless supply of product that they sell to local machine-part fabricators or recycle themselves into car parts, household items, anything.

The graveyard has no fences, and there are no visible markings of any kind to indicate that they may be working in a radioactive wasteland. We test a tank. Nothing. Then we reach a troop carrier. It's almost perfectly intact, with only a small impact hole approximately ten inches wide on its side. The hole is almost perfectly round, surrounded by metal that seems to have liquefied and sprayed outward. It is the telltale sign that it was hit by a "radioactive kinetic penetrator"—a shell tipped with depleted uranium. The Geiger counter tells us we are correct.

"We've got a problem," Raed calls out, as the clicking of the Geiger counter becomes faster. "DU."

Holding the sensor up to the missile's entry hole, the monitor readings increase rapidly, first 200, then 300, then 400 times background radiation levels. As the Geiger clicks and we back away from the tank, one of the scavengers approaches.

Raed asks, "Do you guys cut this?

SCAVENGER: "Yes."

RAED: "You guys just sell it?"

SCAVENGER: "Yes."

RAED: "Do you know that in ten years you might get sick?"

SCAVENGER: "Yeah, God willing (I won't)."

RAED: "But you know this might make you sick, right?"

SCAVENGER: "Yes, it's uranium that they hit the tank with, and it can give you diseases."

RAED: "So why do you work here?"
SCAVENGER: "It's work."

Dangers of DU

The U.S. and UK governments have acknowledged in the past that DU dust can be dangerous. But they claim the danger is localized and dissipates quickly. The worst thing that could happen to you if you inhale it, they contend, is a mild form of chemical poisoning, not irradiation.

There is little definitive science on the long-term health effects of DU exposure. On one extreme of the bitterly contested debate, there are conspiracists who claim DU is part of a genocidal plot to irradiate the Middle East and steal the Arabs' oil.* In the middle is a small, devoted core of activists and vets who claim that there is ample evidence that radioactive weapons are poisoning our troops and pose a very real long-term environmental threat—but acknowledge that there needs to be more testing to fully understand the specific health risks. And on the other extreme, you have the Pentagon, whose stance was best expressed to us by a burly bomb-disposal expert we met on a U.S. military base in Iraq who said, "Hell, DU bullets are only dangerous if you suck on 'em."

DU emits what is called alpha-particle radiation, at very low levels. The radioactivity travels only a short distance—centimeters—before fully releasing all its energy. Alpha radiation can be stopped by something as thin as a piece of paper. But when DU ignites, nothing can protect you. Radioactive

---

*As proof they offer a recently unearthed 1943 Manhattan Project memo written by Brig. Gen. Leslie Groves that suggests using uranium dust as a "terrain contaminant" to irradiate large areas of Germany, as well as a "gas warfare instrument" to poison Nazi troops on the battlefield.

oxides are created that can be easily inhaled or ingested, and the particles are so fine, they can penetrate any known protective air filter. Once DU is in the environment, there is no way to clean it up. DU contaminated dust can spread for hundreds of miles, especially in the dust-storm-prone Middle East. Researchers have found DU soil contamination in the Kuwaiti desert. And according to the U.N. Environmental Program, once lodged in the soil, DU can cause up to a hundredfold increase in uranium levels in groundwater.

In the U.S., areas where the military has tested depleted uranium have been a huge problem. In Jefferson County, Indiana, for instance, when the Pentagon closed a two-hundred-acre proving ground, the lowest estimate for cleaning the site up was $7.8 billion, which didn't include the cost of permanently burying contaminated earth and vegetation eighteen feet underground. Not wanting to pay, the Pentagon military tried to give the land to the National Park Service for a nature preserve. The offer was refused, according to *Le Monde diplomatiques*.[5]

A growing body of science shows that alpha emitters like DU are known to be carcinogenic. Inhalation exposure of low quantities of low-level radioactive material is a well-established hazard. Once you're contaminated, there is no way to get it out of your body.

Anti-DU activists point to the experience of Navajo uranium miners in New Mexico. At the dawn of the atomic age after World War II, the U.S. government began large-scale mining operations on Navajo land, reassuring the Navajo miners there was little danger in handling the yellow ore or its tailings. Today, whole swaths of the Navajo reservation are contaminated, and hundreds, possibly thousands, of miners and their families have been made sick, many with lung cancer, from inhaled uranium dust.

Of the 110 communities on the Navajo reservation, more than one-third are reportedly affected by radioactivity. In 2002, Congress passed the Radiation Exposure Compensation Act (RECA), which acknowledged uranium mining had made the community sick and established a $100 million trust fund. "Already 350 to 400 workers have died from cancer and other diseases. In some communities, the majority of women are widows," Anna Rondon of the Southwest Indigenous Uranium Forum told a Hiroshima, Japan, human-rights group.[6]

Similarly, many believe the real danger DU poses for Iraqis and for U.S. soldiers living and fighting nearby is long-term exposure to contaminated dust or water. Iraqi children, who play in the dirt-filled streets and lack the comforts of basic hygiene we take for granted, are especially are vulnerable. DU can actually become more dangerous over time as it decays. Critics claim that the term *depleted* itself is a misnomer. While the metal is allegedly 40 percent less radioactive than "undepleted" uranium, DU contains the highly toxic U-238 isotope that, when broken down, creates protactinium-234, which in turn radiates nasty beta particles, which can cause cancer. Recent studies have shown that repeated exposure to low-level radiation can actually have more serious effects than one larger, single dose. Once the particles are inside your body, the effects are cumulative, the DU particles release their energy, permanently and irreparably damaging your DNA.*

These effects are exactly what many Iraqi doctors said they began seeing following the first Gulf War.

On February 27, 1991, President Bush ordered what would become the most controversial military action of the

---

*Anti-DU activists claim this long-term hazard is a violation of Article 35 of the Geneva Convention of 1949, which prohibits weapons "of a nature to cause superfluous injury or unnecessary suffering."

Gulf War. U.S. air and ground forces attacked a massive convoy of retreating Iraqi soldiers and civilians on their way back from Kuwait. The U.S. blasted vehicles at the front and rear of a sixty-mile stretch of desert highway south of Basra, then relentlessly bombed and strafed the ensuing traffic jam for hours with DU-tipped bullets fired from A-10 "Warthogs." When it was over, two thousand vehicles and tens of thousands of charred and dismembered bodies littered what became known as the Highway of Death.

For many Iraqi scientists, the highway "blitzkrieg," as one *BBC News* reporter called it, and other engagements throughout the south, directly led to a spike of birth defects in the children of Iraqis living in the region or who had fought there. By the mid-1990s, Iraqi doctors began to voice concern about a "worrying number of anophthalmos cases—babies born without eyes." Statistically, only one in 50 million births should be anophthalmic, yet one Baghdad hospital claimed to have had eight cases in just two years. The Iraqis claimed that seven of the fathers had been exposed to American DU anti-tank rounds in 1991. They also pointed to an increased number of cases of babies born without the crowns of their skulls, and stubs for limbs.[7] As Representative Jim McDermott (D-Wash.) said on the floor of the House, "Iraqi families don't ask if their baby is a boy or a girl anymore, only whether it is normal."[8] Disturbingly, veterans in the U.S. soon began to see similar deformities in their babies.*

A study of American Gulf War veterans showed that 67 percent had children with severe illnesses, missing eyes, or blood infections. In March 2004, British scientists announced

---

**Life magazine, whose November 1995 article "Tiny Victims of Desert Storm" included harrowing photos of the vets' malformed babies, was one of the few mainstream publications to explore the issue in depth.[9]

they had found that children of UK Gulf War veterans were 50 percent more likely to have birth defects than soldiers who weren't sent into the region.

There has only been one soldier whose death has been officially listed as caused by Gulf War syndrome. In April 1999, Terry Riordon, a member of the Canadian Armed Forces who served in the Gulf War, died at age forty-five. Previously a marathon runner, two months after his return from the war he could barely walk. He had all the classic symptoms, loss of motor control, chronic fatigue, respiratory difficulties, chest pain, difficulty breathing, sleep problems, short-term memory loss, testicle pain, body pains, aching bones, diarrhea, and depression. A high level of DU was found in his urine. Shortly before his death, he willed his body to the Uranium Medical Research Centre, a nonprofit group run by a former U.S. Army doctor. Researchers at the Toronto-based organization claim they found high levels of DU in his lungs, thyroid, bones, and elsewhere. The Canadian government confirmed their findings. It was the first official confirmation of a soldier's death due to Gulf War syndrome, though the DU connection was denied by the Canadian government.

Despite Riordon's case, and the mounting body of evidence, the Pentagon has always held firm to its claim that DU is safe. A report on the Department of Defense's DU Web site reads, in part: "Gulf War exposures to depleted uranium (DU) have not to date produced any observable adverse health effects attributable to DU's chemical toxicity or low-level radiation."*

---

*A U.S. Army health spokesman didn't respond to our request for an interview.

Fields of Nasiriyah

It's the day after our graveyard visit. We are more than a little spooked by the previous day's run-in with radioactivity, but we want to do a couple more readings in the south, where the fighting back in March 2003 was the heaviest.

Outsiders historically have never received a warm welcome in Nasiriyah. In 1915, the British battled Ottoman forces here, leaving some five hundred of their troops dead or wounded. In 1991, when Shiite rebels rose up against Hussein's mostly Sunni regime, the result was a bloodbath. Today, the city of some 400,000 (230 miles southeast of Baghdad) is slowly coming back to life, but the scars of war are visible everywhere. During the opening days of Rapid Dominance, Hussein tried to slow the American advance to the capital by placing Russian-built T-72 tanks in dug-in defensive positions all across the city and its environs. He also sent his most elite units, the feared Saddam Fedeyeen, undercover, dressed as civilians to blend in with the local population and threaten them with death if they didn't fight. The battle was fierce. Eighteen American marines* and an estimated eight hundred Iraqis, mostly civilians, were killed, with up to three thousand wounded.[10] A nineteen-year-old private from West Virginia named Jessica Lynch was taken captive.

As we awkwardly head into the brush of a field south of the city, Raed Jarrar jokes to his friend, "Abbas, you be the clearer of mines."

A young goat shepherd points us to an open field down the road where three Russian-made tanks, surrounded by mounds of dirt, are sitting as if frozen in time. At first glance they don't

---

*Up to ten marines may have been killed by "friendly fire" from an American A-10, most likely using DU-tipped bullets.[11]

even look like they've been hit. But as we get closer, we realize we're wrong.

As another goat shepherd and his sons look on nervously, we go to test the first tank.

Our hearts jump.

We are now getting radiation readings of 900, then 1,000, then 1,300 times (9,000 to 13,000 percent) background levels. The readings are localized at the missile entry holes—but it's a strong indication that the entire area could be contaminated.

Later we scrub ourselves and our equipment thoroughly, and some of us throw away the clothes and shoes we were wearing.

Our days as atomic detectives are over.*

The Politics of DU

In Europe, DU is a major issue. NATO forces used DU in Bosnia and then in the 1999 campaign to blast the Serbs out of Kosovo. Subsequent studies found small but significant levels of DU in Serbian drinking water, and a small number of European soldiers and local civilians began to come down with what became known as "Balkan syndrome," complaining of symptoms similar to those afflicting America's Gulf War vets.† In 1996, the United Nations even passed a resolution that classified DU ammunition as an illegal weapon of mass destruction. There is an ongoing and active movement among European Green Party members to ban DU altogether.

---

*Researchers from a Canadian research center, in Iraq at the same time we were, found similar readings in many locations across the country. The two field staff members' urine tested positive for DU.[12]

†Anti-DU activists argue the similarities between the symptoms of sick European soldiers who were never in the Gulf and American Gulf War vets suffering from "Gulf War Illnesses" prove that DU is what is making them sick.

The British press in particular have been especially thorough in covering the issue. Between March 1999 and March 2004, the UK *Guardian*, for instance, ran more than one hundred stories on DU. The *New York Times* ran eight. Log on to the BBC News Web site, and you'll find a whole special section devoted to DU, complete with diagrams, scientific reports, and links to scores of BBC articles. Log on to CNN's Web site, and you'll find a smattering of wire service articles, and the only link for more information will lead you directly to the Pentagon's official DU Web site, where Department of Defense–approved scientists reassure visitors (presumably worried soldiers and their families) that the "alleged" dangers of DU are all hype.

GNN is one of only three American news organizations to have conducted its own radiation tests in Iraq. The others are the *Seattle Post-Intelligencer* and the *Christian Science Monitor*, both news organizations with strong records on environmental reporting.

The *Monitor*'s Moscow bureau chief, Scott Peterson, whom we contacted by phone in Russia, is a veteran of almost every major conflict of the last decade: the West Bank, Gaza, Somalia, Rwanda, Sudan, Chechnya, Afghanistan. He began covering DU in 1998, first in Iraq, then in Kosovo, and then once more in Iraq after the 2003 invasion. He is considered by many to be the top American reporter on the issue. His experience offers an invaluable window into just how difficult it is even for dedicated journalists to get to the bottom of the DU story. As Peterson found out, concrete conclusions are hard to come by in the murky mix of incomplete scientific data, agenda-driven activists, and high-stakes government propaganda.

In 1998, Peterson was in Baghdad working on a story about the effects U.S. economic sanctions were having on everyday Iraqis, when government authorities approached him with an offer. They granted him unprecedented access to report the DU story, setting up interviews with leading doctors and scientists, even a visit to former Gulf War battlefields, including the Highway of Death, where he was able to conduct what would be the first in an ongoing series of a radiation tests. What he found shocked him. His readings showed high levels of radiation across wide areas of the south. In hospitals in Basra, near the heaviest fighting, Iraqi doctors presented him with often horrifying evidence—pictures of deformed babies they said were caused by DU exposure.[13]

Peterson poured himself into the story, spending hundreds of hours going over testimony, scientific studies, and conducting scores of interviews, which often included five-hour conversations with atomic scientists that lasted late into the night. While working on the story, Peterson befriended an Iraqi he called "Khalid," a scientist who headed up an official research center that dealt with DU issues. Khalid helped him organize interviews with Iraqi officials, military officers, soldiers, and doctors.

The closer Peterson got to the story, the more he began to realize there was much more there than met the eye. He began to suspect that Hussein had been using the DU issue for political purposes, and that everything that he was learning wasn't necessarily true. The Iraqi secret police accused Peterson of being a spy, and he had to flee the country. Khalid was arrested and interrogated. It turns out, Peterson had discovered Hussein's dirty little secret about DU.

In the first months after Iraqi forces were driven from Kuwait, Hussein had latched on to the American use of DU as the ultimate example of American criminality. *The Americans talk about human rights but are using radioactive weapons.* The dictator did everything he could to propagate the idea that DU was killing the children of Iraq. International conferences

were held in Europe in which Iraqi doctors brought out horrific pictures of deformed babies as proof that DU was causing
an epidemic. Well-meaning if often naive American and European activists who were moved by the "evidence" began to
mobilize around the issue. In the UK, Labour Party MP George
Galloway started a fund for Iraqi victims in the name of a
young Iraqi girl who was alleged to have been poisoned by
DU. Activists from as far away as Japan, where radiation poisoning is an emotional issue, started campaigns.

Iraqis were getting sick, but what was causing it was
far from clear-cut. Peterson discovered that Hussein had
other reasons for blaming health problems in Iraq on the U.S.
"All of the south of Iraq is a toxic wasteland," Peterson explained to us. "The area north of Basra was a front in the
war with Iran, where chemical weapons were used. And Hussein used chemical weapons against the Shiites in the 1991
uprising."

By blaming DU, Hussein was able to defray attention from
his own human-rights abuses. Hussein even had officials keep
dead babies in cold storage so they'd be on hand for staged
mass "funerals" for foreign TV cameras and activists.[14]

While Hussein's propaganda about DU was getting increasingly sophisticated, the Pentagon and the White House
kicked their own spin machine into gear, trotting out study after study showing DU was safe, and making sure all military
spokespeople followed a carefully prepared script. Colin Powell even included a section on DU in the report he presented
to the United Nations to make the case for war in February
2003. Titled "Apparatus of Lies: Saddam's Disinformation
and Propaganda 1990–2003," the dossier included a section
titled "The Depleted Uranium Scare," which declared DU as
"relatively harmless" and proposed that "scientific evidence"

shows that Iraqi birth defects were most likely caused by "Iraqi use of chemical weapons." It didn't offer any proof. In another section, the report showed diagrams of Hussein's "mobile biological weapons labs," which later turned out to be trucks used for inflating weather balloons. It was just one of a plethora of dubious allegations included in the now-discredited UN presentation.*

Despite the often maddening distortions on both sides, Peterson came away convinced the health threat of DU was real and that the U.S. government was doing everything in its power to cover it up. "The Pentagon has not let a crack of light come through on this from the first day," says Peterson. "The day they do is the day they are hit with tens of thousands of lawsuits and compensation claims."

When Baghdad fell, Peterson returned to Iraq, knowing that the DU story hadn't gone away. Outside the country when the war began, he caught the American invasion on satellite TV and watched images of an A-10 Warthog strafing the Iraqi Ministry of Planning building. He knew there was going to be a problem. The A-10s were most likely using DU-tipped ammunition, and they were blasting away right in the center of Baghdad.

"I knew exactly where to go," he said.

When he finally got into Baghdad, Peterson grabbed his radiation detector and headed straight to the ministry building. Just as he suspected, littering the ground were scores of spent shells, some registering at nearly 1,900 times background levels.

*Many of the WMD allegations included in Powell's report were later found to have originated from a discredited Iraqi defector with ties to Ahmed Chalabi, with the apt code name "Curveball."[15]

The building is just three hundred yards from the heavily fortified main entrance of Hussein's former Republican Palace, now the headquarters for the Coalition Provisional Authority. Peterson also found a three-foot-long DU dart from a 120 mm tank shell lying by the entrance. It produced radiation at more than 1,300 times background levels. He could find only one site in Baghdad where U.S. troops had put up handwritten warnings in Arabic for Iraqis to stay away. We couldn't find any.

Media coverage of Peterson's findings across the world mark a deep lack of concern on the part of U.S. mainstream media outlets. Peterson's findings were headline news in the UK and across the Arab world. Page one of the *London Express* blared DANGEROUSLY HIGH LEVELS OF RADIATION MEASURED AROUND BAGHDAD. Yet here in the U.S., even with a bold headline on Drudge.com linking to the *Express* story, no major mainstream media outlets picked up the story. Not only were his explosive findings ignored journalistically, but when he returned to the gate two weeks later, no one had even bothered to pick up the radioactive shells. They were still sitting right where he had left them.

Rokke's Rules

"You guys don't know what you are messing with. This isn't a game. This is deadly stuff."

It's our first time talking to Dr. Doug Rokke on the phone, and we are being scolded vehemently for going to Iraq in search of depleted uranium readings.

Dr. Rokke is the ultimate DU insider. Prior to and during the Gulf War, he was the director of the Department of Defense's Depleted Uranium Project. It was his responsibility, as he puts it, "to identify, collect, secure, decontaminate, process, and dispose of U.S. friendly-fire equipment struck by uranium munitions." He headed up a team responsible for cleaning up U.S. tanks accidentally destroyed by U.S. artillery laced with DU.

Dr. Rokke is now the Pentagon's most outspoken and controversial whistle-blower. For speaking out, Dr. Rokke has become a focal target for the Pentagon's spin machine and, he claims, its intelligence officers. He is also racked by a level of suspicion we have yet to experience. According to Rokke, shots have been fired into his house, his phone has been tapped, and his every move is being monitored. He tries to keep his schedule known to only a small circle of cohorts.

After months of phone calls and unreturned messages, we finally decide to fly to Chicago and call from the airport. He informs us we first need to meet with Denise Nichols, a former air force nurse and Gulf War Illness victim, an integral part of Rokke's extended network of Gulf War veteran-activists. She lives in Denver. Only after we spend a day with her, getting debriefed on the complex medical tragedy that is Gulf War Illness, are we finally granted permission to meet with Rokke. We turn around and drive the one thousand miles back to Illinois.

Rokke could have simply been using Nichols as a counter-intelligence screener, or what seemed to be a cantankerous, paranoid man may simply have been veteran suffering from Gulf War Illness. As we learned from our research and numerous meetings with veterans, common symptoms of the Gulf War Illness are "chronic fatigue, headache, muscle and joint aches and pains, and cognitive disturbances."[16]

A stocky, blunt man, Rokke has the intensity of someone

who knows he is largely alone fighting one of the most powerful and highly funded organizations in the world: the U.S. Department of Defense.

After he returned from the Gulf, he almost immediately began experiencing the classic symptoms of Gulf War Illness: joint pain, dizziness, and headaches. But it wasn't until two and half years later that military doctors told him he was "thrashed with uranium." His urine had shown five thousand times the acceptable level. Despite fatigue and chronic pain, Rokke spends his time traveling the country, giving lectures and lobbying Washington to halt the use of DU, however unsuccessfully.

Prior to the Gulf War, he had been tasked to create an instructional safety video for troops dealing with DU contamination. But on the eve of the war, Rokke's recommendations and video were scrapped. By its own admission, part of the reason the Pentagon scrapped the program was that "DU training tended to scare people."[17]

Most soldiers went into battle with no idea they were using radioactive ammunition. Yet, as Rokke points out, their training manuals require that anyone who comes within twenty-five meters of any DU-contaminated equipment or terrain wear respiratory and skin protection, and states that "contamination will make food and water unsafe for consumption."

Rokke appealed to the Pentagon to test soldiers as they returned. "When it didn't happen, and my guys started to get sick and die . . . I knew I was sick [and] it was time to speak out. You must speak out and tell the truth, you must as a warrior, and I'm just finishing the job, I am a warrior." Soon he was persona non grata, a military outcast shunned by many mainstream veterans' groups. Thus began a decade-long struggle to get the word out.

"It's obvious today that the military did know, but they

didn't inform anybody," Rokke says. Rokke has two smoking guns that he claims prove the Pentagon knew the dangers of DU and covered them up. One memo is now known as the "Los Alamos memorandum."

The memo reads in part, "there has been and continues to be a concern regarding the impact of DU on the environment. Therefore, if no one makes a case for the effectiveness of DU on the battlefield, DU rounds may become politically unacceptable and thus, be deleted from the arsenal. . . . Keep this sensitive issue in mind when after action reports are written."

A second memo, from the Defense Nuclear Agency, appeared at about the same time. It read in part, "Alpha particles (uranium oxide dust) from expended rounds is a health concern, but Beta particles from fragments and intact rounds is a serious health threat. . . ." For Rokke, the intent is clear: "The United States and the world know about the health and the environmental consequences of using this munition, and they don't care."

In fact, these memos are the just the tip of the iceberg. Anti-DU researchers like the San Francisco–based Dan Fahey have uncovered numerous other instances in which the U.S. military itself or independent organizations under contract with the military have come to similar conclusions. A 1990 report conducted by Science Applications International Corporation (SAIC), a CIA-connected defense technology firm, states, "Aerosol DU exposures to soldiers on the battlefield could be significant with potential radiological and toxicological effects."[18]

The SAIC report went on to conclude that depleted uranium is a:

low level alpha radiation emitter which is linked to cancer when exposures are internal, [and] chemical toxicity caus-

*ing kidney damage. . . . Short term effects of high doses
can result in death, while long term effects of low doses
have been implicated in cancer.*[19]

Yet despite Rokke's battlefield experiences and his trove of
rather shocking documents, he has failed to become a major
force for policy reform. While he is portrayed as nothing short
of a hero in the alternative media, apart from a brief appearance in the spotlight—a 1999 interview on *60 Minutes*—he
has largely been ignored by the big news outlets.

Rokke is a confounding character. His credibility has been
attacked by Fahey, a navy Gulf War veteran who has become
one of the most outspoken anti-DU activists, and one of the
most persistent Rokke "debunkers." He's testified before
Congress and even met with high-ranking Pentagon officials.
While his concerns largely mirror Rokke's, he believes Rokke
overstates many of his claims. For Fahey, Rokke is an impedi-
ment in the struggle to get the Pentagon to change its polices
on DU.

"What is clear is that elements of the U.S. government will
manipulate information and even lie about the health of U.S.
combat veterans to avoid liability for DU's health and environmental effects," says Fahey. He decries, "the willingness of
some anti-DU activists to promote theories as fact," and to
"manipulate statistics."

Fahey, for instance, rips Rokke for his widely reported
claim that "thirty men on his team" had died since the war
ended. In one of the few times the Pentagon directly responded to Rokke, a military spokesman said that only two
soldiers had died who had worked in his unit.

When we confront Rokke on this, he backs off, saying,
"The numbers are not important." He lists off the number of

dead from other units that were in the DU cleanup effort, but refuses to provide us names.

We remember something Peterson told us. "This story is extremely difficult. There is no one involved who doesn't have an agenda."

In December 2003, a group of New Jersey–based Army National Guardsmen who had recently returned from Iraq contacted New York *Daily News* reporter Juan Gonzalez. They were worried. Scores of men in their unit were sick, many complaining of classic Gulf War Illness symptoms: rashes, shortness of breath, nearly daily headaches, and, more ominously, kidney problems—a possible indicator of radiation poisoning. When they asked their superiors to test them for uranium, the army refused.

Gonzalez was the right choice. He is a veteran muckraker. In 2003, he broke the World Trade Center air-quality scandal, uncovering how the Environmental Protection Agency, under pressure from the White House, had changed an air-quality report to conceal serious health risks.

"There was all kinds of pressure on the paper from the White House, the EPA, and the business community," he told us. "So I am used to getting a lot of heat."

Gonzalez convinced his paper to pay for tests on nine of the soldiers. He brought in Dr. Asaf Durakovic, a former chief of nuclear medicine at a U.S. military veteran's hospital and head of the private Uranium Medical Research Center, whose group had tested Terry Riordan and currently performs the only independent testing on American vets concerned they had been exposed to DU. Dr. Asaf Durakovic found that fourteen of twenty-seven sick Gulf War vets he tested had DU in their urine nine years after the war.[20]

On Sunday April 3, 2004, the *Daily News* finally ran the

story, its front-page blaring: "Shell Shock! News Investigation: We find uranium from U.S. ammo in sick soldiers coming home from Iraq" next to a photo of a disheartened-looking Cpl. Anthony Yonnone, of the New Jersey National Guard. Of the ten Guardsmen they tested, six tested positive for depleted uranium. The story ran for five pages and described how someone had dragged a destroyed Iraqi tank onto the former Iraqi airbase where they were living. It sat there for weeks, one hundred yards from where the men slept.

The day after the story broke, the Pentagon immediately went into spin-control mode. The lead of the Associated Press story that ran that Monday made it sound like the army had been responding to the men's concerns, despite the fact they had been refused care:

> "A handful of GIs complained of illnesses after reported exposure to depleted uranium in Iraq. Up to six soldiers from a National Guard unit based in Orangeburg, N.Y., have undergone exams at Fort Dix, and three of them remain there under observation," Fort Dix spokeswoman Carolee Nisbet said Monday. "We are following up on this. We are on top of it. It's not something that has fallen by the wayside," she said.

We tracked down the German scientist Axel Gerdes, who had conducted the tests. Gerdes, an experienced researcher at the University of Frankfurt, confirmed to us that the soldiers' urine had tested positive for uranium, but in fairly small quantities. Gerdes noted that urine tests don't offer an accurate indication of how much DU is actually in a human body—for that you need to do much more intrusive testing, like a biopsy of the lung tissue, where inhaled DU particles would most likely have settled. "I wouldn't be surprised if you found levels thousands times what we found in the urine," he told us.*

High Stakes

Out of nine hundred veterans officially believed to have been exposed to DU in the first Gulf War, only thirty-two have ever been tested. In reality, it's estimated that tens of thousands of soldiers were actually exposed, based on surveys of ten thousand veterans showing that three out of four came into contact with destroyed Iraqi equipment.

Thanks to efforts of people like Peterson, Gonzalez, Rokke, and Fahey, there is an increased awareness that DU could be a problem, that the Pentagon may be treating the issue seriously this time. As of April 2004, over five hundred Operation Iraqi Freedom veterans have reportedly been tested according to the Pentagon, and the results from the first 147 indicate that "several" vets were exposed to DU.[21]

But many anti-DU activists are not holding their breath. Testing is expensive, and the potential liability for the U.S. government is staggering. Just conducting a simple urine test costs a thousand dollars a pop. Detection and treatment could easily tap billions of dollars from an already overburdened VA system. And that's not counting the potential civilian exposures, like private contractors working in security and the reconstruction of Iraq.

The Pentagon knows just how high the stakes are. As a 1994 U.S. Army Environmental Policy Institute study concluded, "When DU is indicted as a causative agent for Desert

---

*In March 2004, the Pentagon announced it had done its own tests on the New Jersey–based National Guardsmen, and found no traces of DU in their urine.

Storm illness, the Army must have sufficient data to separate fiction from reality. Without forethought and data, the financial implications of long-term disability payments and health-care costs would be excessive."*

The tragedy is that the DU saga is nothing new. Between 1961 and 1971, 21 million gallons of Agent Orange, a chemical defoliant containing a known carcinogen (dioxin), were sprayed on Vietnam with the aim of stripping the enemy of dense jungle cover. Like DU, the idea was to give our soldiers a tactical advantage on the battlefield. Up to 2.6 million Vietnam War veterans were exposed, and their resulting ailments would include prostate and skin cancer, type 2 diabetes, leukemia, and birth defects in their children. For more than two decades, their complaints of Agent Orange–related ailments fell on deaf ears. Because Title 38 prohibits veterans from suing the government for injuries suffered while serving in the military, for years the U.S. was legally free of financial responsibility for having sprayed its young men with the deadly toxin.

In 1979, a massive mass tort case was filed on behalf of 2.4 million veterans against the companies that manufactured Agent Orange. By the mid-1980s, the case was whittled away, so that it was finally settled in 1985 for $180 million earmarked for just fifty thousand people—or a pittance of five thousand dollars each—nearly three decades after the first soldiers were sprayed with the deadly bush-killer. Meanwhile, in Vietnam, Agent Orange poisoned the people we came to "lib-

---

*A San Francisco–based private security and "risk management" company called the Steele Foundation advertised DU cleanup services for anyone doing business in Iraq, including the U.S. military. CEO Kenneth Kuntz told us they were finding contamination on former Iraqi military bases they were cleaning up for the U.S. Army to be "a major problem." He declined further comment.

erate" from their Communist oppressors, leading to an increase in cancers and birth defects over three generations. A 2003 study found Vietnamese were still eating contaminated livestock and fish contaminated with dioxin. In one hamlet north of Hanoi, 95 percent of blood samples taken from villagers found evidence of the toxic defoliant.[22]

The U.S. Doesn't Deserve the Blood

Back in Nasiriyah, Raed Jarrar has taken us to Nasiriyah General Hospital. It is probably the most famous medical facility in Iraq. Jessica Lynch was taken here to recover from her wounds and was "rescued" in a dramatic made-for-TV midnight commando raid.

There is a palpable sense of betrayal in the halls. There are still holes in the doors where American Special Forces kicked them in. And her bed where she recovered is still broken from her "extraction" by the commandos. The doctors here saved her life, yet were portrayed by the Pentagon propaganda machine as kidnappers. The doctors explain that they even tried to return Lynch to a U.S. base but were forced to turn back when their ambulance was fired on by U.S. soldiers.

The hospital's director, Dr. Khudair al-Hazbar, graciously allows us to walk into his office with a brief introduction.

Dr. al-Hazbar, who speaks English, confirms that he saw a marked increase in cancers since the first Gulf War, adding that they were forbidden to talk about the cases "because of political reasons."

"There has been an increase in cancer cases in all of Iraq, particularly in Nasiriyah, and the surrounding area. It was the area that was most subjected to the shelling at that time. There is an increased number of blood, bladder and breast, and colon cancers. I have two or three cases weekly of such cancers . . . [and] we lack a center to treat these cancers."

There is no anger in the doctor's voice. He knows that the American soldiers are being exposed to the same toxic battlefield as he and his patients.

"There's a problem both for the Iraqis and Americans. I haven't seen them using any protective gear. They tell us it's a clean war. But it's not clean," he says mournfully, adding, "The American government does not deserve the blood that dropped from Americans and Iraqis."

7

Deadly Jabs and Nightmare Pills

Is the Pentagon's Anti-Biowarfare Program the Real WMD?

■ ■ ■

The AVIP (Anthrax Vaccine Immunization Program)
raises an ominous question: Who protects the force
from ill-conceived force protection?
—U.S. CONGRESSIONAL COMMITTEE
ON GOVERNMENT REFORM, 2000

SIX YEARS AGO, Ronda Wilson was a healthy, head-turning twenty-one-year-old U.S. Army helicopter pilot. She flew the OH-58 Delta Kiowa Warrior, a small, sleek attack helicopter armed with .50-caliber machine guns and Hellfire missiles. Not only was she the only female pilot in her squadron, she was top gun. The military was her family, and she entrusted it with her life. So, when she was ordered to receive a shot in December 1998, she just rolled up her sleeve and didn't even ask what it was. The reaction began immediately, a large painful sore developed at the injection site. The pain extended from her shoulder to her elbow. The military doctors told her this was normal.[1a] In January 1999, she was given a second shot, and according to medical reports, she developed "irritability, loss of memory, fatigue. A month later nausea and diarrhea started. One week after her third anthrax vaccine dose her gastrointestinal symptoms worsened further, evolving into her current disabling state of illness."

By the time she was discharged in April 2001, Wilson had lost a third of her body weight, and was depressed and confused. The young woman once described by her commanding officers as "one of the elite pilots of her generation" could no longer drive a car, suffered severe memory loss, and had such bad stomach pains that she was forced to lie in the fetal position for hours at a time.

Wilson is just one of hundreds, possibly thousands, of American soldiers whose lives have been disrupted and damaged by drugs that are meant to protect them.

U.S. soldiers are being forced, under threat of court-martial and prison time, to take a biowarfare vaccine that may be making them sick, and may not even work against a bio-attack. That may just be the tip of the needle. In addition to the anthrax vaccine, forward deployed troops are shot up with a cocktail of immune system–depleting vaccines, including the controversial hepatitis B and smallpox vaccines. They are also being forced to take Lariam to guard against malaria—a drug that, as we would find out, may or may not work, might be making them crazy, even suicidal, and quite possibly could cause long-term brain damage.[1b]

Like the issue of depleted uranium, these are the stories of the "hidden war"—the real conflict that you don't see on the nightly news. The Pentagon has been tight-lipped, knowing any chink in its armor on these issues could mean millions, if not billions, in potential liability. But these stories expose something else—the troubling nexus between the U.S. military and the pharmaceutical industry, whose dubious drugs may be harming, not protecting, the health of our troops. It's a disturbing saga that will confirm your worst fears about how little the Pentagon appears to care about the fate of America's troops, but it is also a success story, a tale of how one intrepid journalist can bring attention to a story no one wants to talk about.

The Muckraker

Half a block from the Veterans Administration headquarters in Washington, D.C., stands a nondescript concrete building with UNITED PRESS INTERNATIONAL in bronze across the facade. UPI, a wire service that has been around since 1907, lists some of the most renowned names in journalism among its alumni, including Walter Cronkite, David Brinkley, and the cantankerous Helen Thomas. Struggling to achieve profitability and compete with the other U.S.-based wire service, the Associated Press, UPI has changed ownership numerous times over the past two decades, with owners ranging from a Mexican publisher to a California venture capitalist to Saudi Arabian industrialists. In 2000, UPI was bought by an affiliate of the controversial Rev. Sun Myung Moon's Unification Church, which also owns the *Washington Times* and *Insight* magazine.

Despite its "Moonie" connection, and charges that Moon personally skews the *Times'* coverage to the right, UPI has quietly become one of the most outspoken critics of the way the U.S. government has gone about fighting the so-called war on terror. The organization has broken a series of major stories that the larger news outlets missed, including new evidence of Hussein's early links to the CIA, early doubts about the White House's WMD case, and an ongoing series of reports on the plight of the American soldier, written by an aggressive young reporter named Mark Benjamin.

Shortly after Operation Iraqi Freedom kicked off, when the first wounded soldiers began to arrive back from the battlefield, Benjamin began noticing a disturbing pattern. The Pen-

tagon was doing everything it could to cover up what he calls
the true "human cost of the war." For starters, military officials were flatly lying about the total number of wounded—
thousands more men and women were being hurt than they
were admitting, many with serious, horrific injuries. The Pentagon was also facing heavy criticism from military personnel
for the gauntlet of challenges returning solders were facing,
from substandard housing to cuts in their benefits to long
waits for medical care.

"Soldiers in this war, for whatever reason," Benjamin told
us, "are not being treated as well as experienced soldiers tell
me they should."

In late summer of 2003, there was a mysterious outbreak of
pneumonia in more than one hundred American troops deployed in Iraq. Many were completely debilitated, and two
died. Outside experts and veteran groups began to suspect
that the controversial anthrax vaccine, the same one that felled
Ronda Wilson in 1999, could be, at least in part, responsible.

At the same time, Benjamin began tracking another troubling military health story: soldiers were being forced to take
an antimalarial pill that was increasingly coming under fire
around the world for causing serious psychological problems,
including suicidal and homicidal thoughts. Once again, a drug
that was supposed to be protecting the troops against a lethal
threat was proving to be a threat itself.

Benjamin knew a little about vaccines. Throughout the
1990s, he had written a series of articles about problems with
early-childhood vaccinations, specifically the connection between vaccines and the onset of autism. So when he began
hearing rumors about soldiers coming down with so-called
mystery illnesses after getting "the jab," his reporter antennae
went up. He noticed the soldiers were exhibiting similar

symptoms to those of the children that he had studied. Seemingly healthy soldiers were being debilitated with rashes and headaches—some had their entire immune systems wrecked. Some were literally dropping dead.

One story in particular caught his eye: When *NBC News'* star "embedded" reporter David Bloom suddenly died from a blood clot in his lung after collapsing south of Baghdad, the Pentagon told his family and the media that his death was most likely caused by sitting for a long period in a cramped Bradley fighting vehicle. But his family, and many others, had their suspicions.[1c] Later, when soldiers began to get sick with similar lung problems, the Pentagon blamed a combination of desert dust and cigarette smoke, trying to shift the responsibility to the sick soldiers themselves, many of whom had recently taken up smoking.

For Benjamin, none of the Pentagon's explanations added up. By late summer of 2003, he had written a series of investigative stories, and people inside the military had finally taken notice. In August 2003, the army announced it was sending a team of two doctors to investigate these cases of lung illness at Landstuhl Regional Medical Center in Germany, the first stop for most sick or wounded U.S. soldiers stationed in Europe or fighting in the Middle East, admitting for the first time the possibility that vaccinations could be related to the mystery illness.

Control the Body

Like Ronda Wilson, Army Specialist Rachel Lacy was a healthy young woman with a bright military career ahead of her. Then the twenty-two-year-old got the anthrax vaccine. Unlike Wilson, Lacy never recovered. "Lacy died April 4 after what a doctor and her family said was heart and lung trouble, including pneumonia," Benjamin wrote. The reaction began just days after she received five simultaneous vaccinations, including the anthrax and smallpox vaccines on March 2 at Fort Mc-Coy in Wisconsin. Lacy's death was unique in that she fell ill and died prior to being deployed, which meant her case wouldn't be investigated by the team sent to Landstuhl. Since they were only looking at "in theater" cases, Lacy's death left the door open for a truly independent investigation.

As Benjamin told us, "Rachel Lacy was important because the Pentagon essentially lost control of the story. They lost control of the body. They lost control of the doctors and they lost control of the documents, and those are the kind of things that as reporters we need access to." Benjamin had finally found a case where he had a credible, independent source to counter the official version given by the Pentagon. "The autopsy was done by a civilian medical examiner, and the civilian doctors seemed to think that vaccines essentially killed her or contributed greatly to her death," he said. "And so did the medical examiner."

Months after Lacy died, the army still had not included her in its statistics of people whose death was caused by the vaccines. But Benjamin's coverage of her story was beginning to get noticed inside the military community. In November 2003, the army finally admitted that the vaccine could be linked to her death. Only then was Lacy's story picked up by any major news outlet other than UPI. Each was careful to lay out the army's case that the vaccines were FDA-approved, and that Lacy had an underlying medical condition—in this case they claimed she had a genetic predisposition to lupus, an autoimmune disease—absolving the U.S. government of all liability. Dr. William Winkenwerder Jr., the assistant secretary of defense for health affairs, told the media, "There was nothing that could have been done to avoid this most unfortunate event."[2]

It was a classic case of the big media outlets waiting for the "official" line to come before they reported it. There were no follow-ups, no digging, no effort to distinguish the Pentagon's alleged facts from fiction. Like so many complex stories we have investigated, especially ones in which underfunded activists and lower-middle-class victims are facing off against the federal government, it was simply allowed to die on the vine.

But the Pentagon's admission that her death might at least have been triggered by the jabs proved pivotal: the Pentagon was now conceding that its anthrax vaccine could be harming its troops. Which raised a larger question: Why are soldiers being forced to take it in the first place?

Short History of a Mean Spore

Anthrax is an acute infectious disease caused by the naturally occurring bacterium *Bacillus anthracis*. It's most commonly found in wild and farm animals like cattle, sheep, and goats, and humans can get it when they are exposed to infected animals. If your skin is exposed to anthrax spores, infection begins as a raised itchy bump that resembles an insect bite but within one to two days develops into a painless ulcer. Untreated cutaneous, or skin, anthrax results in death in about 20 percent of cases. If you inhale anthrax, that's a different story. Initial symptoms resemble a common cold. But after several days, your lungs shut down and you go into shock. Untreated inhalation anthrax almost always results in death.[3] In other words, if you can figure out how to effectively disperse anthrax into the air, you'll have yourself a very lethal weapon.

In the early 1950s, the Cold War was beginning to heat up. Researchers at the U.S. Army's Medical Research Institute of Infectious Diseases at Fort Detrick, Maryland, were busy trying to figure out ways of turning the world's nastiest germs and viruses into microscopic commie-killing machines—and how to protect themselves if the Soviets beat them to it. The white coats at Detrick conducted a series of tests of an early version of an anthrax vaccine on laboratory workers, but they needed a larger test group to find out if it really could prevent the onset of the disease.

In 1954, Philip Brachman, a young scientist who had just begun working at the Centers for Disease Control (CDC), was given a highly sensitive mission: "Find a population within the United States in which to field-test" a vaccine for anthrax.

Brachman identified four textile mills in Pennsylvania and New Hampshire that were willing to take part in the tests. Since anthrax infection was commonly known as "wool-sorters disease" because factory workers who worked with imported animal pelt made up the majority of the infected, it was a logical choice.

Brachman set up his study to determine whether the vaccine protected against cutaneous anthrax. But something happened at one of the four mills during the study that would raise suspicions in the decades to come. In 1957, a sudden anthrax epidemic broke out at the Arms Textile Mill in New Hampshire. Nine cases were reported, four cutaneous and five inhalation. These would be the only inhalation cases recorded during the entire study. Three of the inhalation cases were unvaccinated workers who had not participated in the study, while two had received the placebo. None of the vaccinated workers developed inhalation anthrax, which implied that the vaccine might have been effective against inhalation.[4] But because the test group was so small, the results were statistically insignificant. Brachman limited his conclusions to cutaneous effectiveness, though he did make a passing reference to the inhalation cases in his final report. Brachman's superiors were pleased with his results and began producing the vaccine.

As is typical of most vaccines that are developed out of Fort Detrick, a commercial partner was found to help manufacture it. The vaccine's first mass producer was Merck, Sharp and Dohme, whose founder George W. Merck had been chosen by President Roosevelt to head the secret program that created Fort Detrick's biological warfare labs. This was the birth of what many critics refer to as the "pharmaceutical industrial complex." But Merck eventually lost interest in the deal. Spore-forming microorganisms such as anthrax require specialized, expensive, highly secure labs. Biological warfare vaccines had low-profit margins and were by their very nature risky. If the vaccines failed, people could die, leaving the company stuck with the liability. Without a commercial producer for the vaccine, the state of Michigan took over production in its Lansing laboratory in 1965.

An important mistake occurred during the transfer of production. The state-run Michigan Biologic Products Institute (MBPI) altered the manufacturing process and began using a different strain of anthrax from Merck. Despite the change, in 1970, MBPI was awarded a license by the National Institutes of Health to manufacture what was called "anthrax vaccine absorbed" (AVA) based on the assumption that it was making a similar vaccine to Merck's and could rely on Brachman's mill studies.

Decades later, the Pentagon cited Brachman's study to justify the use of the vaccine against the threat of an inhaled anthrax weapon—even though his conclusions were admitted to be statistically irrelevant. The move was critical, allowing the Pentagon to justify the vaccine's use to "protect" hundreds of thousands of U.S. troops from the then very real threat of an airborne anthrax attack as the U.S. troops headed into the desert to drive the Iraqi army from Kuwait in February 1991.

Golden Opportunity

What many of the troops didn't realize was that the biological-weapons threat they were facing in Iraq was largely home-grown. According to a 1994 congressional report on the Reagan administration's illegal arming of Hussein in 1986, and then again in 1988, the CDC and a nonprofit biological sample company called the American Type Culture Collection sent microbial seed stock of numerous pathogens, including anthrax, to Iraq for what Iraq called "medical research needs." In 1995, United Nations weapons inspectors linked Iraq's biological weapons program at its Al Salam facility to the 1986 shipment.

In 1988, at the same time we were sending some of the nasty organisms known to man to our then-ally Saddam Hussein, the U.S. Department of Defense (DoD) realized it was woefully short of a sufficient vaccine stockpile. The call went out for bids to provide 300,000 doses. MBPI was the only U.S. producer with a license, and no new producers stepped up given the still limited market size.

By 1990, when our old ally declared Kuwait his nineteenth province and renamed Kuwait City "al-Kadhima," demand for the vaccine skyrocketed, forcing MBPI to rush to make changes to its manufacturing process—changes that would come back to haunt the company. MBPI informed the Food and Drug Administration (FDA) when it changed the original filters used in their vats in order to increase production. After the war, demand remained high. In 1993, the firm upgraded to an even larger filter, this time replacing the steel with ceramic. But this modification was never approved by the agency. In fact, it wouldn't find out about the change for years. Because FDA inspectors weren't vaccinated themselves, they couldn't enter the lab to inspect it. It turns out, for most of the 1990s, when MBPI was pumping out millions of doses for use by America's soldiers, and an increasing number of them were having adverse reactions, the agency responsible for regulating the process was severely out of the loop.

Unbeknownst to the FDA, the DoD had been conducting its own studies on MBPI's process. In 1994, DoD researchers reported finding a hundredfold increase in the level of protective antigen (PA), the protein that causes antibody production in the recipient of the vaccine—a potentially deadly amount. When the DoD questioned the lab about the increase, the lab official attributed the increase to the change of filter. But the FDA claims it was never told of the DoD's finding until the report was presented by a General Accounting Office inspector in 2001.[5]

Across the globe in Saudi Arabia, as MBPI was struggling to ramp up production for the DoD before the first Gulf War, a German banker of Lebanese descent named Fuad El-Hibri saw a golden opportunity. The Saudis also wanted an anthrax vaccine, but because of the problems at MBPI, 100 percent of U.S. supplies were allocated to the 150,000 troops in the Gulf. El-Hibri and his father, Ibrahim, saw the opportunity to meet the princes' request and became investors in Porton International, the commercial distributor for the Centre for Applied Microbiology and Research (CAMR), a UK government–run lab and one of only two in the world capable of producing the anthrax vaccine. El-Hibri would make a fortune off the sales, as *Salon*'s Laura Rozen reported, "Porton sold vaccine to Saudi Arabia at the insanely high price of $300–$500 per dose."

Thanks to a series of savvy business deals and a new Bush administration's obsession with removing Saddam Hussein from power, this was just the beginning of El-Hibri's financial windfalls in the anthrax vaccine game.

The Defector

When allied troops drove Hussein's troops from Kuwait and turned the kingdom back over to the Kuwaiti monarchy, the Iraqi dictator declared victory. He had taught the corrupt Kuwaitis a lesson and survived the Mother of All Battles against the Great Satan. But he had to pay a price. For the next decade, he would be forced to allow intrusive United Nations inspectors to enter his country at will and stick their noses inside his numerous palaces.

Under the auspices of Security Council Resolution 687, the United Nations Special Commission (UNSCOM) first arrived in Iraq in 1992 and began, at least in theory, to supervise the destruction and removal of the country's weapons of mass destruction. Under the UN resolution, Iraq was supposed to declare all chemical and biological weapons both developed and in progress. For nearly four years, UNSCOM inspectors became an almost regular feature on the nightly news, their ubiquitous white SUVs rambling around Iraq in a seemingly endless game of hide-and-seek. They never found a smoking gun, yet it seemed clear Hussein was hiding something. In 1995, Hussein finally admitted to having an "offensive" WMD program, only after one his most trusted generals defected and spilled the beans. At least that's what appeared to have happened. Like almost every twist and turn in the WMD saga, it would later turn out there was more to it than met the eye.

In August 1995, Gen. Hussein Kamel, minister of industry and minerals and Hussein's son-in-law, defected from Iraq to Jordan. He had been responsible for all of Iraq's weapons programs, and brought with him crates of secret documents. Declaring to the world his willingness to help overthrow Hussein's regime, Kamel provided documentation that proved Iraq had been lying about the extent of its weapons programs. According to news reports, Kamel admitted to UN inspectors, the CIA, and Britain's MI6 that Iraq had produced "weapons-grade" anthrax, portraying it as the "main focus" of the biological program.

In the wake of Kamel's accusations, Saddam Hussein admitted to having an "offensive biological program"—though he denied have any "weaponized" stockpiles. The distinction was lost on the U.S. military, which began pushing for a more stable, large-scale vaccination program, for what seemed to them like an increasingly inevitable war.

Over the next nine years, U.S. and UK leaders would use Kamel's 1995 testimony to ratchet up the rhetoric of fear, adding their own spin that painted a dramatically different picture from what Kamel had actually said.

In February 1998, President Clinton, speaking to the Pentagon, recounted, "[Saddam Hussein] admitted to, among other things, an offensive biological warfare capability, notably, 5,000 gallons of botulinum, which causes botulism; 2,000 gallons of anthrax; 25 biological-filled Scud warheads; and 157 aerial bombs. And I might say UNSCOM inspectors believe that Iraq has actually greatly understated its production."

In the buildup to his Iraq war, George W. Bush continued the spin, telling a crowd in October 2002 at the Cincinnati Museum Center, "In 1995, after several years of deceit by the

Iraqi regime, the head of Iraq's military industries defected. It was then that the regime was forced to admit that it had produced more than thirty thousand liters of anthrax and other deadly biological agents. The inspectors, however, concluded that Iraq had likely produced two to four times that amount. This is a massive stockpile of biological weapons that has never been accounted for, and capable of killing millions."

In his now-infamous UN presentation, Secretary of State Colin Powell informed the world, "Iraq declared 8,500 liters of anthrax, but UNSCOM estimates that Saddam Hussein could have produced 25,000 liters. If concentrated into this dry form, this amount would be enough to fill tens upon tens upon tens of thousands of teaspoons. And Saddam Hussein has not verifiably accounted for even one teaspoonful of this deadly material."[6]

Tony Blair went even further. On the eve of the Iraq invasion, he wrote in the *Independent*, "My Christian conscience is clear over war. . . . The UN inspectors found no trace at all of Saddam's offensive biological weapons programme—which he claimed didn't exist—until his lies were revealed by his son-in-law. Only then did the inspectors find over 8,000 litres of concentrated anthrax and other biological weapons, and a factory to make more."

So which was it? Did Iraq have 8,500 liters? Or did it have 2,000 gallons (which works out to approximately 7,600 liters)? Or had Hussein actually produced 30,000 liters, or, better yet, did UN inspectors actually find 8,000 liters? You'd think they would be able to keep their lies straight or at least use the same units of measure. And, yes, all three appear to be lies.

According to the UNSCOM Report S/1995/864 dated October 11, 1995, Iraq had declared the production of "8,500 litres of concentrated anthrax (some 6,500 litres were filled into munitions)." But it wasn't as simple as that. According to the UNSCOM report, Iraq had admitted to field-testing 6,500 of the 8,500 liters it had produced in munitions at the Muhammadiyat weapons test range in 1988 and 1989 and then conducting a failed field test for a biological spray tank in January of 1991. As for the remaining 2,000 liters, the report states, "Of the bacterial bulk agent stored at Al Hakam, Iraq stated that a similar deactivation procedure had been adopted. The detoxified liquid was emptied into the facility's septic tank and eventually dumped at the site. Over 2,000 litres of concentrated anthrax, according to Iraq's declaration, were destroyed at Al Hakam."

In October 1995, after being confronted with Kamel's accusations, the Iraqis admitted to producing over 8,500 liters of anthrax, but they also detailed how the anthrax had either been utilized in tests or destroyed around the time the UNSCOM inspectors entered the country in 1991. And while the Clinton, Bush, and Blair administrations might have had a case that their off-base assessments were "better safe than sorry," a month before the 2003 U.S.-led invasion, it would come out that they had known their claims were bogus.

In a six-paragraph article that got little attention, just weeks before the March 2003 invasion, *Newsweek* broke the story that, back in 1995, Kamel had actually told the UN inspectors a lot more than had been previously reported.[7] A few days later, the entire transcript of Kamel's UNSCOM interview was leaked on the Internet by Glen Rangwala, the same Cambridge Middle East analyst who revealed that Tony Blair's "intelligence dossier" had been largely plagiarized from a graduate student's thesis and other open sources. The following is an excerpt from Kamel's interview where he was questioned by Russian UNSCOM inspector Nikita Smidovich:

KAMEL: However, the main focus was on anthrax and a lot of studies were done.

SMIDOVICH: Were weapons and agents destroyed?

KAMEL: Nothing remained.

SMIDOVICH: Was it before or after inspections started?

KAMEL: After visits of inspection teams. You have important role in Iraq with this. You should not underestimate yourself. You are very effective in Iraq.

Later Kamel would go on to also say:

I made the decision to disclose everything so that Iraq could return to normal . . . not a single missile left but they had blueprints and molds for production. All missiles were destroyed . . . there was no decision to use chemical weapons for fear of retaliation. They realised that if chemical weapons were used, retaliation would be nuclear. I ordered destruction of all chemical weapons. All weapons—biological, chemical, missile, nuclear were destroyed.

According to Kamel, Iraq's entire WMD program was dismantled just after the first Gulf War ended in 1991.* Yet questions lingered about Kamel's revelations. Had he been holding back, or perhaps did not know about Iraq's actual possession of WMDs, including anthrax? Or maybe he wasn't being truthful himself. One UN inspector called him "a consummate liar."[9]

In January 2004, many believe those questions were answered by the discovery of a letter in the Iraqi presidential office after the fall of Baghdad, written by Hossam Amin, who had served as a liaison to the UNSCOM inspectors.[10] The let-

---

*Exiled Iraqi nuclear scientist Imad Khadduri told GNN in 2002 that Iraq's nuclear program was so decimated by war and sanctions that many of his former colleagues were "forced to sell their possessions just to keep their families alive."[8]

ter was written by Amin in 1995, days before Kamel's defection, to brief Hussein on documents Kamel could publicly reveal and what still remained. The contents of the letter, released by the *Washington Post* in January 2004, confirm Kamel's claim that all weapons had indeed been destroyed. These more recent revelations also shed light on why Kamel became so disillusioned after he defected. Not happy with how the information was being utilized by the UN, Hussein convinced Kamel to return to Iraq just six months after he left in February 1996, assuring his brother-in-law there'd be no retribution for his betrayal. As soon as he crossed the border, he was taken into custody and executed shortly after.

Mo' Money, Mo' Problems

Meanwhile, back in the U.S., MBPI finally had its anthrax laboratory inspected by the FDA, and the prognosis wasn't good. MBPI was cited for violations in 1993, 1994, and 1995. After a November 1996 inspection, the FDA threatened to revoke MBPI's license. In a March 11, 1997, letter, the FDA cited twenty-one significant deviations, ranging from equipment malfunctions and lack of temperature control to potency and purity inconsistencies of the vaccines. A year later, the lab was still not able to correct for all the citations, and in 1998, the FDA suspended shipments of the vaccine. With a continued perceived need for anthrax vaccine and a state-run lab not able to transform itself into a high-growth biotech company, MBPI was officially put up for sale.

Ever since his lucrative dealings in CAMR and Porton, Fuad El-Hibri had been keeping an eye on the situation brewing in the United States.

In 1998, El-Hibri formed a new company called BioPort.

His first moves would prove shrewd. Adm. William J. Crowe Jr. was U.S. ambassador to the UK from 1994 to 1997. He also served as chairman of the Joint Chiefs of Staff from 1985 to 1989, the period in which anthrax spores were being sent to Iraq. This apparent irony didn't stop El-Hibri from making the admiral a very lucrative offer—a nearly 13 percent stake in the new company with no investment on his part. El-Hibri desperately needed an American partner if he wanted to win contracts from the DoD, which only awards sole-source contracts to U.S. citizen-controlled companies.* Who better to open doors at the Pentagon than a former chairman of the Joint Chiefs of Staff? Together they would bid for the acquisition of MBPI, and in short order become the sole supplier of anthrax vaccine for the U.S. military.

After Secretary of Defense Cohen's 1997 announcement to vaccinate all 2.4 million troops in the military, BioPort won the auction for MBPI against only one other competitor and purchased the assets and contracts for $25 million in 1998.

At this point, the MBPI facility, now BioPort, was still under suspension from the FDA and needed to renovate its laboratory before resuming its vaccine production. In the summer of 1999, BioPort asked for extraordinary relief from the DoD, which agreed to lower the number of doses and to nearly double the contract value to $49.8 million, effectively almost tripling the per dose price of the vaccine.

El-Hibri admitted in his June 1999 testimony that the company had underestimated the renovations necessary to regain FDA approval, and as part of the contract reassessment, the DoD provided an interest-free advance of $18.7 million to help assist the company's cash flow. Congressman Walter B.

---

*El-Hibris's American wife, Nancy, and an unknown number of employees are also major shareholders.

Jones (R-NC), an outspoken critic of the Anthrax Vaccination Immunization Program (AVIP), the DoD program put in place that requires all U.S. troops to be vaccinated, requested an audit of the company's finances. In December 1999, Jones sent a letter to Defense Secretary Cohen that called for a halt of AVIP, and bitterly criticized the way BioPort was operating:

> *Despite the infusion of more than $160 million dollars of taxpayer funds over ten years, BioPort's production facility is still unable to meet many minimum manufacturing and safety standards. DoD's sole-source provider continues to have great difficulties in creating vaccine lots with consistent potency and antigen levels. . . . Proponents of the program are quick to point out the FDA approval of the vaccine, but fail to mention that data resulting in the license did not arrive entirely from the current licensed vaccine. Instead, the vaccine itself was approved for cutaneous exposure to anthrax in a limited population.*

All of this leads to several disturbing conclusions: The Pentagon is requiring all 2.4 million of our soldiers to take a vaccine whose efficacy is questionable and may be more harmful than protective. The company with a monopoly on this highly lucrative contract has a history of deceptive practices and shoddy production standards,* yet has been able to remain the sole supplier.

The United States is the only country with a mandatory anthrax program, while both the UK and Australia offer it as

---

*BioPort even may have lost one of its own employees to the vaccine in July 2000: Richard Dunn, who monitored test animals for BioPort and its state-owned predecessor, had received eleven doses of the anthrax vaccine. A county medical examiner said Dunn had "an inflammatory response to the vaccine that contributed to his death." BioPort denied the vaccine had anything to do with his death.

optional protection to soldiers, consistent with how an experimental, or unapproved, drug would be handled. As Dr. Meryl Nass, an Arizona-based physician and one of the nation's leading antivaccine activists, told us, "The fact that AVIP has been allowed to operate has been through a series of loopholes. The FDA has always questioned the consistency of the vaccine and only through pressure from the DoD has it issued authorization in numerous ways for its use."

"Trust Must Be Earned"

At the end of World War II, the Allies held War Crimes trials at the Palace of Justice in Nuremburg, Germany. The U.S. tried Dr. Karl Brandt, Hitler's personal physician and head of the Nazi euthanasia program, and twenty-two other doctors involved in some of the most horrendous human experimentation ever conducted. Brandt was found guilty and sentenced to death by hanging in August 1947, and from his ruling a code of conduct was developed for doctors to abide by in future medical research involving human subjects. According to the Nuremburg Code:

> *The voluntary consent of the human subject is absolutely essential. This means that the person involved should have legal capacity to give consent; should be so situated as to be able to exercise free power of choice, without the intervention of any element of force, fraud, deceit, duress, overreaching, or other ulterior form of constraint or coercion; and should have sufficient knowledge and comprehension of the elements of the subject matter involved as to enable him to make an understanding and enlightened decision.*

While the code has never officially made its way into American or German law, its principles have been adopted into the Department of Health and Human Services' Code of Federal Regulations for all government-funded research experiments.

For critics of the AVIP program like Dr. Nass, forcing U.S. military personnel to take arguably experimental anthrax vaccine violates both the spirit and letter of the core ethics defined so eloquently back in August 1947.

During the first Gulf War, the DoD requested a waiver from the FDA to be allowed to administer experimental drugs to the soldiers without prior consent. It was under this waiver that a whole slate of drugs was tested on soldiers without their approval and typically without full knowledge of their potential effects. As a condition of the waiver, the DoD was supposed to track the use of the drugs in the soldiers' medical records and keep detailed records of any reactions. Failure of the DoD to follow through on this waiver condition is a major reason why it has been so difficult to diagnose the causes of Gulf War Illness. A series of congressional hearings on Gulf War Illness in the mid-1990s seemed to pay off with the passage of public law "105-85" in 1997, requiring detailed medical records for every soldier sent to war. This includes a blood draw so that doctors will be able to determine the root cause of any illness that may arise. The only problem: The military didn't implement its own rules. It wasn't until May 2003, thanks to Benjamin's reporting and an ad taken out by the crusading Web site Tompaine.com in the *New York Times* that the military finally announced it was going to begin abiding by 105-85.[11]

Some argue that the military purposefully doesn't track reactions to drugs and vaccines given to soldiers as a way of reducing its potential liability. The General Accounting Office did its own study, and what it found was shocking. The anthrax vaccine's product insert (the brochure that comes with the package) that was in use until 2002 stated that "mild to moderate local reactions" to the vaccine can be expected in 34 percent of recipients while "0.2% should experience systemic reactions." A 2000 GAO survey of National Guard and reserve forces found 76 percent reported local reactions while nearly 24 percent reported systemic reactions.

Ronda Wilson, the former top gun who was disabled by an anthrax vaccine in 1998, had what you'd call a "systematic reaction." After finally being discharged in 2001, her final medical report concluded,

> *There were no other risk factors present . . . that could account for her symptoms. The anthrax vaccination may have adversely affected her immunological balance. There is a clear temporal association with the onset of her illness and her anthrax vaccination. While it is not possible to scientifically prove causality between anthrax vaccination and the onset of her illness, it is impossible to disprove causality.*

These days, Wilson is reluctant to speak about her battle with the anthrax vaccine. When we contacted her, she had no idea of the status of her legal claims and had not talked with her lawyer in months.

"I'm trying to move on," she told us.

Kathy Hubbell of the Military Vaccine Education Center told us about Wilson,

> *For a few years there, we all thought she was dying, since her digestive system was becoming paralyzed. Recently she finally found some treatments that may help. Her desire to*

get on with her life is a healthy one, of course. Many people who are initially active in the movement need a break from the heartache and grief which we deal with on a daily basis.

To others in the military, taking the anthrax vaccine was not as blind a decision as it was for Ronda Wilson. When the first round of shots began at Dover Air Force Base in January 1999, one pilot developed severe arthritis, another began experiencing spells of vertigo, and yet another was diagnosed with lupus, an autoimmune disease. By the spring of that year, concerns over the mandatory program began to grow as soldiers researched the vaccine on the Internet. In the reserve units, where it is easier to opt out of military jobs than in active duty, many were deciding to quit the force instead of taking the jab. By May 1999, morale at the base was being severely affected by the program. Losing a soldier a week, Col. Felix M. Grieder made the bold decision to suspend mandatory anthrax vaccinations at the base and demand answers from the Pentagon on the vaccine's safety.

Two days later, on May 7, 1999, the Pentagon sent some of its top medical officials to the base to answer questions. Soldiers stood up and announced they would rather be court-martialed than to receive another vaccine shot. The brass listened to their complaints and left shortly after. Mandatory vaccinations resumed the next day. Colonel Grieder was relieved of his duty at Dover the following day and was transferred to the Pentagon.[12]

In August 1999, air force pilot Sonny Bates was transferred to Dover from a base in Texas. He immediately felt the tension around the AVIP program. One night he decided to take a DNIF ("Duties Not to Include Flying") list and began to call all of the ill pilots. He found that all fifteen pilots on the list had experienced similar symptoms after their third or fourth anthrax vaccine shot.[13] Bates decided to take the issue up with the base commander and refused to take the shot himself. The air force began court-martial proceedings against him. In February 2000, Sonny Bates appeared on *60 Minutes* to talk about his decision not to take the vaccine. Immediately afterward, the charges against him were dropped, but he lost his pension and was fined nine thousand dollars.

Dover was not the only air force base to experience defections and low morale due to the mandatory AVIP. Travis Air Base in California lost approximately half its fifty-four pilots in its reserve unit due to the anthrax vaccine. The vaccination program continued, with the military brass seemingly lost in the fog of denial.

At a September 1999 House Committee on Government reform hearing on the AVIP, Maj. Gen. Paul Weaver claimed, "We've had 10,700 people inoculated for anthrax in the Air National Guard, with one known refusal documented."

Finally, in April 2000, after five hearings, the Committee on Government Reform had had enough. Its finding read in part:

> *The AVIP should be suspended because it lacks an essential element in a medical program: trust. However well-intentioned, the anthrax vaccine effort is viewed by many with suspicion. It is seen as another chapter in a long, unhappy history of military medical malfeasance in which the healing arts are corrupted to serve a lethal purpose.*
>
> *The fundamental rationale for the AVIP—that something, even an old, questionably effective vaccine, is better than nothing—gives little comfort to those who daily see*

their forebears and colleagues grow sicker from radiation testing, Agent Orange, and Gulf War illnesses. If the noble experiment fails, if the vaccine ultimately causes more casualties than weaponized anthrax, many men and women in uniform do not believe their government will acknowledge their sacrifice or treat their wounds.

Trust must be earned. It can be earned only with a degree of candor and openness that has not been the hallmark of the AVIP to date.

In October 2000, the committee officially recommended the immediate halt of the mandatory program until further testing could be done. Committee member Rep. Christopher Shays, (R-Conn.), was blunt. "I sincerely believe the military is being blatantly untruthful to us. And I believe this program is destroying our readiness. I believe that it must stop."[14]

The AVIP, and its primary supplier, BioPort, were in trouble. The program was shut down. Then September 11 changed everything. One week after the attacks, a still-unknown person began sending letters full of anthrax spores through the U.S. mail system. Letters were sent to Democratic members of Congress, the *National Enquirer*, and NBC's Tom Brokaw. Three people, including a mail handler, died. Congress was shut down for more than two weeks. DNA tests of the anthrax pinpointed the source: Fort Detrick. It didn't seem to matter that it was a homegrown threat. Suddenly there was renewed interest in stockpiling smallpox and anthrax vaccine. With anthrax letters reaching the Hill, AVIP's congressional critics disappeared and the program was saved.

But BioPort was still not receiving passing marks. However, by late December, BioPort's facility, which had been shut down since 1998, was miraculously approved. In January 2002, its license was fully reinstated and the company was allowed to start shipping. As Dr. Nass told us, "Without the anthrax attacks, BioPort would never have gotten back its license."

Meanwhile, a slew of lawsuits were being filed by those affected by the AVIP. Sonny Bates and John Buck, an air force physician who also refused vaccination, sued to have the anthrax vaccine reclassified as experimental. Their suit was dismissed. Ronda Wilson and the family of Sandra Larson, an army specialist who died in June 2000 after receiving her sixth anthrax jab, filed against BioPort for negligence. Their case has since added sixty-nine other plaintiffs affected by the vaccine. (The suit is still pending as of April 2004.) In April 2003, another suit was filed in behalf of six unnamed active members of the military or National Guard and civilian Department of Defense employees who had been ordered to take the vaccine but initially refused. Like Bates's case, they wanted to have the vaccine classified as experimental. They argued that the vaccine had originally only been licensed for cutaneous anthrax based on the Brachman study, and to use it for inhalation anthrax was technically experimental. This time U.S. district judge Emmet G. Sullivan was persuaded by the plaintiffs' arguments.

On December 22, 2003, Judge Sullivan ruled that the anthrax vaccine had never been specifically approved or labeled for use against inhalation anthrax, the stated purpose of the military's use. In his opinion he stated, "This court is persuaded that AVA is an investigational drug and a drug being used for an unapproved purpose. . . . Absent an informed consent or presidential waiver, the United States cannot demand that members of the armed forces also serve as guinea pigs for experimental drugs."

With Judge Sullivan's ruling, the AVIP was officially halted and the anthrax vaccinations were no longer able to be mandated by the military without prior consent. Just when the tears of joy had dried from all those who had been affected by the AVIP, the DoD pulled the ace from their sleeve. Eight days after Judge Sullivan's ruling, on December 30, 2003, the FDA closed a loophole it had left open for over twenty-four years that had allowed the anthrax vaccine to be used without proper testing. In its final ruling, the FDA justified its position on the controversial data that came from the Arms Mill outbreak during Brachman's study:

> *Although there were too few inhalation anthrax cases to support an independent statistical analysis, due to the rarity of this method of exposure during the period of time that the study was performed, FDA noted in the final rule that all of the cases of inhalation anthrax that occurred were in unvaccinated individuals. Therefore, the FDA-approved labeling for the anthrax vaccine does not specify the route of exposure, and the vaccine is indicated for active immunization against* Bacillus anthracis, *independent of the route of exposure.*

Translation: "We admit it's not exactly the best science, but it's all we've got." Ten days later, on January 9, 2004, BioPort announced it had entered into a three-year $245 million deal with the U.S. government to continue to supply the anthrax vaccine.

But the victims weren't giving up. In April 2004, a judge denied BioPort's motion to dismiss, a preliminary victory for Ronda Wilson and the others involved in her suit. If they prevail, BioPort won't be the ones paying the bill. It will be the DoD, that is, the U.S. taxpayer, who will be responsible for any settlement. BioPort received full indemnification as a condition of its contracts with the Pentagon.

In what might be the final and darkest irony of the whole

saga, many critics argue that the development of vaccines for bioterrorism is all a moot point: that the use of vaccine as "force protection" is itself a dangerous fallacy.

In fact, Dr. Nass and others argue, "Vaccines just don't work for biowarfare."

Vaccines work only if your enemy plays by the rules. In 1997, Russian researchers published a report in the British journal *Vaccine* claiming they had genetically engineered a strain of anthrax that their own vaccine was useless against, meaning the MPBI vaccine would most likely be useless as well. Apparently, the Russians had been working on new anthrax strains for years. Recent analysis of tissue specimens from the bodies of victims of an explosion of a bioweapons factory in Sverdlovsk in the former Soviet Union in 1979 indicated that four different strains of anthrax were being developed in the lab. Scientists believe the strains were specifically selected to overcome vaccine protection. A Russian biowar expert named Ken Alibek confirmed that the Soviets had prepared genetically altered strains of anthrax in order to circumvent the use of vaccines against them.[15]

All of which makes perfect sense. If you were the Russians, or, say, an Islamic terrorist, why would you do your enemy the favor of attacking them with the same strain of anthrax against which they had so diligently vaccinated their troops?

Am I Crazy, or Is It Lariam?

Staff Sergeant Georg-Andreas Pogany was sent to Iraq as an interrogator attached to a Special Forces unit. Shortly before leaving for Iraq in September of 2003, Pogany and his fellow troops in the army's Tenth Special Forces group were prescribed Lariam to protect them from the potential threat of malaria. Pogany claims there were no warnings given with the prescription of the antimalarial drug. After three days in Iraq and his third dose of Lariam, Pogany witnessed another soldier dragging a bloody mangled body of an Iraqi man who had been cut in half by U.S. gunfire. The sight shook the sergeant up. He began vomiting and was unable to sleep that night. The next morning, he couldn't get the image out of his head, and reported to his commanding officers that he thought he was having a nervous breakdown and requested counseling. One of the officers told him he should think about what that could do to his career. Pogany told CNN's *American Morning* on November 10, 2003, "His initial reaction to me was that I might want to think about what I'm doing and . . . if I change my mind after lunch, then he's willing to forget that I ever brought it up."

Unable to shake his condition after three days, he was sent by the unit chaplain to see the Combat Stress Management Team psychologist Capt. Marc Houck, who wrote in Pogany's report, "The soldier reported signs and symptoms consistent with those of a normal combat stress reaction." He recommended rest and stress-reduction techniques to Pogany before returning to duty. Pogany was stripped of his gun and placed in a base camp, supervising work detail. On October 7, Pogany was sent back to the U.S. and charged with cowardice, defined as "the refusal or abandonment of a performance of duty as a result of fear" by the military judges' benchbook—and punishable by death.

Back home, Pogany was treated like a criminal. On arrival in Colorado Springs, he was met by military police and stripped of his laptop, his phone, and his Gerber knife. The media immediately ran reports of the "cowardly" soldier who had been sent home from Iraq. Four days before interviewing Pogany on *American Morning*, CNN showed a split-screen image of

Pogany with his "cowardice" charge on one side and a photo of Jessica Lynch on the other. As Trent Gegax of *Newsweek* commented, "The message may not have been intentional, but its impression was clear." On November 6, a military judge dismissed the cowardice charge against him, but his commander immediately then charged him with "dereliction of duty." In mid-November, Pogany began publicly stating that he thinks his panic attacks were triggered by the Lariam pills he was prescribed before leaving for Iraq. After receiving national coverage on television and in print news media, the army finally backed down and dropped all charges in late December.

"Nowhere is this apparent disregard for psychological injuries more apparent than in the case of Sgt. Georg-Andreas Pogany, who was charged with cowardice," Steve Robinson of the National Gulf War Resource Center told the House Armed Service Committee Panel in January 2004.

This wasn't the first case of a soldier allegedly wigging out on Lariam. In the summer of 2002, three Special Forces soldiers allegedly killed their wives at Fort Bragg, North Carolina. All three had recently returned from Afghanistan, and all three had apparently been taking Lariam. All three also committed suicide. The army claims Lariam was not connected to what was actually a spate of killings at Fort Bragg around that time, which included five apparent murders and three suicides, because not all the soldiers had taken Lariam. The army also claims Lariam is not connected to the more recent rash of suicides by soldiers serving or recently returned from Iraq.

William Manofsky, a Naval Reserve commander who volunteered for Operation Iraqi Freedom, became suicidal after returning from Kuwait in March of 2003. Manofsky says he experienced insomnia, aggression, mood swings, acute nausea, severe anxiety, depression, and cognitive disorders, all of which landed him in the emergency room five times. After several attempts to obtain a useful diagnosis from doctors, in May 2003, Manofsky and his wife visited the navy medical clinic in China Lake, California. They again brought up that they felt the Lariam connection was being ignored by the doctors.

According to Benjamin, who originally broke the story:

> A 17-year veteran of the Naval Reserve, Manofsky was handed Lariam last November at China Lake before being deployed. There was no prescription written or warning of possible side effects given, and Tori Manofsky said she has since been told by a base medical worker that there should have been "special instructions for dispensing and documenting" the drug.

During the May visit, Tori insisted that the doctor record her husband's Lariam intake in his medical file, which he did. When the doctor left the room, Tori realized the importance of this documentation and took the paper, which was on a clipboard at the end of the bed, to a copy machine down the hall. When the Manofskys returned to the clinic on June 26 to obtain William's medical records so that he could see a neurologist, they noticed that the sheet was missing from the file. They have since publicly claimed that the navy is covering up use of Lariam and has concealed the documentation that proves it. Benjamin has spoken to other soldiers who have told him that they also had serious problems with the drug and that there is no record of them being prescribed Lariam either, though the military reports about forty-five thousand Lariam pills were prescribed to soldiers from October 2002 to September 2003.

The Nightmare Pill

Malaria is no joke. It's a parasitic disease carried by mosquitoes. Thought to predate man, the disease is believed to have originated in Africa and accompanied humans as they migrated to the Mediterranean, India, and Southeast Asia. Once common to the marshy areas around Rome, hence the name, *mal-aria*, or "bad air" in Italian, it was also known as Roman fever. Around the world, malaria affects some 500 million people in Africa, India, Southeast Asia, and South America and kills nearly 2.5 million people a year, 1 million of whom are children.[16]

According to the CDC, symptoms "include fever and flu-like illness, including shaking chills, headache, muscle aches, and tiredness. Nausea, vomiting, and diarrhea may also occur. Infection with one type of malaria, *Plasmodium falciparum*, if not promptly treated, may cause kidney failure, seizures, mental confusion, coma, and death."

Most people don't know that Lariam is a product of the U.S. Army, conceived and tested at the Walter Reed Medical Center in Silver Spring, Maryland, the army's largest hospital. In 1971, mefloquine, the generic term for Lariam, was developed to replace chloroquine, the long-standing antimalarial drug. Chloroquine-resistant strains of malaria had begun to appear in Vietnam and Cambodia, threatening our troops fighting in Southeast Asia. The drug was then jointly developed by Walter Reed researchers, the World Health Organization (WHO), and Swiss pharmaceutical giant Hoffman-La Roche until it was ready to be manufactured in 1985. First approved for use in Europe, the FDA approved Lariam in the U.S. in 1989, relying on a study by the CDC. The report found the drug to have no serious adverse reactions in the 562 Peace Corps workers he tested. It is now prescribed over

400,000 times each year to travelers going to regions where there are strains of malaria that have become resistant to chloroquine.

But beginning in the early 1990s, Lariam consumers, mainly Western travelers to exotic locales, began complaining to their doctors that the drug was screwing with their heads. The most common complaint was the onset of dark, violent nightmares. Others reported a general change in their mental state, dizziness, irritability, and depression. Some reported hallucinations. One experienced traveler told us she had strange delusions after taking Lariam for a trip to Africa, "I felt small pigs running across my feet." There were no pigs. More seriously, many Lariam takers have reported suicidal thoughts, and there are allegations of suicides linked to the drug, though they've never been a proven correlation. Today, there are Web sites devoted to Lariam's "bad trips," in which people from around the world contribute their personal stories of freaking out while taking the drug. Some experts say that as many as one in four people who take it have serious psychological side effects, though only after a class-action suit did La Roche put a warning inside the package of the American version of the drug.

Celia Maxwell, an FDA official who was responsible in approving the drug, says she doesn't take it, opting for doxycycline, a more mild antimalarial pill. According to news reports, President Clinton favored the alternative as well. Asked why, his spokesman Joe Lockhart told the *Washington Post*, "the usual reasons." He said he chose doxycycline because of "the dreams."[17a]

Dr. Donald H. Marks, a former associate director of clinical research at La Roche, told Benjamin there is "ample reason" to believe Lariam causes suicide. Marks said Lariam can cause "spontaneous neurological activity" and "irritation of certain sensitive areas inside the brain" that could lead to suicidal behavior long after someone stops taking it.

Afghanistan is a high-risk zone for malaria and a chloroquine-resistant zone. But rather than endorse the use of Lariam, the World Health Organization recommends that travelers to the region take chloroquine in conjunction with proguanil, a daily supplement that in combination with chloroquine is effective against newer strains of malaria. The U.S. Army prefers to prescribe Lariam alone, versus this combined remedy, so that its soldiers only have to remember to take a weekly, instead of daily, pill—one less thing to think about when you're getting shot at.

But when the "war on terror" added a second front in Iraq, apparently the DoD forgot to check the WHO Web site. Unlike Afghanistan, Iraq is not in a chloroquine-resistant zone. In fact, Iraq—with a population of 28 million—reported a mere thousand-plus cases of malaria in 2001.* Seventy-five percent of these occurred in northern Iraq, in areas under the control of pro-American Iraqi-Kurds, where few U.S. soldiers are based. Why the military continues to prescribe the controversial drug to soldiers heading to Iraq, where the drug's effectiveness is questionable, is a mystery.

The Lariam fiasco is reminiscent of the Pentagon's use of pyridostigmine bromide (PB) in the first Gulf War. It was given to protect troops against potential exposure to the nerve gas soman. It turns out that Iraq didn't have any soman, but it did have sarin, another deadly nerve gas. PB actually can *increase* the nerve-damaging capabilities of sarin, and up to 100,000 troops may have been exposed to sarin when they blew up an Iraqi chemical weapons depot.

---

*Afghanistan has 937 cases of malaria per 100,000 people. By comparison, Iraq has 14. United Nations Development Program, 2000.

It took more than five years for the DoD to commit resources to investigate PB's potential effects on the well-being of soldiers, and many have expected the same delayed response with Lariam. But in 2004, Benjamin turned up the heat. He questioned the army on the possible connection between Lariam and the higher-than-normal suicide rates that were being observed in soldiers serving in Iraq. Pentagon spokeswoman Martha Rudd told him, "We don't believe there is any connection between Lariam and suicide. There is nothing to indicate that is a factor."

Steve Robinson, executive director of the National Gulf War Resource Center, couldn't disagree more. A week earlier he had told the House Armed Services Committee, "The military is ignoring this drug's known side effects. In some cases, they are lying to family members and acting as if they are baffled by the high suicide and depression rates."

On February 25, Assistant Secretary of Defense for Health Affairs Dr. William Winkenwerder Jr. appeared in front of the same committee panel. The DoD was finally changing its course, after months of downplaying the issue and denying the potential connection to the increase in suicides. Winkenwerder surprised everyone by announcing that the army would begin a study to look into the potential side effects of Lariam that would "include suicide and neuropsychiatric outcomes."

One month later, on April 12, 2004, the VA announced that it, too, would be looking into the potential long-term health and mental effects of Lariam usage, stating it "will need to develop a well-grounded response to concerns among veterans, their families, Congress, the media, and others about possible long-term health effects among Operation Iraqi Freedom and Operation Enduring Freedom veterans from taking the antimalarial drug mefloquine (Lariam)."

In May 2004, Senator Dianne Feinstein, (D-Calif.) made a startling charge. Writing in a letter to Health and Human Services secretary Tommy Thompson, she claimed "six service members have been diagnosed with permanent brainstem and vestibular damage from being given this drug despite the fact that alternative drugs might have been chosen to prevent infection."

Sen. Feinstein wrote that Lariam has "serious risks" that have not been adequately assessed by the Pentagon, the Peace Corps, and other government agencies that distribute it.

Benjamin reported, "According to people familiar with the situation, the six service members were diagnosed in recent weeks by doctors at Naval Medical Center San Diego. Its Spatial Orientation Lab, a Department of Defense facility, specializes in balance disorders. One service member who received a diagnosis is former Navy Reserve Cmdr. William Manofsky, who became severely ill after taking mefloquine in Iraq and Kuwait while deployed for Operation Iraqi Freedom. Another soldier with a mefloquine diagnosis is a Green Beret who served in Afghanistan. UPI reviewed a copy of Manofsky's medical report from the San Diego lab, which includes the notation, 'Lariam induced,' with the word Lariam underlined."[17b]

Without the persistent efforts of soldiers like Pogany, family members such as Tori Manofsky, journalists like Benjamin, and congressional representatives whose duty it is to keep watch over our troops, the DoD would be free to go on mandating Lariam to soldiers. While the DoD's use of Lariam has been stalled, the anthrax vaccine program pushes on.

The final irony, the decision to continue to require mandatory anthrax vaccinations, is in many ways an extension of the illusion that brought us into the war with Iraq in the first place. For the government to admit there is no anthrax threat would be to admit the entire rationale for the war was bogus.

The tragedy is that the politics of war have meant that the only hope is to push for a safer, more stable vaccine to be to put in use.

What Are Journalists For?

In the lead up to the Iraq invasion, the *New York Times*' Judith Miller wrote, or cowrote, a series of explosive front-page articles that seemed to directly back up the administration's case for war. Her articles described an active and dangerous Iraqi WMD program. She quoted Iraqi sources who described, among other claims, a vast network of secret labs "in underground wells, private villas and under Saddam Hussein Hospital in Baghdad."

In the aftermath of the invasion, and the subsequent revelations that her sources included paid informants working for Ahmed Chalabi, the controversial convicted embezzler who U.S. intelligence sources accused of spying for the Iranians in May 2004,[17c] she had become something of a bête noire of the antiwar set. Even some of her colleagues at the *New York Times* were highly critical of her reports. *Slate* editor Jack Shafer asked, "Is the *New York Times* breaking the news—or flaking for the military?" quoting an unnamed *Times* writer who called her reporting "wacky assed."

When pressed to explain the discrepancy between her sources' accounts and the reality of Hussein's missing WMD program, Miller responded, "My job isn't to assess the government's information and be an independent intelligence analyst myself. My job is to tell readers of the *New York Times* what the government thought about Iraq's arsenal."[18]

For many, her comments couldn't have summed up better the state of the mainstream news media. In effect, she was describing one side of what has become two distinct news cultures in America: one that blindly follows the government's official line, and one that actively and aggressively challenges everything it says.

That it was UPI and the *Christian Science Monitor* that broke the major stories of the hidden cost of war is no coincidence. These are privately owned organizations who work outside of the establishment news media. They are not under pressure by investors to cut costs and increase profitability of their news operations. Nor are they tied to twenty-four-hour news channels, where reporters are under constant deadline to generate new stories, which does not allow them to conduct in-depth time-consuming stories. Unlike the network anchors and other big media stars, they don't regularly dine with politicians or attend the swanky black-tie dinners, like the 2004 Radio and Television Correspondents' Association Dinner, where President Bush joked, in an almost surreal display of bad taste, "Those weapons of mass destruction have to be here somewhere!" while a photo of him looking under Oval Office furniture flashed on a big screen.

UPI's Mark Benjamin seems like he's from another universe. As he told us:

> *Part of our job as reporters is to report on what the government is saying. But I like to think that as a reporter I take a very close look at what the government is saying, why they're saying what they're saying, and question what the basis is for their statements. We have a responsibility as a reporter to get to the truth.*

Black Box Democracy

Who's Counting Your Votes?

■ ■ ■

*Number of blank votes recorded by touch-screen machines in a
January 2004 election for Florida's House of Representatives: 137
Votes by which the race was run: 12*
—HARPER'S MAGAZINE, FLORIDA DEPARTMENT OF STATE

Swarthmore, PA

IT'S EIGHT O'CLOCK on a Saturday morning. The Gothic
buildings of the postcard-perfect Swarthmore College campus
are covered in a blanket of deep, fresh snow. Most students are
still snoozing, but in a wood-paneled cathedral, a small band of
digital rebels is downing coffee and crafting conspiracy theories.

Bev Harris, the star presenter for their student-organized
symposium on the perils of electronic voting, hasn't shown,
and they're getting worried.

"We hope she didn't get offed by Diebold," quips one of
the students jokingly.

Harris is the de facto leader of a grassroots campaign against
companies like Diebold, a billion-dollar corporation that
makes ATMs as well as nearly fifty thousand terminals with
similar touch-screen technology that millions of Americans will
use in the 2004 election to choose their next president.

By this point, it should be a familiar narrative: A devoted

corps of ragtag activists toil on the political fringe, while powerful corporate and government interests brand them "paranoid fear-mongers." The mainstream media parrots the corporate line, refusing to take the activists seriously or bothering to do their own homework to validate or disprove the activists' allegations. You'd think that voting, the basic foundation of our democracy, wouldn't get the same treatment we've seen with so many of the stories we've covered in this book. It's just too important. Yet until recently, a small group of so-called conspiracy theorists were the only ones shouting about the wholesale handover of the voting process to a corporation with a documented record of deception. For more than two years, the activists labored in the margins, trying to warn the nation that electronic voting machines and the companies that sell them were a serious menace to our republic. No one seemed to be listening, and now it may be too late.

Bev Harris has been called the "Erin Brockovich" of the anti-electronic voting machine movement, a working-class crusader in a movement of concerned citizens who believes digitizing every aspect of the voting process is a seriously bad idea. For the students at Swarthmore, the Seattle grandmother is more akin to the *Matrix*'s Neo. She doesn't sport a black trench coat or have any time-stopping kung fu skills, but for them, she's a fearless leader in the battle against the evil machines. For Harris's minions, Diebold is a near-mythic villain: a secretive, faceless corporate giant out to take over our nation's most sacred act. The student's quip about Harris's untimely demise was in jest, but this is a conspiratorial bunch. The scary part: they aren't *that* crazy.

Harris was always something of an iconoclast. She drives a Dodge Caravan with a bumper sticker that reads KEEP HONKING, I'M RELOADING. She's always been political. In 2002 she worked with a veterans' group that posted George W. Bush's Vietnam-era military records online. In an ominous sign of things to come, the site was immediately hacked and taken off the Web.

In October of that year, Harris made an astonishing discovery. Intrigued by an article about Diebold's political connections, she started Googling and came across an innocuous-looking Diebold Election Systems FTP (file transfer protocol) site. Upon closer inspection, Harris was shocked to find the site contained nearly forty thousand files, including the entire source code for Diebold's AccuVote touch-screen voting machine, program files for its Global Election Management System tabulation software, a Texas voter-registration list complete with voters' names and addresses, and what appeared to be live vote data from fifty-seven precincts in a 2002 California primary election. Downloading the sensitive files from the unprotected site was as easy as a click of a mouse.

She promptly sent the files to a programmer friend and asked him what they were. He responded, "Incredibly stupid." According to the programmer, the code was full of security flaws, allowing anyone with basic hacking skills to manipulate an election and then easily cover their tracks.

It was a life-changing moment for the fifty-two-year-old literary publicist. Harris soon devoted her life to spreading the word, writing a book, *Black Box Voting: Vote Tampering in the 21st Century*, and launching a Web site, www.blackboxvoting.org, that has become the online hub for anti–"black box voting" activists. Along the way, she became a sort of virtual den mother of the burgeoning movement, traveling the country, talking to scores of community groups, alternative news outlets, and eventually government officials—anyone who would listen to her warnings.

The campaign took its toll. Between visits from the FBI and Secret Service investigating the corporate hacks, she often found herself unable to pay her heating bills and would work late into the night wrapped in a blanket in front of her desk at her computer. "This has been a scary year for me," she told us. "Our income went down drastically, and at the same time I am getting these constant legal threats that I am going to be sued for all this money."

In January 2003, Harris hit pay dirt again. An anonymous whistle-blower released nearly thirteen thousand internal company messages allegedly written by Diebold Election Systems employees.* They were first leaked to a *Wired* magazine reporter, who then handed them off to Harris. If the source code incident was embarrassing, this was a true PR disaster. The documents detail how the company was trying to pass off buggy software, jack up prices, cover up mishaps. According to Harris, these screwups created the conditions in which elections could be stolen outright.

Harris sent the files to everyone she knew—students, activists, and mainstream and alternative journalists—and posted them online, moving them from one server to another, keeping one step ahead of Diebold's cease-and-desist letters.

Students at Swarthmore joined the cause, posting the memos on their school servers in an act of "electronic civil disobedience." Diebold's lawyers threatened the students and the elite Pennsylvania school with prosecution under the Digital Millennium Copyright Act, the same law that was sending hundreds of college kids to court for downloading Snoop Dogg.

"We said, 'All right, this is bullshit, this is corporate censorship, we're going to do something to resist it,'" says a defiant Luke Smith, a mutton-chopped, Jack Black look-alike, and founder of the Swarthmore Coalition for the Digital Commons.

At first, the administrators at the Quaker college, known

---

*Diebold will not confirm or deny whether these messages are authentic.

for its long history of progressive activism from the days of abolition to Vietnam, caved in and ordered the documents taken down. But when the renegades' story hit techie sites such as Slashdot.com, the school reversed itself, and the kids became mini Net-celebs, with an article in *Wired* and representation in a countersuit against Diebold from the cyber-rights crusading Electronic Frontier Foundation. Diebold quietly backed down.

The controversy helped turn the "black box voting" story into an alternative media phenomenon around the world. Reporters as far away as New Zealand were calling it "bigger than Watergate." Here in the U.S., the story seemed to be gaining momentum as respected computer security experts from MIT, Harvard, Johns Hopkins, and Stanford were increasingly backing up everything Harris were saying. Yet as late as the winter of 2003, the mainstream media were still missing the huge implications of what Harris had found. More often than not, she was simply dismissed as a "conspiracy theorist."*

By the spring of 2004, the story became so big, it couldn't be ignored. Lawsuits were filed, members of Congress were introducing bills to force the companies to, at the very least, provide a paper trial for voters. More whistle-blowers were coming forward. The same news outlets that once ignored Harris's persistent e-mails were now busting down her door. But was it too little too late?

Of all the stories in this book, the controversy surrounding black box voting goes to the core of what we are as a nation. Harris and her flock are asking some startling questions: Have we outsourced the most sacred act of our democratic tradition to shady corporations? Are we heading for another Florida-

---

*Even the moderate-liberal *Slate* wrote, "Harris is drawing lots of online links to her black-helicopter claims."[1]

like debacle in which tens of thousands of votes are left un-counted? Or worse, is a right-wing conspiracy out to literally hack American democracy?

Welcome to the Machine

Advocates for electronic voting offer an impressive-sounding list of reasons why electronic voting machines are an idea whose time has come. The systems are as simple to use as an ATM. With the addition of a numeric keypad and head-phones, blind people can now easily vote with little assistance. Electronic machines can easily be set to run any number of languages, at a tiny fraction of the cost of running multi-lingual paper ballots.

"Electronic voting machines save trees," is the favorite pro-machine argument from industry spokespeople and local election officials. *What are you, a tree-hater?* Paper elections involve large print runs, much of which is wasted as voter turnout fluctuates. An election official from San Joaquin County, California, told us touch screens will save taxpayers in his county about $1 million a year in paper costs alone.

Tabulating results is a snap with electronic machines, which is probably why so many election officials have become evan-gelists of the systems. When polls close, an election worker simply inserts an "ender" card in each terminal, instantly counting the votes. The results are saved on each terminal's hard drive and copied onto a flash memory card, just like what you'd use in a digital camera. The official then removes the card and takes it to a central server, where a districtwide count takes place. Media outlets can get results in seconds. No but-terfly ballots, machine jams, or ambiguous chads, hanging, dimpled, or otherwise.

At least that's the way it's supposed to work.

Ironically, most of the opposition against the machines has come, not from Luddites, but from computer-savvy citizens familiar with the fallibility of digital data. A growing number of computer security experts argue that voting is just too important to be left to computers—especially computers made by these companies. In the past, electronic voting machines have been consistently unreliable and chronically insecure, while the biggest producer has been accused of a culture of deception and secrecy.

Thanks to successful lobbying, no one outside the computer company is allowed to examine the software's code, or "look under the hood," should a problem arise. In fact, there is no way to do a real recount. Hitting RESTART only reboots the computer and retabulates the same results. Since the machines provide no paper record, they are, in a word, unauditable.

"There's really no way for the voter to actually, independently confirm that their ballot was recorded correctly inside of the computer," Harris told us. "It's like making everyone blind."

The central irony of this new craze for electronic voting is that it came about as a direct response to the Florida election fiasco in 2000. What most don't realize is that during Florida 2000, electronic voting machines were already being used in some counties in the state and were experiencing serious problems. While the media focused on the problems with paper ballots in Palm Beach and Dade Counties, a major, still unexplained election-night anomaly took place in a Florida county with electronic voting machines that directly influenced how the news media called the presidential election.

On election night November 8, 2000, the state of Florida was the center of the universe. Journalists in New York at Fox

News and NBC were feeling the pressure from powerful political interests to call Florida early for Bush. And down in the Sunshine State the election was going haywire. In Palm Beach, due to a confusing so-called butterfly ballot, elderly Jewish voters were unwittingly voting for a man, Pat Buchanan, who once praised Hitler. In many rural counties, black voters were facing roadblocks, early closings of polling places, and signs saying outstanding warrants would be checked by poll officials. Many other eligible voters who got to the polls were informed they were felons and were turned away as they had been scrubbed from the voter roles in a questionable state-sanctioned process. In Volusia County, home of Daytona Beach and a bastion of black Democratic voters, things appeared to be going more smoothly.

By 2:00 A.M., all the networks, and the voting analysts providing them with data, were beginning to inch toward calling the state for Bush.

According to a timeline created by the Annenberg Center for Communication at the University of Pennsylvania by request of *CBS News*, at 2:09 A.M. Voter News Service (VNS) added the vote count from Volusia County to the state totals. With 171 out of 172 precincts in the county reporting, the addition gave Bush a statewide lead of more than 51,000, according to VNS. What wasn't known at the time is that there was a serious error in the Volusia count.

At around this same time, Ed Bradley, *CBS News'* legendary *60 Minutes* correspondent, reporting live from southern Florida, warned against calling Volusia just yet, "Traditionally, they're . . . one of the last counties to come in. That's an area that has two hundred and sixty thousand registered voters. Many of them are black, and most of them are Democrat."

At 2:12 A.M., Fox News was the first to call Florida for

Bush. NBC followed two minutes later. A minute later, the *CBS News* Decision Desk called Florida, and the election, for Bush. Dan Rather then declared to the nation, "Sip it, savor it, cup it, photostat it, underline it in red, press it in a book, put it in an album, hang it on the wall: George Bush is the next president of the United States."

CNN, who was sharing analysts with CBS, followed suit shortly after. Three minutes later, ABC did the same.

No one was aware that at some point before midnight, a Diebold voting machine in Volusia County subtracted 16,022 votes from Al Gore, and, in some still unexplained way, gave 4,000 erroneous votes to George W. Bush. Later that night, the county officials uploaded the corrected number, but no one noticed until after the spate of election calls had begun. When the nearly 20,000 votes were subtracted, Bush's lead began to evaporate. As more precincts continued to report from southern Florida, as Bradley had predicted, the race quickly reached a statistical dead heat.

At around 3:15 A.M., unaware of his opponent's faltering lead, Gore phoned Bush and conceded the election. Between 3:30 and 3:45, he left his hotel to tell the public he'd lost. Two blocks from Memorial Plaza in Nashville, Gore learned that Bush's lead had all but disappeared. Gore called Bush back and rescinded his concession, adding, "Let me explain something, your younger brother is not the ultimate authority on this." Bush immediately called his cousin John Ellis at Fox News and reportedly told him, "I hope you're taking all this down, Ellis. This is good stuff for a book."[2]

According to VNS, by 3:48 A.M., Bush's lead had slipped to almost six thousand votes. A confused Rather said, "Now the situation at the moment is, nobody knows for a fact who has won Florida. Far be it from me to question one of our esteemed leaders [CBS management], but somebody needs to begin explaining why Florida has now not been pulled back to the undecided category."

By 3:57 A.M., the margin was down to two thousand votes.

By 4:05 A.M., all the networks will have rescinded the Florida call for Bush.

The Florida recount started days later.

It turns out what happened in Volusia wasn't the only anomaly. In Brevard County, also hitched with electronic voting machines, four thousand Gore votes were erroneously omitted on election night, and then later corrected.

Who or what was responsible for the erroneous data is still unclear. But one thing everyone can agree on: The errors had a direct impact on how the election night coverage played out.

In a letter to the congressional commission investigating the media's coverage of election night 2000, CBS News president Andrew Heyward wrote, "a very significant computer error made by the Volusia County Elections Department . . . led to another series of bad calls by the television networks and newspapers across the nation." Yet even with that admission, the news media never followed up on what had happened in Volusia. The big story became the confusing butterfly ballot and the contentious chads, and the battle royale over the manual recount.

As Harris discovered in the thirteen thousand internal Diebold Election Systems electronic memos, the two erroneous county totals came directly from the central tabulating system for each county. In Volusia, the culprit appeared to be a mystery memory card that somehow uploaded the incorrect data.

In January 2001, election officials in Volusia tried to get to the bottom of the incident, demanding an explanation from Diebold. The company's response, as recounted in its own internal communications, says everything you need to know about the company.

First, a Volusia County, Florida, official named Lana Hires frantically wrote the Diebold team:

> *I need some answers! Our department is being audited by the County. I have been waiting for someone to give me an explanation as to why Precinct 216 gave Al Gore a minus 16,022 when it was uploaded. Will someone please explain this so that I have the information to give the auditor instead of standing here "looking dumb."*
> Lana Hires, Volusia County, Florida, January 17, 2001, 8:07 A.M.

Several of the company's key executives and programmers immediately responded to Hires's request for help. Ken Clark, Diebold Election System's research and development manager, wrote back, saying he was as confused as she was. Diebold's John McLaurin said he didn't have any answers either, but added a warning to

> *[keep] in mind that the boogie man* [sic] *may be reading our mail.*

Tab Iredale, the company's vice president of research and development, wrote back offering four possible explanations, one of which was the " 'second memory card' or 'second upload' came from an un-authorised [sic] source."

It was a startling admission. As Harris wrote, "the undeniable fact that a presidential candidate conceded the election to his opponent based on a second card that mysteriously appeared, subtracted 16,022 votes from Al Gore . . . (and) added 4,000 erroneous votes to George W. Bush . . . (and) then, just as mysteriously, disappears."

Ken Clark, Diebold Election Systems R&D manager, wrote on an internal online company message board:

> *If this problem is to be properly answered we need to determine where the "second" memory card is or whether it even exists. Heh. Second shooter theory. All we need now is a grassy knoll.*

The exchange is as shocking as it is revealing. A Diebold executive begins with a warning that a "boogie man" [sic] may be reading their e-mails. Then Iredale admits that one of the possible explanations for the disappearing voters was an "un-authorised [sic]" source inserting their own memory card and manipulating the results. That someone could upload false data to the voting machines and that neither the company nor election officials would have any way of knowing who did it is a dangerous breakdown in the service these companies provide. Yet, to this day, the full story of what happened in Volusia County is still not clear, and neither Diebold nor the county has ever given a full explanation.

Ironically, the public came away from the 2000 Florida debacle with the perception that all the problems in that state were the result of flawed ballots and faulty lever machines. In some ways, that is true. A study by the U.S. Commission on Civil Rights found that "about 7% of the paper ballots in Florida weren't counted correctly. . . . Optical scans had an error rate of about 4%, and lever machines at 1%." Political pressure was intense to find a solution, and find one quick. The commission, unaware of the negative Gore votes in Volusia at the time of their report, concluded that touch-screen terminals had a failure rate of only 0.5 to 1 percent. Almost overnight, electronic voting machines became the magical solution to an embarrassingly antiquated voting system.

In October 2002, Congress passed the Help America Vote Act (HAVA) into law with much fanfare and self-congratulation, pledging almost $4 billion to help states purge themselves of their ancient lever voting machines and enter the brave new world of touch-screen democracy. At the time, it seemed a rare bipartisan success story, but the law was riddled with fundamental flaws. Unlike other countries that use electronic voting technology nationwide, like Brazil and Australia, HAVA made no provisions to standardize all aspects of the process. Each county would be responsible for purchasing the machines, as well as the complicated task of "certifying" the security and accuracy of their individual systems. HAVA, in effect, opened the door to a handful of small private companies, some little more than start-ups—each using a different platform, each out to make the biggest buck—to take control of the most basic act of our democracy. Like the dot-com bust that sent the American economy into a tailspin only a year earlier, blind faith in the virtues of the entrepreneurial spirit and the glories of high-tech, paperless solutions would prove to be a dangerous illusion.

Follow the Money

In the midst of her never-ending research, Harris became intrigued by the story of Chuck Hagel. His story would become part of "black box voting" mythology. In 1996, Republican Chuck Hagel was elected to the Senate in Nebraska in what a local paper called a "stunning upset." He had been trailing in the polls just days before the election. What voters didn't know was that Hagel wasn't just a successful politician—he was also a businessman. Hagel had just stepped down as chairman of American Information Systems (AIS), later called ES&S, now one of the largest providers of voting terminals in the country. ES&S was the only company whose machines counted Hagel's votes in both the 1996 and later in 2002 elections.[3] Like all electronic voting terminals, the machines provided voters with no paper receipts, and had no way of being audited.* To top it all off, the state and the company had signed a confidentiality agreement, which meant the public wasn't told about the relationship between the man they just elected and the machines on which they cast their votes.

The further Harris dug into Hagel's past, the darker it got.

At AIS, Hagel replaced Bob Urosevich, who was a programmer and the CEO. In the early 1980s, Urosevich was a pioneer in the electronic voting biz—financed by a multi-gazillionaire named Howard F. Ahmanson Jr., a member of the highly secretive far-right Council for National Policy, an organization that included Lt. Col. Oliver North, Maj. Gen. John K. Singlaub, and other shady Iran-Contra players. Ahmanson, the heir to a savings-and-loan fortune, is also part of a far-right Christian reconstruction movement. Its philosophy advocates, among other things, "mandating the death penalty for homosexuals and drunkards," according to an article in the Columbus, Ohio, *Free Press*.

Urosevich now runs Diebold Election Systems, and his brother Todd is now a top executive at ES&S. Between the two of them, their companies will play a role in approximately 80 percent of all votes cast in the United States in the 2004 election.[4]

---

*In Hagel's 2002 reelection, several Nebraska ES&S machines malfunctioned. Hagel's opponent filed a request for a hand count. It was denied. A Nebraska law prohibits election workers from looking at the paper ballots, even in a recount. The only machines permitted to count votes in Nebraska are ES&S.

Diebold has deep political ties as well. In 2003, the company's chief executive Walden "Wally" O'Dell hosted a $1,000-a-plate fund-raiser for George Bush at his ten-thousand-square-foot Columbus, Ohio, mansion and then sent out letters soliciting donations with the statement he's "committed to helping Ohio deliver its electoral votes to the president next year."

Forty-two of Ohio's sixty counties use Diebold voting machines.

As *Mother Jones* magazine reported, O'Dell isn't the only Diebold executive priming the Republican coffers:

> *One of the longest-serving Diebold directors is W. R. "Tim" Timken. . . . Since 1991 the Timken Company and members of the Timken family have contributed more than a million dollars to the Republican Party and to GOP presidential candidates such as George W. Bush. Between 2000 and 2002 alone, Timken's Canton-based bearing and steel company gave more than $350,000 to Republican causes, while Timken himself gave more than $120,000.*

In 2004, Timken became one of Bush's campaign "pioneers," and as of March 2004 had brought in more than $350,000 for the president's reelection bid.[5]

Question Marks

Like Cynthia McKinney's heated 2002 congressional race in DeKalb County, Georgia's Democratic senator Max Cleland was in the political fight of his life. Cleland, a Vietnam vet who had lost three limbs in combat, was tagged by his Republican challenger, Saxby Chambliss, as "soft on terrorism" for his opposition to the recently passed Patriot Act. Chambliss even ran a TV ad that featured Cleland, Osama bin Laden, and Saddam Hussein. Democrats across the country were outraged. Just two days before the election, polls in the *Atlanta Journal-Constitution* had Cleland leading by five points. Yet when the final tally came in, Chambliss had won the seat by 7 percent. In just forty-eight hours, he had gained 12 percentage points.

That was just one of several races in 2002 in which Democrats were leading into election day and then lost in tight counts—all in states with heavy electronic voting saturation. In the Georgia gubernatorial race, Democratic governor Roy Barnes lost to Republican challenger Sonny Perdue. It was the first time in 134 years a Republican had won the governor's seat. A *Journal-Constitution* poll just two days before the election showed Barnes ahead by eleven points. In Alabama, Democrat Don Siegelman thought he'd won the election for governor and went home. The next morning, 6,300 of his votes were subtracted, and Republican Bob Riley was given the keys to the statehouse. ES&S officials investigated and later told state officials there was no problem with their machines; it was just a minor glitch.

None of this was hard proof of anything, but added together it formed a troubling picture for many "black box" activists.

Operation: rob-georgia

When Harris discovered the now-infamous FTP site containing Diebold's source code, she also found a series of files that showed how the company was dealing with "certification," the process by which individual counties declare their machines secure and accurate. One file was named "rob-georgia."

As Harris describes her initial reaction in *Black Box Voting*:

> *If you learned that a $54 million order had been placed by the state of Georgia for 22,000 new voting machines, the biggest single voting-machine purchase ever, and that these machines have been installed just prior to the election and then you saw a folder called "rob-georgia," looked inside and found instructions to replace the files in the new Georgia voting system with something unknown, what would you do?*

In the rob-georgia file, Harris made a series of shocking discoveries, including the fact that Diebold was using the same simple password, "1111," to grant access for hundreds of terminals. As it turns out, the *rob* in the title most likely didn't refer to anything as dramatic as a blueprint for stealing an election, but rather to a then Diebold employee named Rob Behler, whose job was to add patches, or fixes, to existing code. Behler later left the company. He alleges that Diebold rigged tests and claims he was part of a last-minute operation to install the patches on 22,000 Diebold machines in the days before the 2002 election—meaning many of the terminals that were used in Georgia were never properly certified by independent testing authorities or cleared with Georgia election officials. Behler told *Vanity Fair*, "Wherever they were headed, we'd get ahead of them and try to lower the failure rate."*

Two years later, Rob Behler, a father of six, is sitting in his well-appointed McMansion north of Atlanta and confirms his

---

*Diebold has denied all of Behler's accusations.

account of what happened in 2002, telling us, "I don't think they set out to do anything corrupt, but in the process they were approaching it as a business and trying to get things done on time and under budget, and things weren't analyzed from the point of view that freedoms were at stake."

Behler added, "I don't have anything vested in it other than making sure my vote is counted. I take that as a serious part of my freedom."

Harris's discovery of the rob-georgia file helped draw the attention of a small group of computer scientists across the country who began to take her suspicions seriously. They started doing their own tests on the company's machines and began raising their own questions.

In Georgia, a former IBM programmer named Roxanne Jekot joined the cause. In a public hearing on the growing concerns about the vulnerabilities of the Diebold terminals, Jekot dramatically challenged the state to a test. She claimed she could hack the system within hours. The state accepted, but then backed down. Shortly after, Jekot told us her garage was broken into, and the brake lines on her pickup truck were cut, although we know of no evidence linking either Diebold or Georgia state officials.

Meanwhile, in academia, many respected computer science researchers joined in. A professor named Avi Rubin at Johns Hopkins University released the first in a series of damning studies to come out of the ivory tower blasting Diebold and its competitors for a lack of basic security precautions. Another study from MIT came to similar conclusions. Rebecca Mercuri, a Harvard computer scientist who has testified before Congress and consulted with several of the Democratic challengers for president on the electronic issue, told us, "Everything that Bev has said has checked out." Yet despite the experts' hefty credentials, as late as the fall of 2003, the national media was still largely refusing to investigate the researchers' concerns, mimicking the companies' and some officials' claims that the critics were "conspiracy theorists" with irrational fears.

A November 11, 2003, CBSNews.com article was typical of the coverage at the time. Titled "Can Voting Machines Be Trusted?" its lead sentence read, "A new conspiracy theory is taking hold across the Internet." Without doing any original research herself, the reporter concluded, "Time will tell if the conspiracy theorists are right or if their criticisms are as easily dismissed as the voting machine companies claim."

The mainstream media's dismissal of the grounded concerns of activists, academics, computer science experts—and even right-wing lobbyists—mirrored the attitude of many election officials, who were increasingly forced to defend their decisions to purchase the multimillion-dollar systems. A public hearing in December 2003 in New Jersey epitomized the increasingly hostile atmosphere, with the activists on one side and the election officials and the corporations on the other. The idea behind the event was to provide a constructive forum for the various parties to discuss their differences. It quickly devolved into rancor.

Stanford's David Dill, who had launched his own campaign for electronic voting transparency in California, told the audience that there was little anti-hacker software could do to identify or prevent the "hundreds of ways" voting software can be compromised. The response from the election officials was denial and then anger. Elaine Ginnold, a local assistant registrar of voters, lashed out, dismissing the critics as "black helicopter people."

The Black Box

One of the most confounding ironies for many black box activists is that Diebold also happens to be the largest manufacturer of ATMs in the U.S.—all of which produce paper receipts. Who would use them if they didn't? Yet the company is leading what has become the central battle in the electronic voting debate—paper receipt or no paper receipt. The companies argue, and many election officials agree, that providing a paper receipt for each voter would be costly and would create more opportunity for malfunctions, like the dreaded paper jam every home computer user is all too familiar with. But the technology for paper receipts is already available, and affordable, activists claim. In the winter of 2003, an entrepreneur named Athan Gibbs, president and CEO of TruVote International, gave a demonstration of his voter-receipt technology at a vendor's fair in Columbus, Ohio.

His system provides two separate voting receipts. The first paper receipt displays under Plexiglas the voter's touch-screen selection on a piece of paper, which then falls into a lockbox after the voter approves it. The second is a paper receipt that includes a unique voter ID and PIN code, which can be used to call in to a voter audit Internet connection to make sure the vote cast was actually counted. Gibbs* argued, "Why would you buy a voting machine from a company like Diebold which provides a paper trail for every single machine it makes except its voting machines?"

Brooks Thomas, coordinator of elections in Tennessee, told reporters, "I've not seen anything that compares to the Gibbs TruVote validation system." The assistant secretary of

---

*Gibbs later died in an unrelated car accident. Nevertheless, his death added more fuel to the hardcore conspiracy theorists' fire.

the state of Georgia, Terrel L. Slayton Jr., called it the "perfect solution."

Despite the enthusiasm, many, including the secretary of state of Ohio, home to Diebold, rejected the proposal, arguing paper receipts were unnecessary, expensive, and weren't mandated by law. They are right about one thing: Nothing in HAVA required electronic voting machines to provide paper receipts. After a series of congressional hearings, which included testimony from many of Harris's allies, in the summer of 2003, U.S. representative Rush Holt (D-NJ) introduced HR 2239, the Voter Confidence and Increased Accessibility Act of 2003, that would require a paper trail for voters and election officials. As of April 2004, it has yet to be voted on. Many states have followed California in passing legislation to require paper ballots on all new voting machines purchased by its counties.

For many, the resistance by the companies to provide paper receipts is baffling. In one of Diebold's leaked internal memos, a Diebold programmer named "Ken" provides at least one clue to the company's motivation. In it, Ken is complaining about a series of news stories in which Delaware state officials had requested paper receipts:

> *There is an important point that seems to be missed by all these articles: they already bought the system. At this point they are just closing the barn door. Let's just hope that as a company we are smart enough to charge out the yin if they try to change the rules now and legislate voter receipts.*

Ken later corrected himself. What he actually meant was: Diebold should charge the state "out the yin-yang," adding, "any after-sale changes should be prohibitively expensive." A more than slightly bemused Delaware state legislator responded, "I'd really like to have [yin-yang] explained to me anatomically, with the assumption that almost any place it would be would be painful."

Criminal Intent?

Bev Harris is convinced that while greed and laziness may be factors in the opposition to paper, there is also something much deeper and darker at work. When most people imagine someone "hacking an election," they think of a Hollywood-like scenario in which an overly caffeinated computer geek sitting in his high-tech lair somehow taps in remotely, punches up 100,000 votes for his favorite comic-book hero, and then covers his tracks with some fancy programming skills. That's about as likely as the plot of a John Travolta thriller, since most machines aren't hooked up to a modem. The other scenario imagines political operatives sneaking into polling places, say the night before the polls open, and taking advantage of an electronic "back door" created by an in-cahoots vendor that allows them to set the machines to spit back out results to their liking. Not impossible, but not likely. The most plausible scenario, says Harris and people like Stanford's David Dill, would be an inside job carried out by a computer-literate, politically motivated company employee, be it a paid operative or just a guy who really loves Ralph Nader, who lands a job at Diebold, ES&S, or in one of the election offices.

And that is why Harris is so concerned about what she found in December 2003.

The date is two weeks after the Swarthmore conference. Harris never made it to Pennsylvania that day. And no, she wasn't abducted by Diebold's secret agents. She had been waylaid by a heavy winter storm.

We're in drizzly, dreary Seattle. We're there because Harris told us we had to be. She's holding a press conference at the Labor Temple, where, she tells us with her trademark flair for the dramatic, she'll be releasing info that "will bring concerns about the security of our voting system to a new level."

Harris begins the press conference that has quickly filled up with journalists and fellow activists with two news flashes: While on a dirt-digging mission in Vancouver, where Diebold's Global Election Systems (GES) subsidiary is based, she and fellow e-voting detective Andy Stephenson discovered that five convicted felons had worked in management positions for GES, including a stock manipulator, a cocaine dealer, and a computer programmer convicted of a sophisticated embezzlement scheme.

Harris's second major allegation of the day is that ten states had used uncertified software in their recent elections—a crime under federal law. To understand why this is important, you have to understand how electronic voting systems are sold.

In the U.S., each county is independently responsible for the purchase and implementation of the election systems for its residents. If you live near a county line, your neighbor may be voting on a Diebold machine while you may be voting on a Sequoia terminal or even a punch-card machine. Since the passing of HAVA, each county has made different decisions and is adopting the newer technologies at varying paces, but all with the mandate to be electronic by 2006.

To ensure that election equipment purchased by state election officials will be "accurate, reliable, and dependable," the Federal Election Commission created the Federal Voting System Standards (FVSS). The FVSS requires vendors to have their software and hardware tested by an independent nationally recognized testing laboratory. The process of these tests is not open to the public, and the laboratories do not take media requests, and in the end only ensures that a voting machine is in physical working order, not whether it's secure. That's part of the next stage of "certification" process, which is left to the individual states.

The testing laboratories are approved by the National Association of State Elections Directors (NASED), which is made up of one elections director from each state or U.S. territory. Since all these people have jobs working for state governments, the administration of the NASED is provided by a nonprofit organization in Houston, Texas, called the Election Center. According to its Web site, the Election Center's purpose "is to promote, preserve, and improve democracy." Its function is to provide information and training for state election workers on the election process. One would think that the organization's role here would be a perfunctory one. However, its strong advocacy for electronic voting machines and its stance against an auditable paper trail have some critics questioning the group's motives.

In a hearing on Voter Verified Paper Ballots, R. Doug Lewis, the director of the Election Center, made a case against voter-verified paper ballots, listing additional weight and cost, printer jams, and ink shortages as three of the nine main reasons in favor of electronic voting machines. His reasons sounded eerily similar to those of the vendors. On March 25, 2004, Linda Harris (no relation to Bev Harris), a reporter for the *Philadelphia Inquirer* got the tax filings of Sequoia, another leading manufacturer of electronic voting machines, and found that the IRS had forgotten to black out the names of the organizations to which it made charitable contributions. It turns out that Sequoia and competitor ES&S had made contributions to the Election Center every year since 1997. Diebold's director of marketing, Mark Radke, admitted to us that

Diebold sponsored Election Center luncheons and rented booth space from the organization to promote its products.

In other words, the only organization in the U.S. responsible for educating election officials and approving the sales of voting systems to election officials was being funded, at least in part, by the electronic voting machine vendors themselves.

March Madness

On the same day as Bev Harris's Seattle press conference, another storm was brewing for Diebold in California. Secretary of State Kevin Shelley revealed that an independent audit in the nineteen Golden State counties using Diebold Election Systems found that not one county had been operating on state-certified software and that three counties, including Los Angeles County, were running software that had not even been tested according to federal standards.

Diebold had already been under close watch by a group of citizen activists who had become inspired by Harris's groundbreaking work. Jim March is Harris's oddball partner. Unlike Harris, who calls herself a liberal Democrat, March is a staunch Republican with a Libertarian bent. March is a six-foot-four, 280-pound suburban John Wayne, who pins one side of his black cowboy hat up so he can talk on his cell phone with his antenna up. He's also a 100 percent certifiable gun nut whose day job is a lobbyist for the Citizen's Committee for the Right to Keep and Bear Arms.*

March and Harris filed a lawsuit against the state of California, including Secretary of State Shelley, calling for the im-

---

*March's hobbies include designing custom knives and swords. His favorite is the "Muskrat," made from buck knives superglued together.

plementation of additional security measures. On election day March 2004, March is determined to keep close watch on the Diebold systems being utilized for the first time in San Joaquin County.

March's archenemies—election officials—spot him as soon as he rolls up on his bike. He pulls off a helmet plastered with political stickers reading BUSH–CHENEY, VOTE FREEDOM FIRST, and diligently locks it to his bike, so he won't violate any election laws governing political advertising inside polling places.

Inside the polling station, March approaches Austin Erdman, the assistant registrar of voters for San Joaquin County. Erdman is not happy to see him. He answers March's question with a few words and a whole lot of attitude. When March catches the eye of a Diebold employee shuttling back and forth between rooms, the man quickly puts on a jacket, covering up the Diebold logo on his golf shirt.

March questions another man who is checking the memory cards and asks him who he works for. The man responds that he works for an asset management company hired by the county. March picks up his cell phone to report his suspicious discovery. The asset management contractor is quickly scolded for speaking to March.

March's lawsuit with Harris has caused quite a stir within the election community around Sacramento. Erdman considers March a pest: "Are they all truthful? No. They are not truthful. He has no idea what he's talking about. He is a gun advocate. He's trying to intervene in areas that he's not very knowledgeable about, which is elections."

Still on the hunt for problems on Super Tuesday, March heads over to a polling station located in a small church on a dark street corner and storms into the room looking for procedural snafus. Conducting a 360-degree inspection of each terminal, March seems almost disappointed to find the location appears kosher—the modems are turned off, and there's no "asset management contractors" tooling around with the machines.

With no more stones to look under, March opens his attaché and begins to read from a leaked Diebold Employee Manual. The only African American poll worker, fifty-one-year-old Leslie Fisher, is all ears. When asked about his impressions of the new machines, Fisher says, "People come in here and they ask, 'Where is my receipt?' and all we have to offer is a[n "I voted"] sticker. You can go to any store, and they will give you a receipt. . . . They say it's because it's too expensive; expense comes from when you don't get the vote right like they did in Florida. That's what's expensive."*

One week after Super Tuesday, Harris, March, and other e-voting activists were joined in their concerns by a bipartisan request from the Senate Election Committee in California, which sent a letter to Secretary of State Shelley urging him to decertify all paperless electronic voting machines prior to the 2004 general election. It turns out there were major problems on Super Tuesday across California, including in Orange County, where machines gave seven thousand voters the wrong ballot, which resulted in more votes being cast in twenty-one precincts than there were registered voters. In San Diego, problems with the machines prevented some polls from opening before 11:00 A.M., resulting in early-bird voters being turned away. Chairman of the Senate Election Committee Don Perata (D-Oakland), commenting on Super Tuesday in California, said it "was a test-flight of widespread use of

*Mark Radke, Diebold's director of marketing, told us the company is willing to give states paper receipts, but said they have not been asked. "If they want a voter-verifiable receipt, we can provide that as well, but again we need some standards to go by. . . . We need specifications, and we need testing to go along with this in order to go along with the requirements of the marketplace."

these machines. I think it's fair to say the test flight crashed and burned. None of us want California to be the sequel to Florida."

On April 20, 2004, March obtained a signed declaration from a new Diebold whistle-blower, whom Harris calls "robcalifornia." The whistle-blower, James Dunn, had worked in Diebold's California offices. He identified March's archenemy, Austin Erdman, San Joaquin County's assistant registrar of voters, cooperating with Diebold officials to cover up the fact that, with the assistance of the county, the company had used uncertified software in the March 2004 elections. The whistle-blower claimed Erdman ordered the workers not to talk to the secretary of state's inspectors about it.*

The next day, California secretary of state Shelly's office held a hearing in Sacramento, giving Diebold one last chance to explain themselves. At the contentious hearing, Diebold Election Services Inc. president Bob Urosevich apologized "for any embarrassment," saying, in what many took as an admission that the company had slipped uncertified machines into the March election, "We were caught. We apologize for that."

Harris, who finally had her chance for a "You can't handle the truth" moment, took the mic and, standing just feet away from Urosevich, declared, "What we have is a company that lies. Yes, I'll say it—lies." When Jim March got his turn, he offered the packed house his recommendation: "It's time to vote 'em off the island."

The next day, Shelly's panel did just that, unanimously recommending to decertify one of Diebold's electronic voting machines in use in four California counties. On the last day of

---

*Austin Erdman denied all of Dunn's accusations, telling us, "This guy that is making these statements obviously is a nut."

the month, giving the counties the necessary six-month advance notice, Secretary of State Shelly confirmed their recommendation so that San Diego, Solano, Kern, and San Joaquin counties are forced to find a new voting system by November—a major disaster for the company and the counties who relied on them. It is victory for Harris and others who have worked against the grain to bring the issue to light. It was the first time a state decertified any of Diebold's fifty thousand electronic voting machines in use in thirty-seven states. The panel also voted to send its findings to the state's attorney general for possible criminal and civil charges against the company for violating state election laws. The California decision reverberated across the country, as other states kicked up their own investigations into the company. If it spreads, states might end up scrambling to replace multimillion-dollar systems at the last minute.

It was a stunning victory for Harris, and, in a way, a day of redemption. Diebold's culture of deception had finally been acknowledged by the state.

But Harris didn't take time out to celebrate. "Other companies are also using uncertified software . . . so I think we still have a long way to go."

On election day 2004, Harris says she plans to have her own small army of twenty thousand independent election observers monitoring electronic voting machines to ensure Americans' most basic right isn't lost in a jumble of zeros and ones.

As whistle-blower Rob Behler told us, "The men and women dying in Iraq to protect our freedom certainly wouldn't want it uprooted here in our own home."

9

Welcome to the
®evolution

Is the Independent Media
Ready for Battle?

■ ■ ■

*With no strong opposition party to challenge such triumphalist
hegemony, it is left to journalism to be democracy's best friend.*
—BILL MOYERS, *Keynote Address, National Conference
on Media Reform*

Minneapolis International Airport, MN

DANNY SCHECHTER, the "News Dissector," is trudging along
a human conveyor belt, dragging his black carry-on bag
stuffed to the max with books and videotapes about the media
revolution. Looking out at the airfield through massive glass
windows, he's waxing poetic.

"Here's the thing: There's no free ride. You have to walk
on the left. But walking on the left is often a lonely walk.
That's the problem. It's a long walk to freedom, said Nelson
Mandela."

For more than three decades, Schechter has trodden a slow
path out from the comfortable mainstream and into the wilds
of the independent media. Beginning as a radio broadcaster at
Boston's WBCN-FM, "the dissector" quickly made the leap
to television news, first joining Ted Turner's fledgling cable

start-up CNN and then ABC's *20/20* as an Emmy Award–winning producer. But once corporate meddlers infiltrated network news, Schechter went indie and started his own production company. A prolific author and documentary film producer, he is now executive editor of mediachannel.org, a Web-based news portal.

This weekend, Schechter is traveling to meet with other leaders of the independent media movement at the inaugural National Conference on Media Reform, in Madison, Wisconsin. Unlike Herb Allen's annual Sun Valley, Idaho, retreat, once considered the world's most prestigious media conference, where CEOs like Rupert Murdoch, Ted Turner, and Michael Eisner hatched their megamergers, Madison is a cold and barren frontier.

Sitting in the Northwest Airlines terminal, waiting for his connecting flight, Schechter munches on a sandwich. We're talking about the media reform conference and whether it is oxymoronic to think that the "media" can ever be "reformed." Schechter is, as ever, optimistic.

"Yeah, I think so. But it will have to be dragged, screaming and kicking. I don't think we're going to find a lot of receptivity unless we can really embarrass, shame, humiliate, and expose what's going on in a way that most Americans can see it, so they will finally say that they won't stand for it anymore."

But isn't this what so-called progressive journalism has been attempting to do for the last two hundred years? Hasn't there been an independent media movement to expose the dark machinations of power since Tom Paine published his seminal pamphlet, *Common Sense*, in 1776? Two centuries later, how much has changed? Sure, there have been moments of brilliant, courageous reporting, where the machinery of national media has ripped itself from the bosom of power and jolted the American political system. But where are we now?

Thirty years after the American government spent $150 billion and lost nearly sixty thousand lives in Vietnam, we are back in a sovereign country fighting a guerrilla war against an enemy that does not directly endanger the American people. What is wrong with this picture?

Clearly, we are in a crisis. Not just because corporate media has become an unofficial outpost of state propaganda, but also because the progressive, independent media have not found an adequate and powerful method of translating the value of their message to mainstream America. Instead of controlling and framing the national political agenda, progressives have consistently been marginalized into a reactionary force with only intermittent potency, a potency relegated to those rare moments when a corrupt government's lies and extortions force citizens to embrace the alternative. And even then, the left is limited to supporting an archaic, superficial alternative presented to them by the economic and political elites. They are resigned to supporting the Democratic Party candidate and forced into an ideological hatred of Ralph Nader because he wants to experiment with the democratic paradigm. These are the default options of a desperate people, not the revolutionary doctrine of a nascent political movement.

Perhaps there is an element of denial in the progressive front as well, one that shifts their attention from the painful recognition of the challenge before them. It's as if they have no sense of what it will take to defeat the deeply entrenched authoritarian force they are battling against. Let's be clear: The national public agenda is dominated by economic and political interests of such power that they essentially own the national media apparatus and currently have at their disposal an entire army to send around the world on a moment's notice. Who is going to challenge them? Are we seriously placing our hopes in this ragtag but ardent group of rebels making their way to Madison? If this movement is to have any power, then it's time to get very serious about the opponent it is facing. This is a battle for control of America's new millennial destiny, and while the progressive movement is still broadcasting from ramshackle studios and marching on Washington with papier-mâché puppets, the corporate military-industrial sector is using every microchip of new technology to directly target the mass consciousness of the American people.

This critique is not lost on Danny Schechter. Shrugging his shoulders, he says, "That's the other problem: There are a lot of people on the left who have a hostile attitude towards media. They don't understand it. Don't know how to use it. Don't have the production values that really hook people and interest them in what's going on, to make it interesting and build an audience. So, the left media, the independent media, needs to be critiqued, as well. It needs to be challenged to do a better job."

Yes, we need a movement to reform the media. But before we can ever hope to reclaim the public resource of communication from the military-industrial sector, we need to overhaul the independent media itself.

Tactically Speaking

Addressing a packed audience at San Francisco's Herbst Theatre in April 2003, *From the Wilderness*'s Michael Ruppert scolded the antiwar contingent for thinking sheer numbers of energized protesters would have any impact on the administration's drive to war. While acknowledging the organizational effort that brought millions into the streets worldwide, he explained that "the energy bounced off because it was directed at a part of the government where they knew that they were not vulnerable. They knew that the war was going to happen anyway."

Furthermore, continued Ruppert, liberals are expected by their conservative opponents to hit the pavement in protest whenever the nation goes to war. "Having a demonstration is not viewed in the rest of the country like it's viewed by the people in San Francisco. Did you know that? It's just those crazy wackos in San Francisco."

Protests have simply become a part of the American political tradition, cynically used by the administration as evidence of the nation's vibrant democratic culture, and then written off as a loud and rambunctious minority.* If the goal is to weaken the administration and erode its legitimate authority, then the progressive movement needs target issues that will unite Americans under a common cause.

"If you want to have a demonstration on something, go out and have a demonstration over the fact that three trillion dollars of your money has been stolen from the Pentagon in two years," said Ruppert.

Referring to the $3.3 trillion reported "missing" and "unaccounted for" by the Department of Defense since 2001,[1] Ruppert painted a scenario that would transform the paradigm of protest culture.

> *Five hundred thousand people in the streets of San Francisco protesting the fact that every American is going to have to spend three, four, or five working years of their lives to pay off their share of the money that's been stolen . . . will scare the devil out of the administration. You start*

---

*Responding to a reporter's question about the impact of antiwar protests, George Bush said, "Size of protest—it's like deciding, well, I'm going to decide policy based upon a focus group."

connecting the dots on money, you start reconnecting the American people instead of separating them along racial, ideological, and political lines. Find out what the American people have in common. And protest that.

The progressive movement often fails to reach a broader audience because it reinforces caricatures of itself, or it allows fringe groups with organizational skills to hijack the momentum of public outrage and use it to advance their own proprietary agenda.

Take the large-scale marches against the invasion of Iraq, the largest of which were organized by International ANSWER (Act Now to End War and Racism). Most marchers had no idea that ANSWER is tied to the communist World Workers Party (WWP), a murky group that in the past has proclaimed its support for such champions of human rights as Fidel Castro, Slobodan Milosevic, and North Korean dictator Kim Jong-il. Most antiwar protesters probably wouldn't have cared had the group not used the events to blare anti-Zionist slogans mixed with a little Free Mumia to boot.* Some participants at the October 2002 march on Washington, D.C., were left feeling that the event focused more on the plight of Palestinians than the Iraqi people. David Corn observed in the *LA Weekly*, the demonstration "was not intended to persuade doubters. Nor did it speak to Americans who oppose the war but who don't consider the United States a force of unequaled imperialist evil and who don't yearn to smash global capitalism."[2]

There is, of course, room for all political persuasions in the antiwar movement. But groups like the WWP are hardly the

---

*Even more alienating were later reports of the WWP's apologist justification for China's 1989 crackdown and murder of pro-democracy protesters at Tiananmen Square.

kind of organizations that will unite the American public under a banner of peace and respect for international law, if that
was ever the point.

Even more mainstream-friendly icons of the liberal camp
have also failed to understand the strategic value of unity. The
past four years have seen a boon in progressive media from the
standpoint of book sales and documentary film attendance. Articulate, funny, and on-message, lefty media stars like Michael
Moore and Al Franken draw more people into the tent than
ever before. But, as is so often the case, underdogs just don't
know what to do once they arrive in the spotlight, showing
they can be just as partisan, just as divisive, just as willing to
paint themselves into a corner as the conservative and religious
fundamentalists who are currently ruling the airwaves.

Al Franken's nationally televised take-down of Bill O'Reilly
at 2003 Book Expo America was a big moment for enemies of
Fox News across America. While O'Reilly sat to his right,
Franken chastised the pundit for lying about a Peabody Award
won by his old program, *Inside Edition*—it was actually a,
nonetheless respectable, Polk Award. But the anger and ferocity
of Franken's ambush, while tame compared with Mr. O'Reilly's
nightly prime-time rampages, only served to mirror and embrace the worst elements of the conservative news culture.
More critically, when all the dust had cleared, what had really
been said? It was a totally inane argument: Polk, Peabody,
who cares? Is that really the most incisive attack the progressive movement can launch against conservative media's top-
rated celebrity?

While Franken's politically insightful and, oftentimes, hilar-
ious broadcasts on financially troubled Air America represent
a high-water mark in the history of U.S. radio, his originality
is often tainted by a personal obsession with the conservative
right. By naming his show *The O'Franken Factor*, Franken is

building his franchise through a ritualized public baiting of Bill O'Reilly. Which, again, is funny stuff, but can only serve to bolster the pundit's cred in the eyes of his supporters. Or worse, make him into a sympathetic martyr for those who don't resonate with Franken's brand of political humor. The inaugural episode of the show featured a skit in which Ann Coulter, brilliantly impersonated by Bebe Neuwirth, is locked in the Green Room, being politically incorrect, uttering obscenities and trashing the place. It's humorous, but in the end, the net result is a petty joke at the expense of less worthy opponents, alienating for anyone not totally sold on the liberal agenda.

Even Michael Moore's acceptance speech for *Bowling for Columbine* at the 2003 Oscar ceremony, while glorious for its momentary capture of Hollywood's most glittering stage, was tainted by an obtuse garishness that did as much to sustain the divide between American political spectrum than bridge it. Over muted boos of the crowd, Moore chose pontification over politesse, claiming:

> *We live in the time where we have fictitious election results that elects a fictitious president. We live in a time where we have a man sending us to war for fictitious reasons. Whether it's the fiction of duct tape or fiction of orange alerts, we are against this war, Mr. Bush. Shame on you, Mr. Bush, shame on you. And anytime you got the pope and the Dixie Chicks against you, your time is up.*[3]

Instead of a pithy and humble critique of the war, the progressive movement was left with a sarcastic and disheveled mascot who ultimately embarrassed and polarized many of the people who had been converted by his brilliant, subversively emotive film.

But there are reasons to be hopeful. In January 2004, the

Academy honored another antiestablishment documentary filmmaker, Errol Morris, with an Oscar for *Fog of War*. Based on a series of interviews with Robert McNamara, one of America's most accomplished militarists, *Fog of War* is an object lesson in the art of self-compromise. Giving McNamara a rope long enough to hang himself, Morris allows his subject to expose the banal evils of war and the realpolitikal amorality of those who wage it. Yet, he also understands there is something of the sage in McNamara, structuring the film around eleven "lessons" from McNamara's life; the first of which is to "empathize with your enemies." At the Oscar podium, the filmmaker was brief and eloquent, giving those who supported the invasion of Iraq pause to consider the future legacy of Bush's reckless and ill-conceived foreign initiative.

"Forty years ago this country went down a rabbit hole in Vietnam and millions died. I fear we're going down a rabbit hole once again. And if people can stop and think and reflect on some of the ideas and issues in this movie, perhaps I've done some damn good here."[4]

Building bridges between ideologically divided groups is a difficult endeavor and one that is often dependent on the olive branch declarations of visionary leaders. But there are those rare times when the poles are driven together in reaction to what is perceived as a common threat, usually as a last-ditch effort to fight the potential loss of rights or freedoms. This was the case in one of the most dramatic populist campaign in independent media history.

On June 2, 2003, the Republican-controlled Federal Communications Commission (FCC), led by chairman Michael K. Powell, son of Secretary of State Colin Powell, voted 3–2 to drastically loosen restrictions on media ownership in the United States.[5] The bitterly contested vote, which divided the commission along partisan lines, green-lighted a new wave of

media consolidation by major corporations. Instead of allowing the FCC's decision to discreetly slide through Congress
and become law, activist groups from across the political spectrum brought the issue of media ownership to unprecedented
visibility, driving a grassroots campaign that generated millions of protest letters to the FCC and Congress.[6]

After news of the FCC decision, public outrage had been
so well channeled that old-school Republican senators Trent
Lott and Jesse Helms joined rebel Representatives Bernie
Sanders (I-Vt.) and Barbara Lee (D-Calif.) in denouncing the
ownership-rules changes. While media monopolization has
long been a core cause of the progressive movement, one of
the major forces behind the unified front was the National
Rifle Association's (NRA) mobilization of its hard-core ultra-
conservative membership. In a May 2003 bulletin, NRA executive vice president Wayne LaPierre implored members to
protest the FCC's relaxation of rules that "have prevented
gun-hating media giants like AOL Time Warner, Viacom/
CBS, and Disney/ABC from silencing [the] NRA when we've
needed to take our message directly to the American people in
critical legislative and political battles."[7] Gun owners responded,
delivering more than 300,000 individual protests, the most of
any group involved in the campaign. On the progressive side,
Web sites like Alternet, CounterPunch, MoveOn, and Common Cause published articulate nonpartisan reports that, in
addition to the NRA, brought the number of Americans who
spoke out against the FCC decision above 3 million.

This storm of citizen opposition was enough to sway the
Senate, which passed a bill to overturn the decision,[8] but at
the time of this writing, the House had still not voted on it.
President Bush declared that he may veto a House bill to
modify the rules changes, effectively rubber-stamping the
FCC's decision.

The corporate media, holding their collective breaths for the FCC-sanctioned gold rush, had "virtually no coverage"[9] of the issue until just one week before the commission was to vote. The only networks to actively report on the rules changes and their potential impact on the country were Public Broadcasting System (PBS) and National Public Radio (NPR), both of which are nonprofit corporations. Beyond that, the independent media was left to spread the message that the FCC, a politically appointed protectorate of a public resource, was planning to allow further consolidation and monopolization of the nation's single most vital conduit for democratic participation.

While it is understandable that Big Media would black out news that could negatively affect their ability to expand and monopolize, it was less clear what justification the commission could have for keeping the public out of the debate. Despite the surge of public interest shown in the issue of media ownership, FCC chairman Michael Powell authorized just one official public meeting*[10] on the proposed relaxation of restrictions. But if the prospect of a compromised FCC, whose decisions could mean billions in new deals for the corporate sector, had the smell of a breaking scandal, the mainstream media didn't go for it. Given the stakes on the table, they were not about to mount comprehensive investigations into potential conflicting interests within the FCC itself. That job was left to the one of the most respected bastions of independent media, the Washington-based Center for Public Integrity (CPI).

Smelling a rat in the FCC's unabashed support of the rules changes, CPI launched a series of probes into the commis-

---

*Despite Powell's refusal to schedule more public meetings, dissenting Democratic commissioners Michael Copps and Jonathan Adelstein organized a series of "semiofficial" meetings across the country.

sion six months before the June 2003 vote. In the true spirit of American muckraking, CPI delved deep into the FCC's culture, showing the darker side of a bureaucracy riddled with conflicts of interest. Saving the most damaging reports for the last weeks before the vote, CPI used its Web site, publicintegrity.org, to break stories that would have once been in the domain of hallowed establishment media icons like the *New York Times*, *Washington Post*, or *60 Minutes*.

On May 22, 2003, CPI published "On the Road Again—and Again,"[11] which surveyed the total value of travel and entertainment expenses FCC commissioners and staff received from telecommunications and broadcast industries. Looking at the eight-year period leading up to the study, CPI found the FCC racked up almost $2.8 million in contributions from the very industries it is supposed to regulate. Of all U.S. destinations, the most popular were Las Vegas with 330 trips, followed by New Orleans with 173. To most observers, it came as no surprise that one of the top beneficiaries was chairman Michael Powell, who "chalked up the most industry-sponsored travel and entertainment among active commissioners during the period covered by the study."

The following week, CPI released another damning report. Titled "Behind Closed Doors,"[12] the study focused on the number of private meetings FCC officials held with the nation's major broadcasters in the eight months leading up to the vote. The study reported "media moguls Rupert Murdoch of News Corp., which owns Fox, and Mel Karmazin of Viacom, which owns CBS,* virtually dashed from one FCC office to another for a series of private meetings with commissioners

---

*Both Murdoch and Karmazin had a large stake in the rules changes, since their companies each own TV outlets that reach more than 35 percent of households, which put them over the limit. Without a relaxation of ownership restrictions, they may have been forced to sell those stations.

and top staff in late January and early February, as the agency was crafting the controversial proposals."

Commenting on the results of his group's investigation, CPI director Charles Lewis said, "The idea that the FCC can render an objective, independent judgment about media ownership is laughable." However, despite the revelations of influence peddling and a severely compromised decision-making process, the FCC was neither censured nor reprimanded by its political bosses. The most significant outcome of the reports, which received extensive media coverage, was the termination of industry-funded travel junkets for FCC officials.[13] A small victory but one that, coupled with the firestorm of public outrage that greeted the FCC rules-change decision, heralded the return of a citizen-based journalism and cemented CPI's status as one of the most vital, and feared, investigative news organizations in America.

The Return of Citizen Muckraking

The Center for Public Integrity was founded in 1989 by Charles Lewis, a disillusioned *60 Minutes* producer who had grown frustrated with the lack of substantive investigative reporting at the network and created CPI as a watchdog organization based in Washington, D.C. Since its founding, CPI has released more than two hundred investigative reports and won several of journalism's top awards.*

One of independent media's most significant journalistic

---

*In 1996, CPI rose to national prominence after it broke the infamous "Lincoln Bedroom" story, profiling the Clinton administration's use of White House sleepovers to reward high-rolling Democratic donors. CPI's subsequent coverage of the 1996 election, which was characterized by a rare nonpartisanship, gave Lewis a reputation for surgical, objective journalism that was unparalleled in the independent media.

coups took place in February 2003, when Lewis got a phone call from an anonymous source asking whether CPI would be interested in secret legislation being drafted by the Department of Justice (DoJ) as a sequel to the Patriot Act. Lewis agreed and within hours received a brown envelope containing the 120-page Domestic Security Enhancement Act of 2003. Dubbed "Patriot II," the legislation would expand the government's authority to diminish or revoke civil liberties, specifically in the areas of intelligence-gathering, surveillance, secret arrests, and expatriation of American citizens accused of being terrorists.

Once CPI had determined the document's authenticity, it contacted members of Congress to gauge what they knew about the drafted legislation. No one, not even those with DoJ oversight, had any knowledge of it. Initially, the Justice Department also denied knowledge of the act but, once it was clear CPI was going to publish the material through its Web site, begged the organization not to reveal its contents to the public. Pleads turned to threats, but undeterred, Lewis pulled the trigger, sending Patriot II live over the Internet. All hell broke loose.

Within forty-five minutes of the document's publication, the DoJ issued a statement reducing the draft to a "proposal . . . being discussed at staff levels." But documents obtained by PBS's *Now with Bill Moyers* showed that a copy of the bill had been sent to Vice President Dick Cheney and Speaker of the House Dennis Hastert. The DoJ attempted to deny that as well, but it was too late. The damage was done. Patriot Act II became the top national story for the next twenty-four hours. If Attorney General John Ashcroft had any hopes of slipping the act through Congress,* he was forced to

---

*The level of secrecy surrounding Patriot II prompted constitutional expert Dr. David Cole to suggest that the Bush administration was "waiting for a propitious

abandon them; CPI's leak created such a controversy that the bill was shelved indefinitely. By providing a credible, ethical, nonpartisan news organization, Lewis set the standard for a new generation of independent muckrakers. He also became their hero. One month after CPI's historic coup, the *Village Voice* called Lewis "the Paul Revere of our time."[15]

So it's not surprising that Charles Lewis is one of the stars of the 2003 Media Reform Conference. He is one of the primary reasons for our trip to Madison, since it is nearly impossible to arrange interviews with him while he is working on one of CPI's multiple concurrent investigations. We are interested in CPI's most recent, award-winning report, "Windfalls of War."[16] Published on October 30, 2003, the exhaustive six-month investigation exposed links between Republican campaign donors and postwar contracts in Iraq and Afghanistan. Using its Web site as a virtual courtroom exhibit, CPI posted over fifty contractual documents including those of Bechtel, DynCorp, and Kellogg Brown and Root, a subsidiary of Dick Cheney's former employer Halliburton, which was "the top recipient . . . with more than $2.3 billion awarded to the company." The report also revealed that $8 billion in contracts were awarded to a block of American companies that "donated more money to the presidential campaign of George W. Bush than to any other politician over the last dozen years." Once again, CPI's work fueled the independent media, giving them more ammunition in their fight to discredit the Bush administration's blatant exploitation of the presidency to reimburse the war profiteers who funded his 2000 campaign.

Needless to say, Lewis has a hectic schedule. Sitting in an empty conference room adjacent to our hotel restaurant, we

---

time to introduce it, which might well be when a war is begun."[14] CPI leaked Patriot Act II on February 7, 2003, just six weeks before the invasion of Iraq.

are given twenty minutes before he has to hit his next meeting. As we prepare for the interview, it is hard to ignore Lewis's atypical persona. He does not affect the posture of a crusading journalist. Instead, he looks like a clean-cut, mild-mannered Midwestern businessman who could be in town for an insurance convention. Until he starts talking:

> *We are a nonprofit, and money is scarce for every nonprofit. If we do a report, it's because we think it's pretty damn important. This is not about celebrities. It's not about ratings. It's because it matters. It affects people's life, their health, their safety, their financial well-being, and their values, too. But the bottom line is we don't do things for no reason. We don't have an agenda. We are not pushing legislation. We don't push candidates or parties. We are nonpartisan. We alienate both parties equally— all parties. We are the skunk at the garden party, essentially.*

In an endearing way, Lewis is the ultimate optimist. He has exceeded all expectations and created a reality in which there are so few limits, he seems genuinely surprised the government goes out of its way to block his attempts to get information.

> *The public has a right to know who is making money from war, and the idea that somebody is going to tell us that we can't get that information is so—I hate to say it, un-American. It's unacceptable. So the beauty of the Web is you can just put that stuff up there. You put up 62,000 words, six sidebars, seventy-one corporate profiles, and five databases. It was a massive effort, and it was very hard for*

*the Pentagon to say it wasn't true. They hated our guts
and they were very unhappy with us, but they couldn't refute it because it was all based on records.*

When we ask him if he feels that CPI's reports get adequate
coverage by the corporate media, he redirects the question.

*Well, you know I have to say we got some coverage. A lot of
the media found it interesting. But the question for me is
not: Was it covered? The real question is: Where the hell
were the traditional journalists? Why didn't they do this?
I mean our budget is four million dollars a year. The* New
York Times *and* Washington Post *have over one thousand
journalists each, and hundreds of millions of dollars in the
budget. We kept thinking someone was going to post [the
postwar contracts] and lay this out, but no one did for six
full months. I am still amazed by it! But I thought that
about Patriot II. We were the first to disclose that Enron was
Bush's top contributor. I don't know how that happened, but
we were the first. Where were the rest of the media?*

When we tell him that this has been the burning question
that has taken us halfway across the world searching for an answer, Lewis smiles knowingly. For him, the responsibility of
gathering information lies with the public and is part of a long
tradition he calls "citizen muckraking." It is one that goes
back as far as the beginning of American democracy, to the
person whom Bill Moyers refers to as "the clarion journalistic
voice of the revolution"—the original political pamphleteer,
Thomas Paine.[17]

A few hours after the Lewis interview, Moyers is delivering
the conference's keynote address to a packed audience in

Madison's Orpheum Theatre. The room is filled with a kind of silent energy so that, even as he is schooling the audience on the origins of revolutionary American journalism, Moyers's every word feels electric. It's the kind of history lesson only the sixty-nine-year-old journalist and broadcaster can deliver.

Speaking of Thomas Paine, Moyers reminds us that it was his solitary mission to bring information to the people, to alert them to the freedom of thought and political action that awaited them on the other side of the American revolution.*

Moyers elaborates, linking past with present, and explains that Paine "had something we need to restore—an unwavering concentration to reach ordinary people with the message that they mattered and could stand up for themselves."

Looking across the plane of upturned heads nodding at Moyers in silent approval, we wonder if the progressive movement has any true understanding of the war that is being fought over the hearts and minds of the American people, or the tactics being used to wage it. If the independent media suffers from anything, it is a profound lack of expertise in the arts of communication and propaganda. Though some may consider these negative and unredeeming skill sets, there can be no serious hope to reform the national media unless the progressives can learn to compete against it, or at least learn from its appropriation of pop-cultural aesthetics. Look at the bland, conservative layout of Alternet.org or the DIY set of *Democracy Now!*, or the anti-Republican partisanship of Air America, and ask yourself whether they are truly reaching out beyond the perimeter of their core constituency, to the mainstream audience who have been weaned on MTV and *Monday*

---

*Paine was America's first pamphleteer. *Common Sense*, which Paine self-published in 1776, had a run of 100,000 copies, and is considered America's first best-seller.

Night Football. Is the progressive sector really ready to take on the spectacle being orchestrated by billionaire globalists with former high-level political strategists running the show? No, it is not.

An entire generation of young people is being neglected and alienated by the very movement that claims to be working for its future. Like the establishment press it claims to rival, the independent media has become a fortressed institution with its own cliques and clichés. Limited by their own inherent biases and constricting conservatism, the progressives are in a form of collective denial that is not unlike that of their peers in the corporate sector. They simply do not see the harder path of self-realization. Or, they don't want to.

Flipping through the Media Reform Conference itinerary, it was hard not to be impressed by the breadth of expertise being offered from some of the greatest minds in independent media.* But there wasn't a single panel or workshop on how to better create, package, and disseminate the valuable information being discussed. Perhaps Moyers, too, senses that the gathering is a little heavy on dogma and slightly void of self-analysis and critique. From his elevated podium, he warns that the conference will have to be more than "a conclave of high-minded do-gooders applauding each other's sermons, because what we're talking about is nothing less than rescuing a democracy that is so polarized, it is in danger of being paralyzed and pulverized."

If ever there was a time for a media revolution, it is now. But before we can transform the external world, we must first

*Some of the progressive luminaries in attendance were dissident FCC commissioner Michael Copps, *Weapons of Mass Deception* author John Stauber, *Paper Tiger* founder Dee Dee Halleck, FAIR's Janine Jackson, *No Logo* author Naomi Klein, Media Alliance's Jeff Perlstein, and conference founders Prof. Robert McChesney and writer John Nichols.

metamorphose ourselves. We must challenge independent media organizations to break out of arcane and ineffective techniques and look objectively at the barricades we have erected across our own paths to self-realization. If the leaders of this movement are happy to lecture the choir who have already congregated around the message, then so be it. But count us out. In our media revolution, we want to reach the widest possible demographic. And to do that, we understand that we have something to learn from the corporate media institutions we have defined as our nemeses.

There is a stark divide between the rhetorical evaluation of corporate media's entrenched monopolistic power and the tactical strategies being offered to combat it. Of course, they possess economic and network superiority, but true revolutionaries know the battle is not controlled by those who wield the largest army or hold the most gold. It is won by those who tap the deepest instincts, ideals, and prejudices of the public mind. These are values that cannot be manufactured. We simply need to find a way to pierce the illusion of lies and deception being cast by the mainstream media. Instead of being marginalized by our disadvantage, we must adopt the tactics of guerrillas, who wage war against an all-powerful totalitarian opponent by using its power against it. The independent media must shift beyond the cloister of irrelevancy, seize the new tools of production, and work to create a spectacle that rivals that of the mainstream media.

In case anyone needed more inspiration to get serious about the battle ahead of us, Moyers has no qualms about laying down the gauntlet:

Never has there been an administration so disciplined in secrecy, so precisely in lockstep in keeping information from the people at large and—in defiance of the Constitution—

from their representatives in Congress. Never has so pow-
erful a media oligopoly been so unabashed in reaching like
Caesar for still more wealth and power. Never have hand
and glove fitted together so comfortably to manipulate free
political debate, sow contempt for the idea of government
itself, and trivialize the people's need to know.

But, as we say, there is reason to be hopeful. Though the
bulk of left-wing and progressive leaders decry the current
wave of corporate empire building, their doomsday prophe-
cies have a silver lining, because monopolization and con-
glomeration are not always signs of strength. Think about it:
Where there was once a spectrum of competing mainstream
media companies, they have now shrunk and become entrenched in a monolithic set of sociopolitical values. Worse,
the once-proud institutions of independent thought have now
internalized the process of censorship, often discouraging or
terminating those journalists or public officials who take on
the work of exposing major cases of governmental and corporate corruption. Big Media has become a servile partner of the
state and lost the power to be innovative, controversial, and
progressive. Huddled together, they resemble a herd of finely
groomed sheep.

Behind them, a vacuum has opened up, and there is suddenly room for a highly branded, charismatic, and controversial set of competitors to accept the challenge and compete
with the din and sparkle of the mainstream spectacle. There
has never been a more fortuitous time to take on the behe-
moth. Like an army of Davids, we have the tools, the techniques, and the will. We have so much vibrant creative energy
within us, and it is precisely because we are on the outside that
we have the edge.

Never before has the security of our world been so reliant

on the freedom of independent, investigative voices to unite the people against those who have nakedly seized the mechanism of American democracy. As the world's dominant superpower, we have the enhanced responsibility of revolutionizing our media system because it is not only framing the debate at home, but it is also doing it globally, and for good reason. The economic and political elites in America know that their survival depends on the rapid absorption of the propagandist media by the nations they seek to dominate and exploit. Fortunately, we have a new generation of independent journalists and citizen muckrakers who will use the unharnessed power of communications technology to fight and win this information war.

What are you waiting for?

Endnotes

■ ■ ■

Introduction

1. John Stacks, "Hard Times for Hard News," *World Policy Journal*, Winter 2003/4.

Chapter 1

1. Megan Garvey, "NBC Balks at Sharing Election Night Tapes," *Los Angeles Times*, September 8, 2001.

2. Henry Waxman, "Did NBC Make Call with Welch in the Backfield?" *Los Angeles Times*, August 13, 2001.

3. Jane Mayer, *The New Yorker*, November 2000.

4a. Eric Boehlert, "Fox Guarding the Henhouse," *Salon*, November 15, 2000. http://dir.salon.com/politics/feature/2000/11/15/ellis/index.html (accessed May 10, 2004).

4b. Letter from Representative Waxman to Bob Wright, chairman and CEO of NBC, September 10, 2001.

4c. Ibid.

4d. Ibid.

5. Associated Press, September 6, 2001.

6. Henry Waxman, letter to NBC chairman Bob Wright, September 10, 2001.

7. Channel Zero, *This Is Channel Zero*, December 1996.

8. Megan Garvey, "Waxman Renews NBC News Assault," *Los Angeles Times*, September 11, 2001.

9. *Meet the Press*, NBC, February 8, 2004.

10. Peggy Noonan, "Philosophy, Not Policy: Why Bush Isn't Good at Interviews," *Wall Street Journal*, February 8, 2004.

11. Jim Rutenberg, "To Many Insiders, Russert Has Hottest Seat," *New York Times*, February 9, 2004.

12. Nicholas Confessore, "Did Jack Welch Call the Election for George W. Bush?" *The American Prospect*, August 1, 2001.

13. Daniel Goleman, *Vital Lies, Simple Truths: The Psychology of Self Deception* (New York: Simon & Schuster, 1996).

14. Noam Chomsky, *Necessary Illusions: Thought Control in Democratic Societies* (Cambridge, MA: South End Press, 1989).

15. Jimmy Breslin, "Their Photos Tell the Story," *Newsday*, December 30, 2003.

16. *Politically Incorrect*, ABC, September 17, 2001.

17. White House Press Briefing, September 26, 2001.

18. David Bauder, "ABC Replacing Bill Maher's 'Politically Incorrect' with Comedy Show Starring Jimmy Kimmel," Associated Press, May 14, 2002.

19. Topic A with Tina Brown, *CNBC*, September 10, 2003.

20. Ken Auletta, "Fortress Bush," *The New Yorker*, January 19, 2004.

21. Michael Wolff, "Russert to Judgment," *New York*, February 12, 2001.

Chapter 2

1. Letter to the Editor, *Stars and Stripes*, October 21–27, 2001.

2. "Our Nation Understands Sacrifice in the Service of Principle. We Will Prevail," Editorial, *Pittsburgh Post-Gazette*, September 17, 2001.

3. White House transcript of President Bush's September 20, 2001, State of the Union address.

4. Todd Spangler, "Jet Crashes in Pa.; Passenger Reported Hijacking in Phone Call," Associated Press, September 11, 2001.

5. Nick Parker, "Ready? Let's Roll," *Baltimore Sun*, September 18, 2001.

6. Todd Spangler, "United Jet Crashes in Pa. After Terror Attacks," Associated Press, September 11, 2001.

7. Mike Wagner and Ken McCall, "Passengers Thwarted Hijackers," Cox News Service, September 12, 2001.

8. "Sept. 11, 2001: Day Torn Asunder; Diary of Tragedy," *Bergen Record*, September 16, 2001.

9. "American Under Attack," *ABC News*, September 13, 2001.

10. "FAA Employee: Hijacked Jets Almost Collided En Route," *Associated Press*, September 13, 2001.

11. Timothy D. May, "Investigators Find Data Recorder, Gather Human Remains at Pa. Crash Site," Associated Press, September 13, 2001.

12. Charles Lane and Philip Pan, "Jetliner Was Diverted Toward Washington Before Crash in Pennsylvania," *Washington Post*, September 12, 2001.

13. *Meet the Press*, NBC, September 16, 2001.

14. Gerard Wright, "On Hallowed Ground," *The Age*, September 11, 2002.

15. Richard Wallace, "What Did Happen to Flight 93?" *The Mirror*, September 12, 2002.

16. William Bunch, "We Know It Crashed, But Not Why," *Philadelphia Daily News*, November 15, 2001.

17. Michelle Malkin, "Just Wondering," *townhall.com*, March 8, 2002.

18. *The O'Reilly Factor*, Fox News Network, March 14, 2002.

19. John Carlin, "Unanswered Questions," *The Independent*, August 13, 2002.

20. Ibid.

21. William Bunch, "Three-Minute Discrepancy in Tape: Cockpit Voice Recorder Ends Before Flight 93's Official Time of Impact," *Philadelphia Daily News*, September 16, 2002.

22. Gail Sheehy, "Stewardess ID'd Hijackers Early, Transcripts Show," *New York Observer*, February 16, 2004.

23. Leon Festinger, *Theory of Cognitive Dissonance*, Stanford University Press, 1957.

24. Ibid.

Chapter 3

1. Byron York, "Bush's Historic Opportunity," *National Review Online*, September 14, 2001.
2. *Special Edition: America's New War*, CNN, September 22, 2001.
3. Associated Press, transcript, August 2, 2001.
4. "Strategic Energy Policy Challenges for the 21st Century," April 2001.
5. William Rivers Pitt, "All Along the Watchtower," truthout.org, June 22, 2002.
6. White House Press Release, May 16, 2002.
7. Matthew L. Wald, "Earlier Hijacking Offered Signals That Were Missed," *New York Times*, October 13, 2001.
8. Matthew Brzezinski, "Bust and Boom," *Washington Post*, December 30, 2001.
9. Mark Fineman and Judy Pastarnak, "Suicide Flights Seen as Threat to '96 Olympics," *Los Angeles Times*, November 17, 2001.
10. "The Media Knew, Too," *National Review*, April 12, 2004.
11. Steven Komarow and Tom Squitieri, "NORAD Had Drills Eerily Like Sept. 11," *USA Today*, April 19, 2004.
12. Ned Stafford, "Newspaper: Echelon Gave Authorities Warning of Attacks," fromthewilderness.com, September 14, 2001.
13. "The Secret War: The European Connection," *The Guardian*, September 30, 2001.
14. Dan Eggen and Bill Miller, "Bush Was Told of Hijacking Dangers," *Washington Post*, May 16, 2002.
15. Dick Cheney's speech to the Conservative Party of New York, March 16, 2002.
16. "Bush: 'We're at War,'" *Newsweek*, September 24, 2001.
17. "Early Fly Ban for Rushdie," *MX*, September 28, 2001.
18. Phillip Matier and Andrew Ross, "Willie Brown Got Low-Key Warning About Air Travel," *San Francisco Chronicle*, September 12, 2001.
19. "How the FBI Blew the Case," *Time*, June 3, 2002.
20. *60 Minutes*, CBS, March 21, 2004.
21. *Meet the Press*, NBC, March 28, 2004.
22. "Cheney to Rush: Clarke 'Not in the Loop,'" rushlimbaugh.com, March 22, 2004.
23. Joshua Marshall, talkingpointmemo.com, March 21, 2004.

24. Condeleezza Rice, "For the Record," *Washington Post*, March 22, 2004.

25. Eric Boehlert, "We Should Have Had Orange- or Red-Type Alert in June or July 2001," *Salon*, March 27, 2004.

26. William Bunch, "Why Don't We Have Answers to These 9/11 Questions," *Philadelphia Daily News*, September 11, 2003.

27. William B. Scott, "Exercise Jump Starts Response to Attacks," *Aviation Week and Space Technology*, June 3, 2002.

28. *Dateline*, NBC, September 23, 2001.

29. Richard Whittle, "National Guard Raced After Two Airliners," *Dallas Morning News*, September 15, 2001.

30. Matthew L. Wald, "After the Attacks: Sky Rules," *New York Times*, September 15, 2001.

31. Gail Sheehy, "Stewardess ID'd Hijacker Early, Transcripts Show," *New York Observer*, February 16, 2004.

32. Paul Thompson, "Failure to Defend the Skies on 9/11," unansweredquestions.org, May 29, 2003.

33. Chalmers Johnson, "Blowback," *The Nation*, September 27, 2001.

34. James Risen and Judith Miller, "The Spies: Pakistani Intelligence Had Ties to Al Qaeda, U.S. Officials Say," *New York Times*, October 29, 2001.

35. Nened Sebak, "The KLA: Terrorists or Freedom Fighters," BBC, June 28, 1998.

36. Marcia Christoff Kurop, "Al Qaeda's Balkan Links," *Wall Street Journal*, November 1, 2001.

37. Chidanand Rajghatta, "U.S. Sees Link Between IA Hijack and Terror Attacks," *Times of India*, October 7, 2001.

38. Michel Chossudovsky, "Bush League," *Philadelphia City Paper*, December 20–27, 2001.

39. Barton Gellman and Mike Allen, "The Week That Redefined the Bush Presidency," *Washington Post*, September 23, 2001.

40. Federal News Service, May 16, 2002.

41. Bob Woodward, *Plan of Attack* (New York: Simon & Schuster, 2004).

42. Barbara Slavin and Bill Nichols, "State Dept.'s No. 2 Has Flair for Blunt Diplomacy," *USA Today*, February 12, 2002.

Chapter 4

1. NAACP Image Awards, March 5, 2001.

2. From a statement released by Rep. Cynthia McKinney (D-Ga.) April 12, 2002, in response to criticisms of statements she made about the September 11 attacks on the United States.

3. Mara Shalhoup, "Big Brother's Little Helper," *Creative Loafing*, December 4, 2003.

4. See, for instance, Associated Press, "Egypt Leader Says He Warned America," December 7, 2001.

5a. "Conspiracy Theories: Uncovering the Facts Behind the Myths of 9/11," Canadian Broadcasting Corporation, October 29, 2003.

5b. Interview with Bill White, "Conspiracy Theories: Uncovering the Facts Behind the Myths of September 11, 2001," *The Fifth Estate*, Canadian Broadcasting Corporation, October 29, 2003.

6. Nathan Vardi, "The World's Billionaires: Sins of the Father?" *Forbes*, March 18, 2002.

7a. Ibid.

7b. "New book says Abu Zubaydah has made startling revelations about secret connections linking Saudi Arabia, Pakistan, and Osama bin Laden: *Why America Slept*, by Gerald Posner, appears to be first description of repeated, explicit quid pro quo between bin Laden and a Saudi official," *Time*, August 31, 2003.

8. Maureen Dowd, "The 'Arab Gatsby' and His Washington Pals," *New York Times*, November 29, 2002.

9. Geoffrey Gray, "Bush Sr. Could Profit from War," *Village Voice*, October 11, 2001.

10. See GNN interview with Greg Palast, "Above the Law: Bush's Racial Coup D'etat and Intell Shutdown," www.guerrillanews.com/counter_intelligence/doc233.html.

11. GNN interview with Greg Palast.

12. Sen. Zell Miller press release, April 12, 2002.

13. Mark Fineman, "Arms Buildup Enriches Firm Staffed by Big Guns Defense: Ex-President and Other Elites Are Behind Weapon-Boosting Carlyle Group," *Los Angeles Times*, January 10, 2002. Fineman wrote, "Carlyle officials say they decided to take the company public only after the Sept. 11 attacks."

14. "Profiting from Disaster?" *CBS News*, September 19, 2001. "Probes into 'Suspicious' Trading," CNN, September 24, 2001.

15. James Ridgeway, "U.S. Ignored Warnings from French," *Village Voice*, May 28, 2002.

16. "Some McKinney Donors Probed for Terror Ties. DeKalb Democrat Said Unaware Any Donors Might Support Terror," *Atlanta Journal-Constitution*, August 3, 2002.

17. Gary Ashwill, "Georgia's New McCarthyism," *Southern Exposure*, Winter 2002/2003.

Chapter 5

1. *New York Times*, October 12, 2000.

2. Irving Kristol, "What It Was, and What It Is," *Weekly Standard*, August 25, 2003.

3. Todd Gitlin, "America's Age of Empire: The Bush Doctrine," *Mother Jones*, January–February 2003.

4. Christine Spolar, "14 'Enduring Bases' Set in Iraq Long-Term Military Presence Planned," *Chicago Tribune*, March 23, 2004.

5. Leon Festinger, Theory of Congitive Dissonance (Palo Alto, CA: Stanford University Press, 1957).

6. Graham Turner, "America the 'Super-duper' Power," *Daily Telegraph*, June 16, 2003.

7. John Stacks, "Hard Times for Hard News," *World Policy Journal*, Winter 2003/4.

8. Niall Ferguson, "American Terminator," *Newsweek International*, January 2004.

9. Transcript of the "United States Is, and Should Be, an Empire: A New Atlantic Initiative Debate," July 17, 2003, as it appears on the American Enterprise Institute Web site.

10. Eric Schmitt, "Rumsfeld Says U.S. Will Cut Forces in Gulf," *New York Times*, April 28, 2003.

11. Nicholas D. Kristof, "The God Gulf," *New York Times*, January 7, 2004.

12. Remarks by Vice President Cheney to the World Economic Forum in Davos, Switzerland, January 24, 2004.

13. David Pratt, "Saddam's Capture: Was a Deal Brokered Behind the Scenes?" *Sunday Herald* (Scotland), January 4, 2004.

14. Richard Sale, "Saddam Key in Early CIA Plot," UPI, April 7, 2003.

15. Declassified British Embassy documents recommending Saddam Hussein to London, 1969; "The Saddam Hussein Sourcebook," National Security Archive, December 2003.

16. Janine di Giovanni, "They came bearing gifts, but now most countries would prefer to forget," *Times* of London, March 10, 2003.

17. Jim Crogan, "Made in the USA, Part III: The Dishonor Roll: America's Corporate Merchants of Death in Iraq," *LA Weekly*, April 25–May 1, 2003.

18. Neil Mackay "Iraq's Arms Revealed: 17 British Firms Armed Saddam with His Weapons," *Sunday Herald*, February 25, 2003.

19. "The Forgotten People: One Man's Battle to Stop Iraq," CBC, March 26, 2003.

20. Ibid.

21. Ibid.

22. "Defense-Garner See Iraq as Long-Term Military Outpost in Middle East," *National Journal*, February 6, 2004.

23. "Turkmenibashi Everywhere," *60 Minutes, CBS News*, January 4, 2004.

24a. "Central Asia and Global Stability: Interview with Martha Brill Olcott," *Washington ProFile* (Russia), January 20, 2003.

24b. Nick Paton, "U.S. Looks Away as New Ally Tortures Islamists," *The Guardian*, May 26, 2003.

25. The National Geographic–Roper 2002 Global Geographic Literacy Survey, November 20, 2002.

26. Human Rights Watch World Report 2003. Uzbekistan, 2003.

27. Richard Gwyn, "Demand for Oil Outstripping Supply," *Toronto Star*, January 28, 2004.

Chapter 6

1. U.S. Department of Defense News Briefing, Col. James Naughton, U.S. Army Materiel Command, Friday, March 14, 2003.

2. Hillary Johnson, "Is the Pentagon Giving Our Soldiers Cancer?" *Rolling Stone*, October 2003.

3. Larry Johnson "Iraqi Cancers, Birth Defects Blamed on U.S. Depleted Uranium," *Seattle Post-Intelligencer*, November 12, 2002.

4. "Depleted Uranium Weapons: Toxic Contaminant or Neces-

sary Technology?" Conference, Massachusetts Institute of Technology, March 2004.

5. Robert James Parsons, "America's Big Dirty Secret," *Le Monde diplomatique*, March 2002.

6. Akira Tashiro, "Navajo Reservation: Health Problems Steadily Increasing," *The Chugoku Shimbun*.

7. Neil Mackay, "US Forces' Use of Depleted Uranium Weapons Is 'Illegal,'" *Sunday Herald* (Scotland), March 30, 2003.

8. Larry Johnson, "Iraqi Cancers, Birth Defects Blamed on U.S. Depleted Uranium," *Seattle Post-Intelligencer*, November 12, 2002.

9. "Tiny Victims of Desert Storm," *Life*, November 1995.

10. Ed Vulliamy, "Iraq: The Human Toll (Part Two)," *The Observer*, Sunday, July 6, 2003.

11. Nick Childs, "Friendly Fire 'Killed US Marines,'" *BBC News*, March 30, 2004.

12. www.umrc.org.

13. Scott Peterson, "A Rare Visit to Iraq's Radioactive Battlefield," *Christian Science Monitor*, April 29, 1999.

14. John Sweeney, "Iraq's Tortured Children," *BBC News*, June 22, 2002.

15. Bob Drogin and Greg Miller, "Iraqi Defector's Tales Bolstered U.S. Case for War," *Los Angeles Times*, March 28, 2004.

16. Testimony of Drue H. Barrett, Ph.D., Division of Environmental Hazards and Health Effect National Center for Environmental Health Centers for Disease Control and Prevention U.S. Public Health Service, Subcommittee on Labor, Health and Human Services, and Education Committee on Appropriations, U.S. Senate, October 5, 2000.

17. Linda D. Kozaryn, "Depleted Uranium: The Rest of the Story," American Forces Press Service, January 2000.

18. Science Applications International Corporation (SAIC), *Kinetic Energy Penetrator Environmental and Health Considerations*, July 1990: Vol. 1, 4–5; included as Appendix D in U.S. Army Armament, Munitions and Chemical Command report Kinetic Energy Penetrator Long Term Strategy Study, July 1990.

19. Ibid.

20. *Military Medicine*, August 2003.

21. "Depleted Uranium Weapons: Toxic Contaminant or Necessary Technology?" Conference, Massachusetts Institute of Technology, March 2004.

22. "Agent Orange Lingers in Vietnam Food—Study," Reuters, August 12, 2003.

Chapter 7

1a. Tim Reid, "The Needle and the Damage Done," *London Times*, November 26, 2002.

1b. Full disclosure: Coauthor Anthony Lappé's father, Dr. Marc Lappé, worked as an expert witness on behalf of the plantiffs in a class-action lawsuit against Lariam maker Hoffman-LaRoche, Inc.

1c. "Smallpox Vaccinations Moving Slowly," *CBS News*, May 12, 2003.

2. CBS, November 19, 2003; MSNBC November 20, 2003; and *Salon*, December 10, 2003.

3. Centers for Disease Control and Prevention Web site.

4. H. P. Albarelli Jr., "The Secret History of Anthrax," World Net Daily, November 6, 2001.

5. "Anthrax Vaccine Changes to the Manufacturing Process," United States General Accounting Office, October 23, 2001.

6. U.S. Secretary of State Colin Powell Address to the U.N. Security Council, White House transcript, February 5, 2003.

7. "Star Witness on Iraq Said Weapons Were Destroyed," Freedom and Accuracy in Reporting, February 27, 2003.

8. Anthony Lappé, "In Search of Saddam's Bomb," GNN.tv, December 19, 2002.

9. Julian Borger, "Iraqi Defector's Testimony Confuses Case Against Iraq," *The Guardian*, March 1, 2003.

10. Seth Ackerman, "A Legacy of Lies," *Mother Jones*, February 20, 2004.

11. Steven Rosenfeld, "Too Little, Too Late?: New Policy Announced Under Pressure," Tompaine.com, May 2, 2003.

12. Scott Miller, *Direct Order*, documentary film, 2002.

13. Arthur Allen, "A Cure Worse Than the Disease?" *Salon*, http://

dir.salon.com/health/feature2000/10/27/anthraxindex.html (accessed May 10, 2001).

14. Jamie McIntyre, "Congressional Report Says Anthrax Vaccine Large Part of Air Force Exodus, CNN," October 11, 2000.

15. Ken Alibek statement before the Joint Economic Committee United States Congress hearing on Terrorist and Intelligence Operations: Potential Impact on the U.S. Economy, May 20, 1998.

16. RPH Laboratory Medicine Web site, http://www.rph.wa.gov .au/labs/haem/malaria.

17a. Keith Epstein, "The Lariam Files," *Washington Post*, October 10, 2000.

17b. Mark Benjamin and Dan Olmsted, "Drug Causing GIs Permanent Brain Damage," United Press International, May 26, 2004.

17c. Evan Thomas and Mark Hosenball, "The Rise and Fall of Chalabi: Bush's Mr. Wrong," *Newsweek*, May 31, 2004.

18. Michael Massing, "Now They Tell Us," *New York Review of Books*, February 26, 2004.

Chapter 8

1. Paul Boutin, "Hack the Vote: How to Stop Someone from Stealing the 2004 Election," *Slate*, July 31, 2003.

2. Associated Press, "Fox Executive Spoke Five Times with Cousin Bush on Election Night," December 12, 2000.

3. Alexander Bolton, "Hagel's Ethics Filings Pose a Disclosure Issue," *The Hill*, January 29, 2003.

4. Lynn Landes, "Two Voting Companies & Two Brothers Will Count 80% of U.S. Election," Ecotalk.org, April 27, 2004.

5. Bob Fitrakis and Harvey Wasserman, "Diebold's Political Machine," *Mother Jones* online, March 5, 2004.

Chapter 9

1. "The War on Waste," *CBS News*, January 29, 2002; Kelly Patricia O'Meara, "Investigative Report: Rumsfeld Inherits Financial Mess," *Insight on the News*, August 10, 2001.

2. David Corn, "Behind the Placards: The Odd and Troubling

Origins of Today's Anti-war Movement," *LA Weekly*, November 1–7, 2002.

3. www.michaelmoore.com.

4. www.oscar.com.

5. Kenneth L. Gilpin, "Senate Votes to Repeal New Media Ownership Rules," *New York Times*, September 16, 2003.

6. Bernie.house.gov, the official Web site of Congressman Bernie Sanders (I-Vt.).

7. Ted Hearn, "FCC's Media Roster Plan," *Multichannel News*, May 19, 2003.

8. Ibid.

9. Charles Layton, "News Blackout," *American Journalism Review*, December 2003–January 2004.

10. Bob Williams and Morgan Jindrich, "On the Road Again—and Again. FCC Officials Rack up $2.8 Million Travel Tab with Industries They Regulate," Center for Public Integrity, May 22, 2003.

11. Ibid.

12. Ibid.

13. Ibid.

14. Charles Lewis and Adam Mayle, "Son of the Patriot Act," Alternet.org, February 7, 2003.

15. Nat Hentoff, "Red Alert for Bill of Rights!" *Village Voice*, March 7, 2003.

16. Ibid.

17. Bill Moyers, Keynote Address to the National Conference on Media Reform.

True Lies Netpendix

■ ■ ■

FOR MORE INFO on the stories and characters in the book, see the following sites:

Representative Henry Waxman (D-Calif.)
www.henrywaxman.house.gov

Flight 93
www.flight93crash.com

9/11 Truth Alliance
www.911truth.org

Cooperative Research (9/11)
www.cooperativeresearch.org

Mike Ruppert's From the Wilderness
www.fromthewilderness.com

Michel Chossudovsky's *Global Research* Magazine
www.globalresearch.ca

Alex Jones's Info Wars
www.infowars.com

William Rivers Pitt's Truthout
www.truthout.org

National Commission on the Terrorist Attacks Upon the
United States
www.9-11commission.gov

Cynthia McKinney for Congress
www.cynthiaforcongress.com

Greg Palast
www.gregpalast.com

Project for the New American Century
www.newamericancentury.org

Talking Points Memo
www.talkingpointsmemo.com

National Security Archive's Saddam Hussein Sourcebook
www.gwu.edu/~nsarchiv/special/iraq/index.htm

Information Clearing House
www.informationclearinghouse.info

Association for the Study of Peak Oil and Gas
www.peakoil.net

Human Rights Watch
www.hrw.org

Noam Chomsky's blog
blog.zmag.org/ttt

Raed Jarrar's blog
raedinthemiddle.blogspot.com

The Christian Science Monitor
www.csmonitor.com

Depleted Uranium Education Project
www.iacenter.org/depleted/du.htm

Uranium Medical Research Centre
www.umrc.org

Depleted Uranium Information Library (U.S. Department of
Defense)
deploymentlink.osd.mil/du_library

United Press International
www.upi.com

Dr. Meryl Nass, M.D.
www.anthraxvaccine.org

Black Box Voting
www.blackboxvoting.org

The Election Center
www.electioncenter.org

Media Channel
www.mediachannel.org

Center for Public Integrity
www.publicintegrity.org

Tom Paine
www.tompaine.com

Free Press
www.mediareform.net

NOW with Bill Moyers
www.pbs.org/now

Get Involved

■ ■ ■

LOG ON TO GNN's Web site, www.gnn.tv, to follow up with all the *True Lies* stories, read more about our journeys, check out full transcripts of the interviews we conducted for the book, and learn how you can launch your own investigations so you can start disseminating the news yourself. On the site, you can also purchase GNN DVDs and tapes, get info about the *True Lies* documentary film, and find out about upcoming GNN book signings, screenings, and other events.